W9-DHT-286

JOHN WILDMAN

By the same Author

FINANCIAL AND COMMERCIAL POLICY UNDER THE
CROMWELLIAN PROTECTORATE

OLIVER CROMWELL: THE CONSERVATIVE DICTATOR

MARLBOROUGH

LOUIS XIV AND THE GREATNESS OF FRANCE

NIL ADMIRARI

JOHN WILDMAN
From an engraving by W. Hollar, 1653

JOHN WILDMAN

Plotter and Postmaster

A Study of the English Republican Movement
in the Seventeenth Century

by
MAURICE ASHLEY

NEW HAVEN
YALE UNIVERSITY PRESS
1947

PRINTED IN GREAT BRITAIN

CONTENTS

LIST OF ILLUSTRATIONS

CHAPTER I

A DARK AND RESTLESS SPIRIT

Major Wildman . . . the soul of English politics . . . from 1640 to 1688.
DISRAELI *Sybil*

'LET posterity know,' Major Wildman instructed his son in the last decade of the seventeenth century, 'that in this age lived a man who spent the best part of his days in prisons without crimes, being conscious of no offence towards man for that he so loved his God that he could serve no man's will; and wished the liberty and happiness of his country and of all mankind.'

For many years, however, posterity remained ignorant not merely why John Wildman spent 'the best of his days' in prison and about what his conception of the 'liberty and happiness of his country' might be, but even who John Wildman was. A few diligent readers might perhaps have remembered him from Lord Clarendon's vivid *History of the Rebellion*, but, if they did, they would have had a prejudiced and incomplete picture.

Henry Hallam, the Whig historian, was the first nineteenth-century author to direct attention to Wildman. His name, he wrote in his *Constitutional History*, published in 1827, 'is not very familiar to the general reader, but occurs perpetually for about half a century . . . one of those dark and restless spirits who delight in the deep game of conspiring against every government.' In 1845 Wildman appeared for a few lines in Thomas Carlyle's best seller, *The Letters and Speeches of Oliver Cromwell*, as 'a stirring man, very flamy and very fuliginous: perhaps . . . the noisiest man in England.' Thus the Scottish mystic. It was left for Carlyle's contemporary, Benjamin Disraeli, later Conservative Prime Minister of Great Britain, to discover something more far-reaching about John Wildman.

'A remarkable feature of our written history,' observed Disraeli in the third chapter of his novel *Sybil* (1845), 'is the absence in its pages of some of its most influential persons. Not one man in a thousand, for instance, has ever heard of Major Wildman; yet he was the soul of English politics in the most eventful period of this kingdom and one of the most interesting to this age, from 1640 to 1688, and seemed more than once to hold the balance that was to decide the permanent form of our government. But he was the leader of an unsuccessful party.'

Wildman's party was the republican party and his goal the establishment of a democratic English republic. For this he conspired for fifty years and through five reigns. With unusual discrimination he planned the murders both of Cromwell and of Charles II. He was imprisoned in turn by the Long Parliament of Charles I, by Cromwell and by Charles II. A fifth of his active political life was passed in prison. A warrant was made out for his arrest by James II and, if the hopes of his political opponents had been fulfilled, he would have died on the scaffold instead of full of years and honours, one of the richest aldermen of London. His cause was admittedly an unsuccessful one in his own lifetime— and may appear to have been so since. For we have never had a democratic republic in England; we have had a republic, but it was not democratic; and we now have a democracy, but it is not republican. Nevertheless it cannot be doubted that the middle-class democracy under which we lived during the Victorian heyday would have approached his ideal. To Cromwell and to William III alike parliamentary democracy was another name for anarchy. Major Wildman marched hard in advance of his age.

So far as we have been able to discover, Wildman did not leave behind him written material about his life entirely adequate for the edification of posterity. None of his family letters has survived; he wrote no memoirs; he made no confessions. Even his official and business letters are few and far between. The story of a conspirator's career is necessarily obscure. It has to be pieced together out of scattered and often contradictory documents. The words of public informers have to be weighed; the lies of stool-pigeons must be sifted; the accusations of State prosecutors either accepted or gainsaid.

To bridge the gaps and to make this study of a curious man as full as possible, we shall not only trace the steps of Wildman's remarkable adventures, but also see him in terms of the 'unsuccessful party' of which he was a leader. The republican movement in England had two brief triumphs in 1649 and 1659, but between those dates and during the generation that succeeded the restoration of Charles II the Republicans were driven into the background or underground. Yet Wildman and his fellows kept the republican idea burning, and in their own often peculiar way taught the notions of political freedom and constitutional rights. They helped to build the settlement of 1689 out of the failure of 1660.

Wildman was born in 1623 and was therefore only nineteen years old when the foundations of England were rocked by the great civil war. He was educated at Cambridge and studied law in London. Nothing is known of his ancestry. Since his first wife came from Berkshire and he bought an estate in Berkshire, perhaps he was born in that part of England. To his contemporaries Wildman was always known as the Major. Exactly when or why he was promoted to that rank is not known. Nor are the details of his army career at all clear. The royalist historian, Clarendon, asserts that Wildman was made an officer by Cromwell during the first civil war. Another political opponent, writing in 1648, described him as 'a pretended gentleman of the Life Guard to his Excellency Sir Thomas Fairfax' (Fairfax was the commander-in-chief of the Roundhead army); as the same pamphleteer also calls Wildman 'the curate of Windham' one is not inclined to take his evidence too seriously. The references made to Wildman during the debates in the council of the Roundhead army in 1647 indicate beyond any real doubt that he was not a soldier at that time. On the whole, it may be assumed that Wildman did not achieve military rank until after the execution of Charles I. In 1649 his name was down as an officer in Sir John Reynolds's regiment which was selected for service in Ireland. From 1653 Wildman is regularly referred to as a major. In 1655 he planned a cavalry rising against Cromwell and in 1659 he seized Windsor castle in the name of the English republic. At the beginning of 1660 he appears once in the records as a colonel. Apart from these efforts his military career was undistinguished, or at any rate indistinguishable in contemporary narrative. His claim to a place on the pages of history is both that of a remarkably peaceable man of war and of a singularly warlike man of peace. Still, he was always known as the Major or as Major W—. Only on his election as a City alderman in the winter of his life did he shed this soldierly guise.

Wildman was an early riser and appears to have enjoyed good health. He studied medicine as a hobby and acted as his own and his wife's doctor with some success—at least Lucy Wildman thought her husband an excellent doctor and he himself lived to be threescore and ten, which was a rare accomplishment in the seventeenth century.

On occasion Wildman could show a fierce temper, but his ordinary mood was one of extreme caution. Henry Ireton, namesake and offspring of Oliver Cromwell's son-in-law, bore emphatic witness that this was his characteristic attitude. He also cast some light on Wildman's conversational powers: 'I am sure,' he observed, that Wildman 'was always such a cautious Sir Politick to me, that if ever he told me any piece of common news, though of no greater moment than what one might hear in the street, he would talk of a giant, a horse, a cock and a bull, and such kind of stuff, and then say he used that way of talking, and that they who had not wit enough to understand him, he cared not for conversing with . . .'; 'which humour,' adds Ireton—reasonably enough— 'was enough to keep me from being ambitious of much of his conversation.' The language, of course, was that of the professional conspirator. It may be that Wildman, who apparently did not trust Ireton, preferred to provide him with cock-and-bull stories instead of intelligible conversation.

What some saw merely as caution in Wildman, others regarded as low cunning. Samuel Pepys, who never met Wildman, repeats in his diary a remark of the statesman Sir William Coventry that he had been 'a false fellow to everybody.' Another unfriendly witness, Colonel Nathaniel Wade, who disliked the part taken by Wildman in the Duke of Monmouth's rebellion of 1685, asserted that 'according to the character I have had of him' he was 'a man of cunning, very able to draw others into snares and keep out himself.' Both these opinions were second-hand. Two men who knew Wildman personally—Bulstrode Whitelocke, the Cromwellian lawyer, and Gilbert Burnet, sometime Bishop of Salisbury— speak of him as a consistent Republican who never betrayed anyone who trusted him. In the storm and stress of the seventeenth century, above all under the Cromwellian dictatorship, during the royalist reaction, and in the reign of the fanatic James II, a Republican with democratic leanings had to be supremely cautious and betray neither himself nor others by speech or action. Except for his occasional bursts of temper against those who despised the cause which he served, he preserved his composure under the gravest provocations. He took as his motto *nil admirari*—'nothing ever surprised him.'

In spite of the pious thoughts inscribed on his tombstone, John Wildman was an agnostic. Adequate proof that he was no sectarian puritan may be found in the fact that different contemporaries placed him in different sects. Samuel Pepys refers to him as a 'Fifth Monarchy Man,' that is, a member of the sect which believed that God was about to appear on earth as the personal ruler of the world, as was prophesied in the Book of Daniel. Other informants called him respectively a 'notorious Anabaptist,' a Quaker and a Presbyterian. He was none of these. Clarendon in his *History* says that Wildman 'was inspired with the spirit of praying and preaching' only 'when those gifts came into request,' or, in other words, that he adopted the puritan cant in order to make a name for himself when the puritans were in power. Indeed although, like all the writers and speakers of that age of Christian soldiers and frenzied prophets, he made good use of biblical phraseology, those who listened to his oratory in 1647 or were familiar with the company he kept after 1659 can hardly have doubted that he was indifferent to religion except in so far as he could invoke it as a sanction for political freedom. His intimate friendship with men like Henry Nevile, Henry Marten, Algernon Sidney, and the second Duke of Buckingham, all men who were notoriously unaffected by the current religious enthusiasms, is a reliable clue to his religious outlook. At the revolution of 1688, when a scheme for a comprehensive Church of England was put forward, a Church which should have so elastic a doctrine as to attract all the nonconformist sects as well as the Anglicans, it was opposed by Wildman because he was afraid that the Church would become too united and powerful. 'No bishop, no king' was a doctrine to which all good Republicans subscribed, and that was why they worked for twenty years through the sects who hated the bishops. Bishop Burnet, himself a good friend to the idea of religious comprehension, suspected, probably not without justice, that Wildman and his friends were 'in their hearts enemies to the Christian religion.'

11

Further evidence of Wildman's religious views is afforded by various speeches made by him in the army debates of 1647. In one debate, after the fundamental principles of government had been under discussion for some time and a point had been reached where sharp differences between the democrats and anti-democrats were plainly discerned, Oliver Cromwell thought to settle the issue by a proposal that 'a smaller committee should be set up to seek God in a uniting spirit.' This plan won the earnest approval of the assembled puritans, who were truly beginning to forget their political disputes when Wildman could stand it no longer and begged that they should 'return a little to the business in hand.' Later in these debates, after Cromwell and others had selected texts from the New and Old Testaments to sustain their particular points of view, Wildman came out with the frank but disconcerting statement: 'We cannot find anything in the Word of God what is fit to be done in civil matters.' There were certain conceptions, he added, that were invariably associated with the idea of God, such as justice and mercy, which were admirable general principles of political conduct, but, he said, they could not hope to find in the Holy Writ a complete political constitution for the English people.

In 1648 Wildman took part in a debate specifically about religion, or, to be precise, on the functions of the State in relation to religion. Should the magistrate be given power to coerce people into accepting religious principles? Wildman strongly denied (in harmony with the common puritan attitude) that the magistrate had any possible right to direct or order individual thought. Such a procedure, he said, is incompatible with the very essence of liberty. 'God hath made you instruments of liberty,' Wildman told the council of the army. 'In matters of religion that's preferred to us before life. Let's have that or nothing.' Finally, in the same debate, Wildman declared that there are no possible agreed principles of religion which a magistrate has the right to enforce. To the argument that magistrates should forbid conduct which violates the light of nature he retorted, 'It is not easily determinable by the light of nature what is sin.' He went even further: 'It is not easy by the light of nature to determine there is a God.' The Sun or Moon, he said, may be God. The magistrate is as liable to error as the people whom he judges. He is as likely to destroy good as to prevent evil. Thus in religion, as in politics, Wildman was in advance of his time.

It was the habit of political debaters of the seventeenth century to use not only biblical texts but also legal lore as embellishments to their argument, just as the eighteenth century employed classical quotations and the twentieth century uses blue books. Wildman, like the rest, found illustrations if not justifications in the Bible, but he was far more at home when deploying legal precedents. He seems to have been even more comfortable with the text of Magna Carta than with that of the Book of Daniel, and he was just as capable of perverting and misconstruing mediaeval instances as others were of misrepresenting the moral code of the early Jews. Those who knew him well in later life commended his wide knowledge of English law. He is 'very learned in law,' wrote Bishop Burnet; he is 'esteemed excellently versed in the laws of England,' noted the Reverend Robert Ferguson.

Whether Wildman derived his considerable knowledge of English law in the course of a professional training or as a pastime is not absolutely clear. Professor Pease, the American historian of the Leveller movement, refers to him as 'a young barrister,' but this is an assumption which cannot be confirmed from the records of the London Inns. It is, however, possible that, like most of his middle-class contemporaries, he took a course in law at an early age. It is memorable that men like John Pym, who were intended for a business career, and Oliver Cromwell, an hereditary land-lord, studied law before settling down to their predestined occu-pations.

Apart from this possibility, it is plain that when various parties called upon Wildman at different stages of his life to act as their legal representative they would scarcely have done so unless he were known as an expert in law. Like Socialist barristers in our own day, he would have been invited to assist in democratic legal processes firstly because he was a sympathizer with the interest concerned, but nevertheless, secondly, because he was definitely a lawyer. Thus in 1647 his public career begins when at the age of twenty-four he is asked to put the case of the democrats before the council of the army. Next year he defends Sir John Maynard, himself a lawyer of distinction, apparently with Maynard's approval, in a pamphlet. Another pamphlet was written by him with the significant pseudonym of 'John Lawmind.' In 1650 he acted as the representative of the freemen of London in a purely legal contest with some of the most eminent lawyers of London. Again, he was called in by the freeholders in the Isle of Axholme when they wished to embark upon a legal struggle with the drainers of the fens. Finally, he was made the legal agent and executor of the second Duke of Buckingham. In one of the cases which he dealt with for Buckingham he was definitely referred to as an 'attorney.' We may rest on the broad assumption that although Wildman may not have been a barrister, he was certainly a recognized attorney or 'solicitor,' especially familiar with questions of land tenure and the laws of real property.

Whether, if he had chosen to devote himself completely to the legal profession instead of to the more exciting life of plotting and speculative finance, John Wildman would have been successful, we cannot tell, but we may guess. His conduct of the few cases that have been named was neither particularly effective nor convincing. He was lacking in tact and willingness to compromise. He allowed himself to be wrapped up in subtle and ingenious but unconvincing arguments derived from dark precedents. As a politician this may have been unavoidable and even necessary. For these precedents were the small change of seventeenth-century political debate and were bandied about as much by well-known statesmen as by the smaller fry. But the point is that these elaborate precedents, which Wildman garnered as a youth and in which he engrossed himself during his many leisure hours in prison, often served to confuse rather than illuminate the causes for which he strove. It is in spite of, and not because of, such laboriously acquired knowledge of legal history that Wildman's political arguments have merit and give him a claim to be regarded as an advanced and intelligent political thinker. Yet the historian must not altogether discount the importance both to Wildman himself and to his audiences of these legalistic reasonings. It is indeed a commonplace that the irreconcilable conflict in the English civil wars was (in theory at least) because one side maintained that Charles I had broken the fundamental laws of the kingdom, while the other side urged that Parliament, and not the King, had violated the Constitution.

As an advocate and orator therefore Wildman was seldom

successfully persuasive and hence came to prefer plotting to rhetoric. He was handicapped as an orator, moreover, because he always felt obliged to promote such advanced views. Although the student of the army council debates, who reads carefully the profound controversies between the first Henry Ireton and John Wildman, may feel, with such an eminent modern political philosopher as Lord Lindsay, that Wildman failed to solve the problem of how to reconcile liberty with authority, his sympathies, if he is a democrat, will undoubtedly lie with Wildman rather than with Ireton. But to-day is three hundred years later. In those solemn conclaves and in the Parliaments of Charles II or William III Wildman could scarcely have hoped to influence his fellows with ideas so entirely out of tune with the time; but where he had a congenial audience he appears to have been an effective speaker. After 1660 men of his views were actively discouraged. Indeed they soon found their way into prison. During the twenty-five best years of his life (1653–1678) Wildman was unable to indulge his rhetorical talents because what he had to say was disliked by the ruling powers.

If Wildman's legal and constitutional studies were of little help to him as a debater, they earned him a considerable reputation as an author of State constitutions at a time when constitution-mongering was the prevailing fashion. His reputation in this respect may even be compared with that of Napoleon's protégé, the Abbé Sieyès, in the early years of the French Revolution. Unlike Sieyès, he had the opportunity to exercise his talents at widely different times and circumstances; but Wildman's constitutions were never given the chance to prove that they were workable. Sieyès had the wit to find a place for Napoleon in his constitutions; Wildman's schemes either eliminated a dictator or pared the powers of the throne.

The first of Wildman's constitutions or outlines of constitutional principles was known as 'The Case of the Army' (1647); this was widened into the first and second 'Agreements of the People.' These were the first written democratic constitutions known to the modern world and were scattered in various forms throughout Europe during the mid-seventeenth century. One or two of their minor clauses were embodied into the first Cromwellian written constitution. When there were prospects of setting up a republic in

1659, Wildman was invited by the army to help to frame a scheme of government, and he was a leading member of two clubs that met in London at that date to dissect and discuss constitutions. In 1681, when the overthrow of Charles II was envisaged, he was credited with another 'framework of government.' In 1688 when he arrived at the conspirators' centre in Holland he at once announced his disapproval of the constitutional declaration which had been drafted for William of Orange and protested so vigorously that ultimately the declaration was modified to meet his wishes. The famous Bill of Rights (1689) also failed to secure his approval; and just before he died he was writing to complain that William III had violated the Constitution, if not the Constitution as it was interpreted by Ministers of State at least the ideal constitution framed in the fertile mind of Major John Wildman.

As a writer Wildman confined himself to pamphlets. It was at one time popularly supposed that he was engaged upon a great work on the laws of England for which he had collected materials in prison, but if it were ever completed, it was never published. Lord Clarendon maintains that Wildman had a 'smooth pen,' by which presumably was meant the ability to pour out a flood of persuasive argument in a short space of time. This was no unusual gift in his age. But it is certainly significant that he was called upon by the rank-and-file of the republican army and by the Levellers to draw up their 'cases' for them. Perhaps as 'a scholar bred in the University of Cambridge' and as a London attorney, it was felt that he was bound to be capable of producing accurate and convincing prose.

Wildman's ability as a pamphleteer does not in fact compare with that of the first-rate English pamphleteers of the seventeenth century—not merely with that of outstanding figures like Milton and the Marquess of Halifax, but even with men on a lower intellectual plane, like William Prynne and John Lilburne. Lilburne, for instance, wrote at the same time and on the same subjects as Wildman; the material on which they drew was identical; but Wildman lacked the vivacity and wit of Lilburne, although he was not far behind him in ferocity, enthusiasm or variety of illustrative texts.

Nevertheless Wildman wrote two celebrated pamphlets— *Putney Projects* (1647) and *The Memorial to Protestants* (1688)—

which helped and supported the revolutions of 1649 and 1689 respectively. Perhaps the best thing he wrote was the 'Declaration against Cromwell' (1655), which was only published in full many years after it was completed. It was a succinct and telling indictment of the Cromwellian dictatorship, established in violation of all the promises made during the civil war. Cromwell did not lightly forgive him for it and indeed threatened him with the scaffold.

As a business man Wildman was both shrewd and successful. Although, except at the outset of his career, he never allowed his business interests to interfere with his political faith, he was able to build up a substantial fortune. He had the reputation, common to most wealthy men until they have made their pile, of being careful with his money. He could never be persuaded to invest big sums in dubious causes. He astutely took advantage of the way in which large parcels of land were thrown on the market during the Interregnum to speculate in property with profit. He bought himself a nice estate in Berkshire which he protected with constant suits in Chancery. His appointment as one of the executors of the wealthy second Duke of Buckingham points to his reputation as a business manager also during the reign of Charles II. When he was in prison frequent appeals were made for his release on account of the damage caused by his absence to the interests of his clients and creditors alike. Since he remained rich enough to buy the position of Postmaster-General in 1689—a position which was open only to a man of capital—it may be assumed that his affairs did not suffer unduly from his devotion to plotting.

Wildman's family affairs can in all the known circumstances have occupied but a small part of his active life. He was twice married. His first wife, Frances, was the daughter of the Roman Catholic Sir Francis Englefield, a Berkshire baronet. The marriage must have taken place during the civil wars, and it is characteristic of Wildman's indifference to the religious bigotry of his age that he should at such a time have married a Roman Catholic's daughter. There was one son by the marriage, but as no mention of Frances is to be found either on Wildman's tombstone or memorial tablet, and as he must have married again soon after her death, he cannot have felt the same measure of devotion towards her as he did towards his second wife, Lucy.

B

Lucy Wildman (daughter of Lord Lovelace) shared her husband's fortunes and misfortunes for thirty-seven years. She tended him in his periods of outlawry, looked after his business affairs when he was in prison, and lived to enjoy his triumph at the Court of William III. She was married to him some time before 1655, went abroad with him in 1670, and died at the age of sixty-three, predeceasing him by only six months.

Wildman's only son, John, by his first wife, shared his father's first term of imprisonment in the reign of Charles II and acquired a captaincy when he joined his father on William of Orange's invasion of England. Not only did the younger John Wildman raise a company of foot to serve William III, but later he displayed zeal by spying on the Jacobites, an inherited family trait. He fell foul of his commanding officer, a Colonel Stuart, whom he treated sufficiently badly to be assaulted by Colonel Stuart's nephews. The last we hear of him is in 1698, complaining that 'the want of money and employment has reduced him to very poor conditions.' But in fact when he died in 1710 the younger John Wildman was wealthy enough to endow handsomely a branch of the English aristocracy. The younger Wildman married Eleanor Chute, the second daughter of a Kentish gentleman, but she died in August, 1677, at the age of nineteen. Perhaps she died in childbirth, for Major Wildman was never a grandfather. His son did not marry again, but stuck with his father and stepmother. According to his adopted son, the second John Wildman was 'a very strict observer of all public and private virtues, a great lover of the English Constitution, and had an utmost abhorrence of all oppression and tyranny.' 'The sweetness of his temper and the modesty of his behaviour,' added his epitaph, 'rendered him a most agreeable husband, master, neighbour, and acquaintance.' Epitaphs are not usually impartial, but it seems that John brought up his only child in the way that he wished him to go.

Thus there is every reason to suppose that the family life of the elder John Wildman was happy. With his wife Lucy and his widower son together they surmounted the stormy days of the Rye House Plot, of the Monmouth Rebellion, and of the Glorious Revolution, to emerge into the brighter and warmer light of William and Mary's reign. We may contrast the story of the professional plotter and agnostic agitator, the would-be political assassin of saturnine countenance and mystic utterances, with the family man who gained a fortune and settled down as a country gentleman in a stately Elizabethan manor, a hundred yards from the parish church of which he was the patron. What little is known of his private life and personal characteristics has now been set out. Henceforward our concern with him is almost entirely as a public figure. First, we must consider the rise of the English republican party, of which John Wildman was to become a leader.

CHAPTER II

THE FIRST REPUBLICANS AND DEMOCRATS

The worst of rebels never arm
To do their King and country harm,
But draw their swords to do them good,
As doctors use, by letting blood.
                    SAMUEL BUTLER *Miscellanies*

THE last big battle of the first civil war was fought on the clay hills by Naseby in June, 1645, and the surrender of Charles I's stronghold of Oxford a year later marked the completeness of the Royalists' defeat. The King was now in 'honourable captivity' with the Scottish army and the destruction of the Established Church for which he had risked his throne was under way. The bishops were abolished and the Westminster Assembly, appointed by the House of Commons, was framing a fresh constitution for the Church of England. It was generally expected that this reformed Church would be on a Presbyterian pattern, with a hierarchy of assemblies, pastors, elders, and deacons, since the Presbyterians were in a majority both in the Westminster Assembly and in the House of Commons. On the other hand, the victorious Roundhead army was predominantly 'Independent,' believing in the right of individual congregations to govern themselves without any hierarchy. Both the Independents and the Presbyterians tried to negotiate with the King for his return, offering to guarantee his throne if he would but accept their constitutional principles and promise security to their respective religions. The King naturally hoped to play off the two parties against each other. It was in this period of uncertainty and intrigue, when everything was in the melting-pot, that the origins of the English republican movement may be found.

As happened with the French republicans during the French Revolution, the republican party in England developed with surprising rapidity only after the civil war began. Its ultimate triumph was the product of circumstances, of the sheer inability of the Roundhead leaders, themselves never Republicans by conviction, to come to terms with the defeated King. But the way for a republican constitution had been prepared by a number of examples and intellectual and religious influences which, as the opportunities of the time began to invite new ideas and schemes, converted different groups and individuals to the republican or democratic cause. Among the puritans, notably among the Anabaptists (forerunners of the modern Baptists), and to a lesser extent among the Independents, what must have counted for much was the democratic internal organization of their own congregations, members of which had in the reign of James I sailed to America to set up what were in effect small republics there. Again, for the traveller and the reader of the traveller's tale there were the impressive contemporary examples of the Dutch, Swiss, and Venetian republics, particularly the Dutch republic, which was becoming a rich and flourishing State, although some intellectuals were more impressed by the ingenious oligarchic constitution at Venice. Thirdly, famous pamphlets which had been published by the Presbyterians to undermine the power of Mary, Queen of Scots, or by the Jesuits to provoke revolt against Queen Elizabeth, had taught the doctrine that a monarch might legitimately be deposed, although that was not of course the same as saying that a republic ought to be substituted for the deposed sovereign. In such an atmosphere select passages from the Old Testament (such as the Book of Samuel) carried weight among the sectaries, while educated country gentlemen found republican inspiration in the classics and the early histories of Greece and Rome.

Nevertheless, in spite of such influences there were scarcely any Republicans in England at the outbreak of the civil war. Neither the Short Parliament nor the Long Parliament (both of which met in 1642) contained a single Republican. The opposition to the King was originally concerned simply to assert the supremacy of the law.

Henry Marten, who was born at Oxford in 1602 of a respectable county family, may perhaps be called the first avowed English Republican. A witty and outspoken orator, he married a rich widow and was described as 'a great lover of pretty girls to whom he was so liberal that he spent the greatest part of his estate.' Certainly his sexual behaviour scandalized the puritans and his extravagance later brought him to bankruptcy. Charles I called him a 'whoremaster' (as Oliver Cromwell did later), and turned him out of Hyde Park. In August, 1642, the King complained that Marten had declared 'our office is forfeitable and that the happiness of the kingdom does not depend upon us, nor any of the regal branches of that stock.' In 1643 Marten was said to be guilty of 'scandalous utterances about the King and the House of Lords.' In August of that year he defended a pamphlet by a clergyman named John Saltmarsh which may perhaps be considered the first English republican pamphlet. Saltmarsh had written that 'it were better that one family should be destroyed than many.' Marten said that he saw no reason to condemn the author for such an obvious statement of fact. He was expelled from the House of Commons for his audacity and was not re-admitted until January, 1646. By this date conditions had so changed and distrust of the King was so deep that Marten was able to become with impunity the leader of a definite republican group. Included among his followers were Edmund Ludlow, a stupid but honest soldier; Robert Blake, the famous admiral; Algernon Sidney, destined to be executed for his republican faith; John Skippon, who was to become one of Cromwell's Majors-General, and Colonel Hutchinson, a solid Nottinghamshire gentleman, who lives yet in the pages of his wife's biography. A proposal put forward in September, 1647, that all negotiations between the Parliament and the King should be ended received thirty-four votes in its favour, and this may be taken to be the maximum membership of the republican party in the House of Commons under Marten's leadership.

It may well have been from Henry Marten that John Wildman imbibed his strong republican principles. Both Marten and Wildman lived in Berkshire; Wildman married a Berkshire girl, and there is evidence of close intimacy and even relationship between the two families (although at a later date). Wildman was afterwards to buy as his permanent home a house that had formerly belonged to Marten and was sold by him to help to meet his large debts.

Outside the House of Commons republican ideas began to gain support between 1642 and 1645, at any rate among the non-Presbyterian puritan sects. The Presbyterians, who formed the majority of the puritans, were and remained throughout the

seventeenth century open-minded about the best form of government, but on the whole they tended to be monarchists. The
Independents, on the other hand, inclined towards republicanism.
It is doubtful how strong the Independents were before the civil
war. The Reverend Richard Baxter said that the number in
London was very small, but an Anglican vicar wrote in 1640
that they were 'a not inconsiderable party and that they grow in
many parts of the kingdom.' When Baxter visited Cromwell's
New Model Army, which consisted mainly of Independents and
sectarians, after the battle of Naseby, he was surprised by the
republican attitude of the ranks.

The republican ideas which were beginning to grip the soldiers
of Cromwell's army were less subtle and more democratic than
those advocated by the small republican group in the House of
Commons. Most of the Republicans in the Commons—especially
men like Algernon Sidney and Sir Henry Vane—were far from
being democrats. The republic which they envisaged as re-
placing Charles was an aristocracy of the 'chosen' or 'virtuous.'
They took as their model the Sanhedrin—the Wise Men of the
ancient Jews—or the Council of State in contemporary Venice.
Far different were the political notions of the man to whom
Cromwell's soldiers looked for guidance, John Lilburne, nicknamed 'Freeborn John,' the first important advocate of democratic republicanism.

Lilburne began his political career at an early age when he was
imprisoned by Charles I for helping to publish libels against the
bishops. Released from prison in 1642, he fought as an officer in
the civil war. He was, however, an unquenchable controversialist,
and he soon attacked the Earl of Manchester and other Presbyterian commanders for mismanaging the war; for this he was
committed to prison by the House of Lords. He appealed to the
House of Commons, but was imprisoned by them for criticizing
the King. Pamphlets written by him when he was in Newgate
prison in 1645 gradually formulated his republican views as well
as what were later called 'Leveller' opinions. In his *Regal Tyranny
Discovered*, which was published in January, 1647, he 'punctually
declared the tyranny of the Kings of England from the days of
William the Invader and Robber and Tyrant, alias the Con-
queror, to this present King Charles, who is plainly proved to be

the worst and more tyrannical than any of his predecessors.' He produced a confused medley of republican arguments. The Scriptures showed that God had not 'approbationally instituted' but only 'permissibly suffered kingship'; Charles had violated his 'contract and agreement' with the people and broken his coronation oath; had not Cato said that 'no man can be an honest man but he that is a freeman'? and, after all, 'were not our sovereigns sprung from bastards?' Whatever Lilburne was driving at (and a close study of his pamphlets does not completely prove that he was opposed to some kind of monarch as a figurehead) it is clear that the ordinary soldier or sectarian must have interpreted what he wrote as a downright plea against the institution of monarchy. Lilburne's works spread extensively throughout the army in 1645 and 1646; and at the same time they were eagerly bought in London and the provinces. The doctrine, which Lilburne also taught, that the ultimate sovereign power in the State rested not with Parliament but with the people gave his disciples the name of Levellers—a name which was perhaps invented by Cromwell— and by the autumn of 1647 there were reported to be about ten thousand Levellers in London and from fifteen to twenty thousand in the country. Throughout the period between the imprisonment of Charles I and the restoration of Charles II the Levellers took up an independent attitude both to Parliament and to the parliamentary Republicans. In the words of Professor Pease they 'generally favoured a republican form of government; but they regarded it always as a means to an end, and were not drawn from their (democratic) principles into supporting the Commonwealth with the so-called republicans.' Yet it should be noticed that a 'remonstrance' published in London early in 1646 against the imprisonment of Lilburne is the first pamphlet openly to ask for the abolition of monarchy.

Such was the composition of the republican movement when, in January, 1647, the Scottish Army abandoned King Charles I, who had fled to them for protection after the battle of Naseby, to the mercies of the English Parliament. There were Republicans among the junior officers and rank-and-file of the New Model Army—Cromwell's army—Republicans among the followers of John Lilburne, principally in the City of London, and the group led by Henry Marten in the House of Commons.

From that date for the next two years events moved rapidly. On the one hand, conviction grew among the victorious Round-heads that the nominally reigning monarch would have to be deposed and perhaps the monarchy abolished at the same time. On the other hand, the dissatisfaction felt by the army with the incomplete and unrepresentative House of Commons caused crude but genuine democratic ideas to be aired. Had these two trends intermingled, England might conceivably have attempted to set up a democratic republic a hundred and fifty years before the experiment was tried in France. It is for this reason that the history of the republican agitation in the army deserves to be followed in some detail.

Although at the beginning of 1647 the future of monarchy in England had become an acute problem, neither the Presbyterians, who dominated the House of Commons and the House of Lords, nor General Fairfax and Lieutenant-General Oliver Cromwell, who led the army, had yet given up hope of a compromise between the constitutional demands of the Roundheads and the wishes of their prisoner, King Charles. But the political position at this date was complicated by a growing rift between the army as a whole and Parliament. The army's grievances were that Parliament had failed to pay the soldiers their arrears, had planned to disband a large part of them, and intended to ship the rest off to Ireland, but not under the command of their most trusted general officers. Lilburne's propaganda urging that Parliament was unrepresenta-tive thus spread rapidly in the army, where, according to more than one contemporary account, it was widely read or discussed during 1647. In the spring of that year the regiments began to elect agents or 'Agitators' from their ranks to express their grievances; and although these 'Agitators' had as their first duty the representation of certain specific complaints of the soldiers, they were constantly under the spell of Leveller ideas. The earliest 'Agitators' were the representatives of eight regiments of horse and they became active in April, 1647, although the first paper which survives signed by Agitators is dated 17th May and has reference to a meeting at which officers appointed to represent the grievances of their regiments fell out among themselves. The leading Agitator at this date was Edward Sexby, who advocated 'keeping a party of able pen-men at Oxford and the Army where their presses be employed to satisfy and undeceive the people.' He was also in favour of holding 'correspondence with soldiers and well-affected friends' in different parts of the country for the purpose of resisting the Presbyterians' plans, of keeping a close watch on the King, and of forcing the general officers to stay with the army. Finally he proposed that they should draw up a list of their demands which should include a 'reformation of civil justice,' an act of indemnity, and punishment of the guilty.

Provoked by the attitude of the Commons to the army, even the leading officers for a time toyed with the ideas and accepted the point of view of the Agitators. Soldiers and officers alike forwarded petitions both to the House of Commons and to their generals detailing their complaints; Parliament was confronted not with a few malcontents but with an entire army. Under these circumstances the House of Commons capitulated; six weeks' arrears of pay were offered to soldiers on their disbandment and four officer members of Parliament were sent to the army headquarters to investigate. These commissioners, of whom Cromwell was one, did little good. The mutual distrust of the Presbyterian House of Commons and of the Independent army was too deep. On 25th May the House of Commons took the bull by the horns and gave orders that every soldier must make up his mind instantly either to accept disbandment or go to Ireland. Sexby advised the Agitators to resist and to arrest their officers if they tried to lead their soldiers to Ireland. Fairfax, the commander-in-chief, who now resumed his duties after a prolonged absence owing to illness, ordered the soldiers 'to forbear any further acting by themselves without their officers in any irregular ways.' He was too late to reassert discipline. The army was angry and resentful. The regiments had formed councils and appointed Agitators, resolving to work 'in unison for their rights.' Some of the officers, too, began to petition against disbandment and to work in collaboration with the Agitators, although Cromwell and Ireton (according to Wildman) prophesied 'confusion and ruin' and tried to suppress the soldiers' petitions. The Agitators advised the soldiers to stand by their officers and all refused to disband. Fairfax gave way before the storm and agreed to a 'general rendezvous' or public meeting of the whole army at Newmarket on 5th June. Oliver Cromwell, a realist and an opportunist, always anxious to accept the compulsion of circumstances as divine guidance, now decided also to throw in his lot with the army. To obtain an important pawn in the coming conflict with Parliament, Cromwell ordered Cornet Joyce to seize King Charles I. The King, whom Joyce found on a Northamptonshire bowling green, became a not unwilling victim of abduction and was removed to army headquarters. On 5th June officers and men agreed to 'A Solemn Engagement of the Army,' refusing to disband until all their grievances had been settled; on 12th June the entire army marched on London and forced the Presbyterian leaders most obnoxious to them to withdraw; and two days later they agreed to a 'Declaration of the Army,' setting out their point of view in lucid terms: 'We are not,' ran this challenging statement, 'a mere mercenary army, hired to serve any arbitrary power in the State, but called forth and conjured by the several declarations of Parliament to the defence of our own and the people's just rights and liberties.' This declaration, which virtually claimed that the army was a more representative and democratic body than Parliament, showed how deeply Lilburne's doctrines had struck. But although Cromwell was now prepared to side with the army against Parliament, neither he nor the other 'Grandees,' as the high army officers were nicknamed, were yet ready for revolution by force or for the destruction of monarchy. When on 16th July the Agitators urged that the army should march back to London and impose their terms on Parliament, this was opposed by Cromwell, who wanted to arrive at an agreed treaty with the Presbyterians. His son-in-law, Ireton, a man of real intellectual distinction and the driving force among the Grandees, therefore drew up a draft scheme called the 'Heads of the Proposals' as the basis of such a treaty, which also was to be submitted to the King.

The 'Heads of the Proposals,' the first English written constitution to be conceived, while it made the King's power subservient to that of Parliament, also lessened the power of Parliament by making it more amenable to the control of the constituencies and by establishing liberty of conscience as a fundamental right. These proposals were referred by General Fairfax to a committee of twelve officers and twelve Agitators. The revisions agreed by the committee were:

(1) That restrictions should be placed upon the King's power to veto parliamentary bills; a Bill passed by two successive parliaments could become law without the King's consent.

(2) That all who had fought against the Roundheads should be excluded from office for ten years, unless Parliament decided otherwise.

(3) That an Act should be passed to abolish the bishops.

(4) That another Act should be passed confirming the sales of the bishops' lands.

For the moment the army was united. The 'Heads of the Proposals' were published and sent to the King. Then at the beginning of August the army marched on London and overthrew the Presbyterian majority in the House of Commons. But Cromwell and Ireton built their hopes on a final settlement with the King, and even accepted some important modifications in the 'Heads of the Proposals' to meet Charles I's objections. This was not in the least to the taste of the Levellers or army republicans. The alliance between the Grandees and the Agitators thus proved to be only temporary.

As early as July Lilburne had warned the army from his prison cell in the Tower of London that Cromwell would betray them, and he had appealed to Oliver himself not to be seduced either by the sums of money voted to him by Parliament or by 'the covetous earthworms who were his friends.' In the autumn the movement to restore the monarch upon terms was in full swing. Cromwell entered into direct negotiations with Charles I. The combined meetings of officers and soldiers' representatives were dropped. In the purged House of Commons Cromwell successfully opposed Henry Marten's motion that no more 'addresses' should be sent to the King.

The result of this debate infuriated the Levellers, who described it as showing the sense of the army to be in favour of further negotiations with the King when it was only the 'sense of Cromwell.' The continuance of the interviews between Cromwell and Ireton and the King's representatives added fuel to the flames. The growing republican party inside and outside the army was determined to oppose this 'desertion of their cause' and massed its forces and 'pen men' for resistance: 'Why,' demanded the Republicans, 'are Cromwell and Ireton so familiar with Ashburnham and others, the King's chief agents? Why permit they so many of his deceitful clergy to continue about him? Why do they themselves kneel, and kiss, and fawn upon him? . . . Oh shame of men! Oh sin against God!' 'You have robbed by your subtlety and shifting tricks the honest and gallant Agitators of their power and authority . . .' wrote Lilburne to Cromwell. The dissatis-faction and suspicion aroused by all the complicated political manoeuvres and fruitless constitutional negotiations of 1647 pro-duced grave unrest in the army. Meetings took place among the soldiers and several regiments elected new Agitators. Five regi-ments, including those of Cromwell and Ireton, took the lead in putting forward democratic and republican views; they signed a statement of their attitude called 'The Case of the Army' on 9th October.

The author of 'The Case of the Army' was a rising young lawyer and politician, an intimate associate of John Lilburne, who acted as a link between the London Levellers and the Agita-tors in the army. His name was John Wildman, and he made his first appearance on the stage of history in the army council held at Putney in October, 1647, to resolve the unsettled problems of the first civil war.

CHAPTER III

WILDMAN AGAINST CROMWELL

I consider that's the undeniable maxim of government: that all
government is in the free consent of the people.
JOHN WILDMAN, 1647

WHEN in October, 1647, John Wildman appeared at Putney
church to defend the cause of democratic republicanism, the
question whether the future government of England was to be by
a king or a republic had become a live issue. The democratic
republican movement was growing steadily more popular in the
army. Six weeks earlier Henry Ireton had presented his 'Heads
of the Proposals' to the council of the army, and had secured its
approval only in the teeth of considerable opposition. Lilburne, still
in prison and disgusted with Cromwell, who had once been his
hero, threatened what the 'hobnails and clouted boots' of the
'private soldiers' might do for the cause of democracy. Wild
rumours, originated, or at any rate propagated, by the Levellers,
circulated about the promises and rewards which Cromwell had
obtained from King Charles I for his support. Matters were not
improved when on 20th October Cromwell delivered in the House
of Commons a three-hour speech in favour of monarchy. The
menace of mutiny in the army was real. The Putney meeting of
the General Council of Army, to which representatives of the
soldiers were invited, was approved by Cromwell to avert anarchy.

Wildman's first task on arriving at army headquarters was to
crystallize and to make articulate the political ideas of the republican soldiers. He helped to draw up 'The Case of the Army Truly
Stated' for presentation to General Fairfax and also to frame a
document called 'The Agreement of the People,' which embodied
in succinct form the constitutional programme of the Levellers.
'The Case of the Army' and 'The Agreement of the People' to
some extent cover the same ground, but whereas the 'Agreement'
is concise, the 'Case' is prolix; the former is concerned with principles, the latter with desirable practices.

'The Agreement of the People', 'for a firm and present peace upon grounds of common right,' after a preamble explaining how the late war had proved the justice of the Roundhead cause and describing the 'high rate' at which they valued their 'just freedom,' declares in the form of four points:

(1) A redistribution of parliamentary seats 'according to the number of the inhabitants.'

(2) The dissolution of the existing Parliament on 30th September 1648.

(3) That the people 'do, of course, choose themselves a Parliament once in two years.'

(4) 'That the power of this, and all future representatives of this nation, is inferior only to theirs who choose them' and extends 'without the consent or concurrence of any other person or persons' to the control of ministers, officers, magistrates, the making of peace or war and all foreign policy.

There is no mention of the King, and clause four is clearly republican. Five reservations were made in regard to the completeness of Parliament's powers:

(1) Freedom of conscience was to be guaranteed to all: 'matters of religion . . . are not at all entrusted by us to any human power.'

(2) Military conscription was to be prohibited.

(3) An act of indemnity was to be passed.

(4) All laws were to be binding on every citizen alike, charters or other property rights notwithstanding.

(5) All laws were to be equal and good, 'not evidently destructive to the safety and well-being of the people.'

These clauses were described as establishing 'our native rights' and were to be maintained against all opposition.

'The Case of the Army' 'added a number of particular demands': industrial monopolies were to be declared illegal and all trade made free; no man was to be obliged to testify against himself in a court of law; all laws were to be codified; usurped privileges were to be abolished; enclosed lands were to be restored to the poor; and sinecures were to be swept away. The theme of 'The Case of the Army' was that the Roundhead soldiers had been betrayed by their officers, who were conspiring with the House of Lords and with the Presbyterian party; and it was stated that the most pressing grievances of the rank-and-file were that their pay was being withheld from them because the public finances had been mismanaged and that the profits from the sales of bishops' lands had been dissipated through corruption.

These two declarations were plainly provocative and revolutionary in the extreme. ❨The strangeness of the times in which John Wildman lived is revealed by his daring to submit such startling ideas to the English generals and by the council of the army's readiness to discuss them. At this council seven representatives of the soldiers were invited to defend their point of view, since the officers had decided 'to send for those persons concerned in the papers.' Sexby, Allen and Lockyer, three of the original Agitators, presented themselves together with two 'soldiers' and two 'gentlemen.' John Wildman and Maximilian Petty were the 'gentlemen.' At the meeting Cromwell, although himself a participant in the debate, took the chair as senior officer, for Fairfax was not well.

The decision of Cromwell and Ireton to call the representatives of the soldiers into political consultation and to hear their grievances showed how conscious they were of the dangers of mutiny. Clearly—as the debates and their procrastinating tactics proved—they had no intention of conceding the republican and democratic demands of Wildman and his colleagues. Indeed after some brief preliminary skirmishing Henry Ireton launched a violent dialectical attack on 'The Agreement of the People.'

The debate was opened by Sexby, who summed up the existing political situation admirably from the Leveller point of view: 'The cause of our misery is upon two things. We sought to satisfy all men, and it was well; but in going to do it, we have dissatisfied all men. We have laboured to please a king, and I think, except we go about to cut all our throats, we shall not please him; and we have gone to support an house which prove rotten studs [props] I mean the Parliament which consists of a company of rotten members.' Cromwell and Ireton, he continued bluntly, had been especially guilty in intriguing to please King and Parliament, and their reputations had been 'blasted' in the army. 'These things I have represented as my thoughts,' concluded Sexby modestly, 'I desire your pardon.'

Cromwell indignantly denied that he had acted independently of the army council except in his other capacity as a member of the

House of Commons. When he spoke as a member of Parliament, he was speaking not for the army but only for himself and he was not ashamed of what he said. Ireton added that he refused to have anything to do with people that 'do seek the destruction of either Parliament or King.' In any case, he said, he was not there to give an account of his actions but to listen to the Levellers' proposals.

The Agitators' papers were then read. Cromwell immediately attacked 'The Agreement of the People' as academic, theoretical, impracticable, and, worst of all, 'tending to anarchy.' Nevertheless, he said, he wanted the discussion to continue in a spirit of Christian unity; he would first of all point out that the army was already committed by certain engagements and declarations that it had made and they would have to consider whether the new scheme could be reconciled with their former commitments. Like Ireton, Cromwell believed that John Wildman was the real author of the army's 'Case' and observed severely: 'You that are not soldiers you reckon yourselves at a loose and at a liberty, as men that have no obligations upon you.'

Wildman at once replied. He neither affirmed nor denied that he wrote the 'papers'; he merely accepted them. He was the 'mouth' of the soldiers. He took up Cromwell's point about engagements by demanding whether 'dishonest engagements' must be kept. If not, then surely, he argued, their business must be to consider whether the engagements which had been made by the army or in the name of the army were honest or not. The soldiers were entirely confident that their present proposals did not contradict any honest engagements which had been undertaken in their name.

Ireton answered by pointing out that 'The Case of the Army' had in fact started by outlining ten 'breaches' that had been recently made in the army's declarations or engagements; and he went on to assert that the fulfilment of contracts was the basis of all law and all government: supposing I promise to pay you a sum of money and then consider that my promise was exacted unfairly, have I the right to refuse to pay? As to the Agitators' papers he agreed with some things in them and disagreed with others, but —like Cromwell—he repeated that they must first discuss how far they were already pledged by their previous undertakings. If

C

Wildman, who was not in the army, 'held himself absolved from all engagements,' surely the Agitators, who were soldiers, would stand by the declarations of the army?

Vice-Admiral Rainsborough, a Republican who had delayed taking up his duties in the navy in order to participate in the debate in his capacity as a colonel in the army, replied to Ireton. One must, he thought, put one's 'bounden duty to God' and one's conscience before everything else. Neither dangers nor difficulties nor even the argument that 'The Agreement of the People' would alter the laws of the kingdom as they were 'ever since it was a kingdom' should deter them if they felt that it was the proper constitution for free men to live under. Cromwell now intervened with the proposal that a small sub-committee should be formed in which the officers should discuss with the Agitators which of their engagements were righteous and which were not. Colonel Thomas Goffe, an enthusiastic sectarian, suggested that, better still, they should all adjourn and seek God's help in composing their differences. The representatives of the soldiers felt a little suspicious about this; Cromwell assured them that they knew better than to make use of 'religious meetings as covers for designs or for insinuation amongst you,' but Wildman refused to be diverted from 'the business in hand.'

Wildman now tried to answer Ireton's telling criticism that, whereas in 'The Case of the Army' the soldiers had laid stress upon the importance of the army's engagements, they were at present arguing that engagements need not necessarily be kept. Wildman attempted to draw a distinguishing line between a mutual contract which could not be violated without the concurrence of both contracting parties and a general engagement to accept anything that another might command. For example, suppose 'a true Parliament . . . make an unjust law, though they make an un-righteous law,' must we obey? Surely, he said, that cannot be the case. Indeed had not the army itself declared 'that they stood upon principles of right and freedom and the laws of nature and nations'? Suppose that the Presbyterian Parliament now came to terms with the King and forced upon them the restoration of the monarchy, were they to consent to such an arrangement merely because they felt under a general obligation to obey Parliament? Ought they not, rather, to return to the principles which the army accepted on

14th June, namely that the rights of the people in parliament be 'absolutely insisted on.' If a thing is the people's due, no engagement can prohibit it.

Ireton expressed deep indignation that Wildman had reverted to mundane matters when, as Colonel Goffe had proposed, they should have been turning their minds to higher things. Indeed, if he did not think that there was 'venom and poison' in Wildman's words, he would not have answered them. He then argued that Wildman was playing with terms. Whatever might be true of divine justice, the basis of human justice was 'that we should keep covenant one with another.' In other words Ireton argued, as Thomas Hobbes, the philosopher of despotism, was arguing about the same time, justice and legality were interchangeable terms. If it is 'just' that I should keep my engagements, how can anyone talk of an unjust engagement? Wildman had invoked the law of nature, but that is a meaningless phrase: 'If you will resort only to the law of nature,' Ireton said, 'you have no more right to this land or anything else than I have.' If by the law of nature one may break a contract, why should any contract ever be kept? Wildman's democratic doctrines therefore undermined the whole fabric of civilized society.

Wildman wriggled somewhat under this analysis and began to shift his ground. He said that he doubted whether there could be a true engagement to an unjust thing, but he begged the army council to lay engagements aside and consider 'whether it be unjust to bring in the King in such a way as he may be in a capacity to destroy the people.' Evidently some of the younger members of the council were growing bored with the theoretic arguments (fascinating though they may be to the political theorist three hundred years later), for one of the captains remarked: 'Mr. Wildman says, if we tarry long, if we stay but three days before you satisfy one another, the King will come and say who will be hanged first.'

Ireton, however, was anxious that the council should appreciate the essentials of political philosophy. He once more explained his theory of justice and grappled with Wildman's formula: 'We are not bound so absolutely to personal obedience to any magistrates or personal authority that if they work to our destruction we may not oppose them,' by asking how one was to define the word 'destructive.' Any man will conceive anything destructive to himself if he happens to dislike it. If a general turns his guns on his soldiers, the soldiers have a clear right to resist him, but they had no right to disobey his orders whenever they fancied that they were unjust. Cromwell now interposed with a magisterial speech from the chair, calculated to wind up the debate or at any rate to postpone it. They ought, he said, now to adjourn and consult God. 'I shall speak only two things to Mr. Wildman.' Wildman had urged that while they were debating the King and Parliament would come to terms behind their backs. But the soldiers' representatives, including Wildman, had also said that they came to the council only as delegates; they could not compromise or do anything else without consulting their principals. If this were so, surely it was a far more fruitful cause of delay than anything else? He therefore begged the Agitators to come to the next meeting, not as delegates but as plenipotentiaries. After some further desultory discussion, in which Wildman reiterated his point about unjust engagements, the meeting broke up.

On the following day, in accordance with Goffe's proposals, officers and Agitators met and prayed while some preached in turn, all through the morning. When afternoon came there had been no time for the sub-committee set up to consider engagements to meet. Cromwell therefore urged the council to postpone its consideration of 'The Agreement of the People' until the next day. But his motion was defeated, and as both he and Ireton swore that they had given no private or personal promises to the King or Parliament, it was agreed to be reasonable that they should all consider whether 'The Agreement of the People' violated the public pledges of the army.

The first clause of 'The Agreement,' which was in favour of manhood suffrage, was then read, and Ireton at once asserted that it was contrary 'to the fundamental and original civil constitution of this kingdom.' This argument did not appear to cut much ice, and Colonel Rainsborough intervened to define the democratic point of view: 'I think,' he said, 'that the poorest he that is in England hath a life to live, as the greatest he; and therefore truly, sir, I think it's clear, that every man that is to live under a government ought first by his own consent to put himself under that government; and I do think that the poorest man in England is not at all bound in a strict sense to that government that he hath not had a voice to put himself under.'

Henry Ireton now fired his full anti-democratic batteries: 'I think that no person hath a right to an interest or share in the disposing of the affairs of the kingdom . . . that hath not a permanent fixed interest in the kingdom.' A man without property, he argued, has no concern with national stability and therefore is a menace to all governments. The franchise, he thought, must be a property franchise and be limited to those with a stake in the country. No man without land or goods had a right to a vote. And although he was not against the redistribution of parliamentary seats according to numerical equality he 'would have an eye to property.'

In a conciliatory manner Cromwell threw his weight on to Ireton's side:

'The consequence of this [democratic] rule tends to anarchy, must end in anarchy: for where is there any bound or limit set if you take away this [limit], that men that have no interest but the interest of breathing [shall have no voice in elections]?' Colonel Rich also argued on the same side: 'You have five to one in this kingdom that have no present interest. Some men [have] ten, some twenty servants, some more, some less. If the master and servant shall be equal electors, then clearly those that have no interest in the kingdom will make it their interest to choose those that have no interest. It may happen that the majority may by law, not in a confusion, destroy property; there may be a law enacted that there shall be an equality of goods and estates.' Democracy was therefore evil, for it led inevitably to communism.

At this point Wildman took up the debate. They had been arguing, he said, about the difficulties that might arise from manhood suffrage 'judging the justness of a thing by the consequence,' but what they had failed to decide was whether manhood suffrage was or was not right in itself. Let us forget our past constitution, he said. We have been slaves, our laws made by our conquerors; now we are engaged for our freedom: 'Every person in England hath as clear a right to elect his representative as the greatest person in England. I conceive that's the undeniable maxim of government: that all government is in the free consent of the people . . . [can any person] justly be bound by law, who doth not give his consent that such persons shall make laws for him?'

Ireton answered this last question by saying that resident foreigners were in fact so bound, a debating point to which Wildman boldly answered that a naturalized foreigner ought to have the same voting rights as a native. For some time the debate continued to circle round the argument that democracy means the destruction of property and ultimately a reign of anarchy, while from the chair Cromwell, although believing Ireton's arguments unanswerable, urged a compromise or a sub-committee. Finally the decision was postponed.

Ireton then reverted in a singularly uncompromising spirit to the thorny question of 'engagements.' He said that he thought that so far the army had kept its engagements pretty well. Take, for example, their engagement 'not to divide.' Were not the Agitators themselves the only breeders of division? Rainsborough pertinently observed that he was unaware that when the army swore not to divide they had all promised to hold the same opinions. Ireton then said that he saw no fundamental difference of opinion between his 'Heads of the Proposals' and the Agitators' 'Agreement of the People.' One of the Agitators pointed out that 'The Agreement' did not set up the King and House of Lords in their old glory as the 'Proposals' seemed to do, and Wildman pleaded the Agitators' right to advocate 'more speedy vigorous actings.' He urged that there were many items in Ireton's scheme contrary to the causes for which they had fought: Ireton, he said, would give King and Lords control over the army, and was prepared to restore the King's right of veto, 'thus making Parliament so many round O's.' Hence they must come back and meet the need, stressed by 'The Agreement,' for a clear definition of the inalienable rights of the people. Unless these were defined, any act of indemnity could be nullified by the King and some future parliament. Ireton said acidly that there was no doubt Wildman knew 'The Case of the Army' by heart, but it was a violent attack on the army council and therefore the council could not stomach it. As to the King and Lords the army had engaged itself to uphold them, but it was quite untrue to say that the 'Proposals' maintained the King's right of veto. In a long speech he defended the army council's actions and denied that they were incompatible with any of the army's joint declarations. Wildman replied: 'I do not know what reason you have to suppose I should be so well acquainted with "The Case of

38

the Army" and the things proposed in it,' and quoted the text of the 'Proposals' to prove that the King's veto had been reduced only 'in one particular,' namely that he could not overrule the House of Commons' decisions about the redistribution of the constituencies. Otherwise the King was to be restored to all his personal rights. That, argued Wildman, is his full restoration and a restoration accepted before the people's grievances have even been considered. With this speech the day's debate closed.

It is clear that Wildman felt rather bitter at the way in which the debates had been going and, in particular, at the manner in which Cromwell had conducted the proceedings from the chair; for on 29th October he issued a lengthy broadsheet which he addressed 'to all the soldiers of the army' from 'the free people of England.' He warned them to 'take heed of crafty politicians and subtle Machiavellians' and to be 'sure to trust no man's painted words'; one of the 'surest marks of the deceiver,' he continued, 'is to make fair, long and eloquent speeches.' He broke no bones over explaining of whom he was talking. It was Cromwell and Ireton who were 'holding forth to you the bloody flag of threats and terrors, talked on nothing but faction, dividing principles, anarchy,' and the like. He begged the soldiers not to be frightened by the word 'anarchy': for was it not flaunted only by those who had a love for monarchy which was but 'the gilded name for tyranny'? Indeed since Cromwell and Ireton had already accepted in the House of Commons the decision to carry on negotiations with the King, was not the whole procedure of debating the Levellers' proposals at Putney but an elaborate hypocrisy? That was why the representatives of the soldiers at Putney found that their hopes of realizing their 'joint and just cause' 'daily died within them.' Let them deal plainly with Cromwell and Ireton before it was too late: 'If Cromwell instantly repent not and alter his course, let him know also that ye loved and honoured just, honest, sincere, and valiant Cromwell that loved his country and the liberties of the people above his life, yea, and hated the King as a man of blood, but that Cromwell ceasing to be such, he ceaseth to be the object of your love.' Let them stick together and be of good courage and they might yet achieve the Levellers' millennium.

It must be remembered that Wildman was a young fanatic, reluctant, as young men are, to trust experience or to compromise.

Moreover the continued support of the rank-and-file, who were in fact always keener on obtaining their 'just rights,' including their back pay, than on erecting a revolutionary form of government, was the only weapon which Wildman had to use against Cromwell. In reality the trend of the debate had not yet gone against the Levellers and Cromwell was more than willing to meet them half-way if he could but unify the army. Indeed on the very next day when the sub-committee of the army council and of the Agitators, which had been proposed by Cromwell, met, it agreed on a number of important points about the election and duration of Parliaments over which there had been differences between Ireton and the Levellers. Wildman was not on this sub-committee. A compromise was also reached over the suffrage question, the soldiers who had fought in the civil war being promised a vote, although the principle of manhood suffrage was not accepted.

On Sunday, 1st November, the General Council, including Wildman, again met, and after prayers and several sermons Cromwell opened the proceedings with a plea that the army must recognize the validity of the existing Parliament because it was the sole legal basis of authority left in the State, and he begged the army to be united within itself and to maintain war-time discipline. After some desultory talk Cromwell came to the point left untouched by the compromise of the sub-committee, namely the future of the King and of the House of Lords. He urged that although all parties were agreed that they could not be restored to their former rights, only the Agitators were in favour of their complete abolition. In these circumstances the only way in which they could reach an agreed solution was for them to let their minds be guided by a Christian spirit and trust that 'God will lead us to what shall be His way.'

Wildman felt doubtful whether their differences could be solved by reference to God, since every man interpreted the mind of God in his own way. The best that they could do was to apply the divine standards of justice and mercy to the matter in hand. Is it, he inquired, 'demonstrable by reason or justice [that it is right] to punish with death those that according to his [the King's] command made war . . . and then [to say] that there is a way left for mercy for him who was the great actor of this, and who was the great contriver of all?' Wildman spoke as an unrepentant and convinced Republican.

Then came a misunderstanding, fruit of a deeper antagonism, between Cromwell, hitherto the consistent supporter of monarchy, and Wildman the Republican. Wildman had asserted that Cromwell had drawn a distinction between those who wanted to 'preserve' and those who did not want to preserve the King and Lords.

CROMWELL: 'Sir, I did not speak of the *destroying* of the King and Lords—I have not heard any man charge all the Lords so to deserve punishment—but [of] reserving to them any interest at all in the public affairs of the kingdom.'

WILDMAN: 'Then, sir, as I conceive, you were saying the difference was this: that some persons were of opinion that the preservation of the power of King and Lords was paramount to all considerations and might keep them from any giving them what was due and right.'

CROMWELL: 'I said that while some men did apprehend that there might be an interest to them [the King and Lords] with safety to the kingdom, others do think that no part of their interest could be given without destruction of the kingdom.'

WILDMAN: 'For the matter of stating the thing in difference, I think that the person of King and Lords are not so joined together by any; for as yourself said, none have any exception against the persons of the Lords or the name of Lords. But the difference is whether we should alter the old foundations of our government so as to give to King and Lords that which they could never claim before.'

He then argued that the King by his coronation oath, which binds him to grant such laws as the people shall choose, implicitly denies his own right to make laws. To give the King the right to veto laws is therefore to give him a right which he had never possessed but had in fact usurped. As for the Lords, 'seeing the foundation of all justice is the election of the people,' it is unjust that a non-elective body should have the power to make or veto laws.

Henry Ireton then defended at length the position of the King's veto in the 'Heads of the Proposals.' Wildman thought that their differences were as wide as ever and that the act for triennial parliaments, advocated by Ireton, would establish the powers of the King and Lords more firmly than they had been established before. 'I conceive,' he added later, 'that whilst we thus run into such particulars there is very little probability of coming to satisfaction. The case, as there it is stated in 'The Agreement,' is general; and it will never satisfy the godly people in the kingdom unless that all government be in the Commons, and freely.' It was all very well for Ireton to say that no law could be made without the consent of the Commons, but that presupposed some other lawmaker besides the Commons. So long as no law can be made without it being sent to the King and Lords for review, 'the kingdom cannot be in safety' and the King's party 'may get up and do what he will.'

Ireton asked Wildman what evidence he had, apart from his dubious interpretation of the terms of the coronation oath, for saying that the King and Lords never had any real constitutional rights. After some squabbling over early history and political maxims, Wildman summed up their differences as being over whether or not they should permit the King to resume his functions in such a way that the House of Commons had to petition him for confirmation of every Act that it passed. One of the speakers had said that they were fighting over shadows. Wildman retorted that it was no shadow but a substance 'when nothing shall be made but by address to the King. This will be very shameful in future chronicles, that after so much blood there should be no better an issue for the Commons.'

'Do you think we have not now laws good enough for the securing of the rights of the Commons?' demanded Ireton.

'I think,' answered Wildman, 'that according to the letter of the law, if the King will, he may kill me by law.'

Ireton assured him that they would see that the King did not kill him or any other man except by due process of law.

'I shall be glad of it,' retorted Wildman, and 'if not, I am but a single man; I shall venture myself and my share in the common bottom.'

So closed these remarkable debates in so far as they have survived for later generations to read. But the meeting and committees continued for several days longer, during which the Levellers temporarily gained the upper hand and Ireton eventually walked out in a huff. In spite of the acrimony of the debates—an acrimony more superficial than real—some progress at length had been made towards reaching an agreement. On 2nd November a committee representing both officers and Agitators recommended:—

(1) that in future the House of Commons should have the final decision in the making and execution of all laws affecting the commoners of England except in such fundamentals as were reserved:

(2) that no law should be made or repealed which affected the commoners of England without the consent of the House of Commons:

(3) that the House of Commons should be the supreme court of appeal for all commoners:

(4) that all officers of justice and Ministers of State should be accountable to the Commons, but that peers [except in an official capacity] should be judged only by peers:

(5) that no persons could be pardoned by the King without the consent of Parliament:

(6) that the people hold as fundamental principles which Parliament could not upset:—

(a) matters of religion—'not to be trusted to any human power':

(b) no commoner to be forcibly enlisted except for the immediate defence of the kingdom:

(c) no commoner to be prosecuted for the part that he took in the civil war (without the consent of the Commons):

(d) the laws about electing Parliaments and the regular meeting of Parliament could not be altered.

The recommendations of the committee represented a reasonable compromise which, it was decided, should be submitted for the approval of Parliament—a decision about which the Levellers took the poorest possible view. And indeed it was plainly unlikely that the House of Commons would take much notice of a scheme which restricted its own powers. Nevertheless the scheme is of importance as showing the prevailing feeling in the army which was in the end to determine the structure of the new Government.

On 4th November the council moved forward again and accepted the Leveller principle of manhood suffrage. Moreover, on the 5th, Guy Fawkes Day, the council went so far as to send a resolution to the House of Commons dissociating the army from any further scheme for reopening negotiations with Charles I. This resolution represented the peak of the Levellers' success—the summit of John Wildman's hopes. Three days later Oliver Cromwell, who apparently had been absent from these meetings, turned against Wildman and the Agitators. Under his influence the decisions of 4th and 5th November were reversed; the Agitators were sent back to their regiments and, inspired by Oliver's powerful direction, the next meeting of the full council was postponed indefinitely.

So the final result of the Putney meetings was that only a partial reconciliation had been effected between Ireton's and Wildman's constitutional programmes. On two points, however, the general officers, after a momentary wavering, became adamant: first, they would not agree to accept manhood suffrage—it tended, in Cromwell's words, 'too much to anarchy.' Secondly, they refused to try the King for murder as 'a man of blood.' Yet these were the two essential preliminaries to Wildman's brave new world, the two necessary measures without which, he believed, his democratic republic could not be established. Oliver Cromwell was to give way over the trial of King Charles I after the second civil war. But so far from this ushering in democracy, it was to pave the way for military dictatorship, a dictatorship which Wildman was to resist to the end.

To the student of political ideas these three-hundred-year-old debates have a peculiar interest because for the first time in our history one man came forward to advocate *both* democracy *and* republicanism. Throughout the Middle Ages writers and preachers had asserted that a ruler's absolutism must be qualified on the ground that the secular arm should always be subject to the spiritual. The Reformation did not, as Montesquieu maintained, make for republicanism. On the contrary, the first result of Protestantism was to strengthen the system of monarchy by allowing the ruler to choose his country's religion. But after the monarch's power had temporarily been strengthened in England by the King becoming Supreme Head of the Church, critics of the State religion again began to maintain that the monarch had no right to order consciences. The great forward impulse to liberal political ideas came from the religious minorities. A 'law of nature' overruling established laws and customs was invoked by many different authors to permit resistance to the sovereign. And once it was admitted that subjects might disobey or even depose their sovereign by an undefined law of nature a democratic tendency became observable. The Levellers pushed the 'law of nature' argument to its logical conclusion by claiming that there were many principles of government to which not only the King but any sovereign power must be subject.

Republicanism, on the other hand, as we have seen, usually arose from more pragmatic causes and on more practical grounds— in the Netherlands from the tyranny of Philip II of Spain, in England from the obstinacy of Charles I. An active minority seized political power, as is customary in time of revolution, but without the slightest intention of sharing it with the common people.

Wildman was convinced before Cromwell that Charles I and the majority of the existing House of Lords would never accept those qualifications upon the absolute exercise of sovereignty which were necessary to guarantee liberty of conscience and freedom from restraint of trade. Consequently he supported both democracy and republicanism simultaneously. That was his unique contribution. The democratic movement made little or no progress during the seventeenth century and, as we shall see, Wildman himself became persuaded that it was not practicable. On the other hand, republicanism, that is to say, government not by one individual but by a limited ruling class, was to be introduced for an experimental period, and never again in our history after the Puritan Rebellion was a sovereign able to claim as wide powers as did James I or to exert such sweeping control over affairs of state as the Tudors had done.

CHAPTER IV

LEVELLER AND SCAPEGOAT

If Cromwell be an honest man, then I will never trust an honest man again.

JOHN WILDMAN, 1648

THE final result of the Putney debates therefore was to make the Levellers profoundly dissatisfied with the leaders of the army. John Wildman's ambition when he came to Putney had been to induce the army to assent to a written democratic republican constitution, which it should impose on Parliament, ignoring and deposing the King. Instead of that, Parliament had been allowed to continue negotiations with Charles I and was merely to be invited to accept what, in his view, was only a watered-down version of Henry Ireton's scheme, 'The Heads of the Proposals'; and 'The Heads of the Proposals' were distasteful in the extreme to Wildman, for had they not been modified to suit the susceptibilities of a guilty monarch?

According to the rough draft of 'The Heads of the Proposals,' Wildman complained, there was to have been a restriction on the King's veto, no Royalist who had taken part in the civil war could hold public office for ten years, and the King was to approve the abolition of the bishops. But the amended scheme was allowed 'to depend upon the King's absolute will.' The King's right of veto was upheld, Royalists were to be admitted to power in five years or less, and only the coercive powers of the bishops were abolished. Oppressive courts, tithes, monopolies, and forest laws were also retained. 'The Heads of the Proposals,' he said, embodied in a new form all the old 'enslavery principles' of kingship. 'Is this, O Cromwell,' asked Wildman, 'the right of the people in their Parliaments which you would engage our lives to secure?'

The anger of the Levellers, which was vented by Wildman, determined Cromwell to take strong measures. He persuaded Fairfax, the nominal commander-in-chief, who had returned to Putney when the constitutional debates were almost finished, to split the army into three brigades and to put a stop to all further

46

discussions, although to compensate the soldiers for their agents being sent back to their regiments they were promised a periodic 'rendezvous' or general meeting at an indefinite future date: and, as a sop to the Levellers, yet another sub-committee was appointed on 9th November, including Cromwell and Wildman, to consider the old question whether the proposals of the Agitators were compatible with the 'engagements' of the army. But this was a mere piece of procrastination, and the sub-committee never appears to have met. Indeed Oliver Cromwell knew that he had given a challenge to the Levellers. For at about the same time he wrote off to warn his cousin, Colonel Whalley, who was in charge of Charles I, now a prisoner at Hampton Court, to be on his guard lest the Levellers attempted to lay hands on the King as a counter-measure. The consequence of Cromwell's high-handed actions was to persuade the King to escape from Hampton Court the better to fish in troubled waters and to incite mutiny in the army.

On 12th November Charles I, to whom Whalley had shown Cromwell's letter, fled from Hampton Court to Carisbrooke castle in the Isle of Wight whence, he announced, he would in due course emerge from his 'cloud of retirement' and show himself the true 'Father of his Country.' On 15th November, when the army discovered that so far from being granted a general rendezvous, they were only to air their grievances in separate brigades, a mutiny broke out at Ware near Cambridge, two regiments appearing there without orders, the soldiers wearing 'The Agreement of the People' in their hats and the motto: 'England's Freedom, Soldiers' Rights.' Their intention, it is said, was to arrest Cromwell as a traitor. The mutiny was successfully suppressed, one officer being cashiered, and a soldier shot there and then on the field of war. The soldier was Trooper Arnold and he was the first martyr of republican democracy: 'It was death to observe the army's engagement, or but speak for the Agitators,' wrote Lilburne two years later. 'O let that day never be forgotten! let not the blood of that innocent person be here had out of remembrance till justice be had for the same.'

Once the Agitators had been dismissed, the army split up, and a ruthless example made of Trooper Arnold, the General Council of Army Officers was able to pursue its discussions in 'sweet harmony,' save for occasional critical interpolations by Vice-Admiral

Rainsborough, who was still reluctant to leave the scene of political intrigues and put out to sea.

Wildman returned to London—he had an office in St. Martin's le Grand—and, together with Lilburne, organized a campaign of speeches and propaganda directed both against the army chiefs and against the two Houses of Parliament. In December he published his able pamphlet, *Putney Projects* or *The Old Serpent in a New Form*, for the purpose of proving to the rank-and-file of the army how Cromwell and Ireton had abandoned their cause and been seduced by the temptations held out to them by the King. The pamphlet was published anonymously as 'presenting to the view of all the well affected in England the serpentine deceit of their pretended friends in the army endeavouring to introduce tyranny and slavery by a new method.'

Wildman's experiences in the debates at the council of the army had by no means altered his opinion expressed on 9th October that the army 'are betrayed by their officers who are entering into combination with the House of Lords and the Presbyterians.' In *Putney Projects* his information was obviously sufficiently accurate to sting Cromwell. It was probably supplied to him by Rainsborough, one of the representatives of the army who, together with Ireton and two others, negotiated with the King about 'The Heads of the Proposals' in July. The proclaimed object of the pamphlet was 'to unfold plainly the mystery of Cromwell's and Ireton's deceit.' Its motto was taken from Amos v. 19: 'It is with us as if we fled from a lion, and a bear met us, and fled from a bear, and leaning our hands on the wall a serpent bites us.' The language was sharp about Cromwell and Ireton—'these promising patriots' who 'were only sweet-mouthed courtiers' and whose conversations with the royal agents had demonstrated their 'palpable hypocrisy.' Had not the King's flatteries 'proved like poisoned arrows which infected all the blood in their veins?'

'O once much-honoured Cromwell,' Wildman appealed, 'can that breast of yours which was the quondam royal palace of principles of freedom and justice! can that breast harbour such a monster of wickedness as this regal principle?' Not only, said Wildman, was Cromwell a supporter of monarchy but also of the House of Lords, although in 1644 when he was infuriated by the military incompetence of the Earls of Manchester and Essex he had asserted that England would never flourish nor would public affairs be successfully managed as long as a House of Peers existed. 'O how much is he changed from that man!' observed the learned Wildman in Latin, 'O see your liberties prostrate at the feet of usurpers.'

Putney Projects contained yet another accusation against Oliver Cromwell: 'Had he not suffered that gallant champion for English freedom, Lieutenant-Colonel John Lilburne, to consume in prison by that usurped lordly power?' It was indeed so; since 1646 Lilburne, the Leveller chief, had languished in the Tower of London, although he had not been deprived of pen, ink, and paper, and had therefore been able to pour out a spate of pamphlets to assist Wildman's campaign condemning Cromwell's and Ireton's bargaining with King Charles I. The story, whether true or false, that Cromwell had been offered the Earldom of Essex as a payment for his services to Charles I was completely credited by Lilburne and given wide circulation by him. Nevertheless, in spite of verbal attacks of unmeasured violence launched against him by Lilburne, Cromwell had visited Lilburne in the Tower and had tried to extract from him a promise that if he were released he would not stir up further unrest in the army. Lilburne refused to give any promise, but on 9th November 1647, the last day of the Putney debates, he had been permitted by the House of Commons 'to go abroad from the Tower' on bail. It was not long before he was in trouble again.

Lilburne directed all his energies into the campaign which had been started by Wildman against Cromwell. Literature was disseminated and meetings held. One such meeting was arranged at Smithfield in January, 1648. Smithfield, lying to the north of the City, then, as now, was the great cattle market of London. The high excise duty, which had been imposed upon meat to help to pay the costs of the civil war, had aroused grave discontent among the butchers and buyers of the market. In February, 1647, a dangerous riot had broken out there, in which the excise collectors were cudgelled when a purchaser had refused to pay the excise on a bullock. It was therefore a suitable centre from which to carry on propaganda against the Government. The meeting was called to protest against Cromwell's whole handling of the political situation and was to take place in a private house on Monday, 17th January.

Meanwhile decisive political events were happening. Although, according to one of his courtiers, when Charles 1 left Hampton Court for the Isle of Wight he still hoped to come to terms with Cromwell, from his new refuge the King at once opened discussions with a number of commissioners who had been sent from Scotland to offer to restore him to his throne if he would promise in return to guarantee Presbyterian supremacy in England for three years and to suppress the Independents and all other rival religious sects. The English Parliament at the same time dispatched to Charles an ultimatum known as the 'Four Bills' which demanded control of the militia by Parliament for a period of ten years. The King did not hesitate for long over his choice between these two alternatives. By 28th December 1647 he had rejected the Four Bills and signed an 'Engagement' with the Scots. Although the 'Engagement' was buried deep in the garden of the castle where the King now dwelt, Cromwell was well aware of what was on foot. Angered by Charles's double-dealing, he determined to seek a means of settling the government of England without the King. Thus, while *Putney Projects* was being published, Cromwell and Ireton were actually abandoning the policy for which Wildman condemned them. On 3rd January 1648, with their approval, the House of Commons, reversing its previous vote, carried a motion that no further addresses should be made to the King, and a reconciliation between Cromwell and Rainsborough took place. Cromwell no longer ruled out the possibility of establishing a republic. The road thus appeared to be open for the Levellers to press upon the country and upon the army their plan to set up a republic and put the King on trial for his life. The meeting called at Smithfield formed part of their campaign to promote this policy.

A letter written by Lilburne, Wildman, and other Levellers to their adherents in Kent at the beginning of 1648 throws some light on the character of their campaign. 'Our bowels are troubled and our hearts part within us,' the latter ran, 'to behold the diversions, distractions, heart-burning and contentions which abound in this distressed nation.' 'Rumours and fears of war,' it continued, 'hath so wasted our trading and exhausted the prices of all food and clothing that famine is even entering our gates.' Let them, urged Lilburne and Wildman, determine now, after seven years of vainly waiting for justice, peace and freedom, that they would permit no denial of their demands. The Leveller headquarters 'appointed several active men in every ward and division of London and in the adjacent centres' to be campaign committees. Petitions were circularized for signature and meetings of support were organized.

The Smithfield meeting was held in a house belonging to a gardener on Ratcliffe Highway, Wapping. The object of its promoters was to collect signatures for a petition to the House of Commons in favour of the Leveller views. The petition attacked in particular the powers of the throne and the privileges of the House of Lords. The King, it urged, must be entirely deprived of his right of veto and the House of Lords of its legislative powers and criminal jurisdiction (except over its own members).

Lilburne opened the Smithfield meeting by explaining to the audience that Parliament had ordered them five years before to fight for their liberties but had never told them what their liberties were. They had been commanded to take up arms against their sovereign because he had betrayed the trust placed in him by the nation, and yet they had been informed in the very same breath that the King was the fountain of justice and could do no wrong. No wonder, he exclaimed, the people were bewildered and began to think that they had been fooled into waging war against the King. He urged them to sign the petition if only to 'beget knowledge and understanding' and to encourage people to read it and talk about it. The petition asked that all power should be derived from the House of Commons alone, that all limitations on the Commons' power of making laws should be abolished, and that the franchise should be extended to all males over twenty-one except beggars and criminals; that the law should be written in English and that there should be no court fees or bribery and that trials should be speedy; that monopolies and oaths should be done away with, taxation reduced, excise abandoned, and the poor law reformed. Lilburne boasted that the House of Lords had offered him £30,000 to lay the petition aside. But the petition was to be used in the main for propaganda purposes so as to convert the general public to the Leveller cause and convince those members of the House of Commons who really 'intended good to the Commonwealth.'

Wildman then took up the argument. He pointed out that unless quick settlement of the government were reached, the civil war would break out again—a strikingly accurate forecast. He argued that discontent was rife at that time not only because of the political anarchy but also on account of the economic instability; and he went on to quote the case of the Wiltshire clothiers who 'professed trading was so dead that some of them who set at work formerly a hundred [employees] did now set at work not above a dozen.' The unemployed could be seen gathering in groups on the roads and seizing the corn on its way to market because they were so short of food. The presence of the army in the City was also discouraging to business, for merchants were unwilling to send their goods to the shops out of fear that they would be requisitioned without payment. And he ended with the provocative statement that 'if Cromwell were an honest man, then he would never trust an honest man again.' And both Wildman and Lilburne made use of the argument that the delay by the House of Lords in passing a Bill in 1642 to put the control of the militia into the hands of Parliament had encouraged the King to veto the Bill and had so brought about the civil war.

One other speech was delivered at the meeting by a certain Mr. Hunt, who revived the story of the rewards held out to Cromwell by the King and added that Henry Ireton was to be made a Field-Marshal and Ireton's son a bedchamber man to the Prince of Wales. Mr. Hunt affirmed that he would rather become another Felton (the assassin of the first Duke of Buckingham) than 'allow all honest men to be destroyed.'

Wildman subsequently pointed out in a pamphlet called *The Triumph Stained*, which he wrote about this meeting, that these outspoken expressions of anger were due to the lack of trust now felt for Cromwell because of his change of attitude between October and January. In October, 1647, he had defended monarchy in a long speech in the House of Commons. As late as 15th November he had maintained that the King could not be held responsible for the civil war. But that same January he was arguing convincingly against any further negotiations between Parliament and the King. Yet surely Wildman must have known the real reason why Cromwell had suddenly shifted his ground. He must have guessed—it was evidently common knowledge at the beginning of 1648—that Charles I had rejected Cromwell's overtures in favour of those of the Scots who were willing to guarantee the royal right to veto

Bills and the power to control the militia in return for their 'special privileges' and a Presbyterian church government. Nevertheless suspicion over Cromwell's honesty or the honesty of his motives lay at the root of the agitation. The meeting appeared to be a success, for it did not end until a motion had been carried in support of the republican petition for which Lilburne and Wildman were seeking signatures.

Their propaganda campaign, however, was destined to go no further. A neighbouring Presbyterian minister, George Masterson by name, stigmatized by Lilburne as 'the lying shepherd of Shoreditch,' who had been present at the meeting, preferred a complaint before the House of Commons, accusing Lilburne and Wildman of using words 'tending to the dishonour of Parliament.' The main—and just—point in his charges was that they were trying to undermine the powers and prestige of the House of Lords.

Now it happened that on this very day the army had posted troops in Whitehall mews in order to coerce the House of Lords into accepting the vote of no further addresses to King Charles I. What could be a more admirable means of pleasing the House of Lords than to arrest these troublesome Levellers who had insulted the Upper House so grossly? After all, the subversive and anarchical doctrines of Lilburne and Wildman were just as menacing to the Grandees of the army and the country gentlemen in the House of Commons as they were to the peers of the realm; let them then become scapegoats, pledges of a better understanding between all those who had a stake in the country and an ambition to achieve full political supremacy in the kingdom. On 18th January the Serjeant-at-Arms was commanded to arrest Lilburne and Wildman, and on the following day they were ordered to be committed to the Tower and the Fleet prison respectively, there to await trial for sedition.

Lilburne and Wildman, however, refused to give themselves up quietly, and on the next day (20th January) the Houses of Parliament learned that they had not yet been captured and 'that some of their party had given out words that they should not go to prison.' A monster protest meeting was called in Deptford, Kent, to uphold the justice of their cause and the arguments of the republican petition. Guards were ordered out to assist the Serjeant-at-Arms in the performance of his duty, and the

Parliamentary Committee in Kent was instructed to suppress all meetings in the county and to prevent riots. In London the militia was called out to prevent any protest meetings in the City.

This employment of force was successful, although Lilburne managed to convert one of the soldiers who had been sent to arrest him. The two prisoners were brought before the bar of the House of Commons on the afternoon of 20th January. They both refused to recognize its jurisdiction and demanded to be tried by common law. 'Mr. Speaker,' said Wildman, 'I come not here in reference to this informer or on legal warrant but out of respect to the House.' He quoted Mr. Justice Coke and other authorities to prove that an arrest on the evidence of a single informer was illegal, and after describing what had happened at the Wapping meeting, he argued that neither his discussion of the unrest among the poor of Wiltshire nor of the privileges of the House of Lords was treasonable within the meaning of the Act of Edward III or was contrary to Magna Carta. After the House had considered Lilburne's and Wildman's pleas until it was dark and candles had to be brought in, they were each duly committed to their separate prisons, there to remain without trial—in spite of many petitions for their release—for a period of six months.

Later in 1648 a rumour began to go the rounds that in order to obtain their political ends Wildman and Lilburne had not been content merely to summon meetings and to collect signatures for petitions but had made up their minds to stop at nothing. Denzil Holles, M.P., who had been one of the eleven Presbyterians to be expelled from the House of Commons by the army, wrote in his *Memoirs*: 'The Leveller party, as appears by that business of Lilburne and Wildman, even resolve to take Cromwell out of the way and murder him for an apostate.' This was written during February, 1648, and obviously refers to the Smithfield affair. It may indeed have been directly copied from a pamphlet by George Masterson, called *Truth's Triumph* (which Wildman answered in *The Triumph Stained*), for Masterson asserted that at the meeting Wildman had said he knew three other men besides himself who had resolved to kill Cromwell. Although this story was accepted by Godwin, a respectable nineteenth-century historian of the British Commonwealth, Holles's evidence, even when strengthened by that of Masterson, would of course not hang a dog. Other stories which were current at the same time were that Henry Marten, that licentious Republican, was planning not only to depose the King but also to murder Cromwell. The Leveller leaders were also said to have been ready to assassinate the King if they but had the chance. So impressed was Henry Lilburne, a brother of 'Freeborn John,' with this last story that during the second civil war he decided to betray Tynemouth castle, which had been entrusted to his charge, to the Royalists.

Although there is only a shred of evidence against him at this date Wildman's participation during later years in murder plots against Cromwell and James II obliges his biographer, if he would be conscientious, to curb his moral indignation at historians who have ventured to believe that Wildman was ready to let one man die for the people.

CHAPTER V

THE MAN IN A MASK?

God hath made you instruments of liberty. In matters of religion
that's preferred by us before life. Let's have that or nothing.
                                        JOHN WILDMAN, December, 1648

D URING the course of his first term of imprisonment in the Tower
of London John Lilburne had met Sir John Maynard, an old
friend, although he belonged to an entirely different political party.
Maynard had begun his political career by attaching himself to the
first Duke of Buckingham, the unpopular Minister and favourite of
Charles I. Maynard had not entered the House of Commons until
January, 1647, when by reason of his obvious abilities he had at once
become prominent as a member of the parliamentary Committee
of Safety. In this capacity, because he was a sturdy Presbyterian
and a suspected secret Cavalier, he incurred the hostility of Cromwell and Ireton. He was named one of the eleven members most
obnoxious to the army Grandees, charged by them with 'unlaw-
fully levying an armed force in the City' in order to protect the
integrity of Parliament, and finally committed to the Tower in
September, 1647, when he met Lilburne. At this particular point
of time Lilburne was in the unusual position of having been
deprived of ink and paper, but as he appreciated that Maynard's
case was a useful stick with which to beat the army leaders and
their creature, the 'purged' House of Commons, he asked John
Wildman to write a pamphlet on Maynard's case.

It is necessary to understand why Wildman undertook this piece
of special pleading for a man who did not belong to the republican
party. Maynard's case was exactly the same as Lilburne's and as
Wildman's was soon to be. All three were put into prison without
trial by mere order of an unrepresentative House of Commons and
'during the pleasure of Parliament.' All three had been singled out
as victims of the special dislike of Cromwell and of Ireton. The
pamphlet was in fact one of those instances where political principles yield place to political tactics.

The Law's Subversion or Sir John Maynard's Case Truly Stated was published by Wildman under the pseudonym of John Howldin shortly before his appearance at the Wapping meeting. It explained that what had kindled the indignation of Cromwell and his son-in-law, that 'puny colonel,' who had been advanced by favouritism after the battle of Naseby, was Maynard's bold declarations against the partiality, ambition, covetousness, and injustice of the Grandees of the army. Merely because he was a conscientious Presbyterian (and who was Wildman, ever the tolerationist, to gainsay another man's religion?) he was impeached, illegally arrested, and expelled the House of Commons. Had not the Commons, demanded Wildman, arrogated to itself jurisdiction above the common law? To throw a man into the Tower for his political opinions simply because they were opposed to those of the army leaders—was that the liberty of the subject for which the civil war had been fought? Although Maynard (like Wildman himself later) had pleaded Magna Carta and the Petition of Right, the House of Lords, 'tools of the swordsmen,' had rejected his defence. Oliver Cromwell had chosen to disregard the ancient liberties of the land: 'O that every Englishman would hearken to the graves of dying liberties!' exclaimed Wildman in a mixed metaphor straight from the heart. Sir John Maynard was soon to demonstrate his gratitude for this surprising advocacy.

But for a time Wildman and Lilburne had to remain in their respective prisons while events moved slowly but certainly in the direction of a second civil war. Since the failure of Parliament and the army to reach agreement over a new constitution for the kingdom, people generally, or at any rate the politically conscious, had grown more and more dissatisfied. Had the first civil war, they asked, been fought for nothing? Were the victories of Marston Moor and Naseby meaningless? Were the Cromwellians content to have destroyed the Royalists and imprisoned the King, and put nothing in their place?

At Christmas, 1647, it had begun to seem as if puritanism in its political aspect was a purely negative creed. The 'pagan' festivities of holly and mistletoe were forbidden, no plays might be performed in London, all teachers with a taint of royalism were banned—such were some of the manifestations of the puritanical 'no.' But no positive plan to rehabilitate a divided country had been accepted. The Levellers had a plan, as outlined in Wildman's 'Agreement of the People' and in the Wildman-Lilburne petition of January, 1648, for a democratic government without the King. And in March Henry Marten had proposed that the House of Commons should depose the King to clear the way for a republic. The Royalists had their plan to take advantage of the growing political confusion and discontent against the puritans to rescue the King and win back his throne. Even the King had a scheme to regain his ancient glory, although it were a little tarnished, by calling in the aid of the rigid Scottish Covenanters.

But Cromwell, it seemed, had no concrete plan. Although in February he had made 'a severe invective against monarchical government' and had even attacked a lawyer for questioning the view that Charles 1 had acquiesced in the (alleged) poisoning of his own father, by April he was again vainly attempting to induce the King to accept a modification of 'The Heads of the Proposals.' At length, however, Cromwell was drawn away from ineffective diplomatic negotiations to work he knew how to do—fighting; for in May, 1648, a discontented colonel had raised the standard of revolt at Pembroke castle and in July the Duke of Hamilton's Scottish army had invaded England in the King's name.

The attitude of Parliament, the nominal ruler of the country, to the ensuing conflict was most peculiar. A large section of the House of Commons was not unsympathetic to the Scots' desire to enforce the Covenant at the point of the sword and thereby make England into a realm governed by a Presbyterian Church. The House of Lords even refused to declare the Scots to be national enemies. And while heavy fighting was in progress, parliamentary commissioners calmly continued to negotiate in the Isle of Wight with the royal prisoner on whose behalf the war had been revived. Indeed while Cromwell and his army were battling with the Scots, Parliament was plotting to overthrow him.

On 3rd June Sir John Maynard was released from the Tower and at once took a leading part in the latest campaign against Cromwell, advocating a personal treaty with the King. Ten days later Lilburne, now in Newgate, optimistically sued his gaoler for unlawful imprisonment. He was allowed to put his case, but on 23rd June he was recommitted and again deprived of pen and paper and of access to his friends outside.

Lilburne and Wildman were not, however, to remain in prison

much longer. Once more a powerful petition was drawn up in the City and on 2nd August a grateful Sir John Maynard addressed the House of Commons on their behalf. He urged that their committal was more worthy of a prerogative court like the Star Chamber than of an enlightened assembly. Let them, he urged, henceforward imprison none but their own members and avoid these 'old Council Table warrants.' It was true, he added, that Lilburne, 'this brave, invincible spirit,' had made some ill-conceived remarks about them, but did not Solomon observe with justice that 'oppression will make a wise man mad'? After this the Commons unanimously agreed to their release and the House of Lords promptly concurred.

Samuel Gardiner many years ago drew attention to the remarkable fact that the Lords and Commons, who agreed with each other about nothing else, should at this time have unanimously consented to the release of these two obstreperous Leveller leaders. We cannot doubt his explanation that this act of clemency was part of the movement against Cromwell. As pawns they had been imprisoned and as pawns they were now released. Justice slept, as is customary in time of civil war. On the very same day as their release—2nd August—two other things happened. A committee was appointed by Parliament to wait on the King with proposals for a personal treaty and Major Huntington, who had once been in Cromwell's confidence, charged his former chief with high treason. We have Lilburne's own view of the reason for his release. He was offered, he said, his chance to revenge himself on Cromwell by joining in Huntington's impeachment. 'I scorned it,' he wrote, 'and rather applied myself to help him [Cromwell] up again, as not being favourable to a Scottish interest.' On 3rd August, 'the second day of my freedom,' Lilburne dispatched a letter of warning and encouragement to Cromwell. This letter, Lilburne was informed, was 'not a little welcome to him' and, with the letter in his pocket, Cromwell proceeded to overwhelm Hamilton's superior army at the battle-and-rout of Preston. In the following month Lilburne went north and talked to Cromwell, but was gravely disappointed with the result of his interview. For he found him 'more self-exalting than really and heartily prepared to advance our liberties and freedom.' He therefore returned to London, where Wildman was awaiting him.

The scheme now decided upon by the Levellers was to exploit Charles I's 'treachery' in bringing about the renewal of the civil wars by rallying converts, especially among the Independents in the army, to the cause of a democratic constitution. A meeting in support of this campaign was arranged at the Nag's Head Tavern by Blackwell Hall, at which (according to Lilburne) 'we had a large debate of things, and where the just ends of the war were as exactly laid open by Mr. Wildman as ever I heard in my life.' The meeting declared itself against cutting off the King's head and in favour of an immediate constitutional settlement. This decision was reached on Lilburne's advice. He argued that even if they admitted that both the King and Parliament were evil and tyrannical 'yet there being no other balancing power in the kingdom against the army but the King and Parliament, it was our interest to keep up one tyrant to balance another, till we certainly know what that tyrant that pretended fairest would give us [as] our freedom.'

A committee was now set up to frame another 'Agreement of the People.' The committee consisted of five Independents (including Henry Marten), four army officers (including Ireton), and four Levellers (including Lilburne and Wildman). A preliminary understanding was reached at the Nag's Head on 15th November. This provided that the 'well-affected people' in each county should send delegates to army headquarters in order to sign a contract defining the limits of the future powers of Parliament and that the existing Parliament should subsequently be dissolved and be replaced by a new one elected according to the terms of the fresh 'Agreement of the People.' A series of meetings followed, and finally in December they all gathered in Whitehall to debate.

On 10th December, on the eve of these debates, Lilburne's committee had completed and passed by a majority its new 'Agreement of the People' which Lilburne also described as the 'Foundations of Freedom.' The 'Agreement' proposed that the franchise should be confined to householders assessed for poor relief, that the powers of Parliament should be drastically revised, and that a single-chamber Parliament should be elected. There was a list of eight reservations on the powers of Parliament, including a prohibition against Parliament interfering with the free exercise of religion. The scheme was a compromise, for certain Leveller proposals about further restrictions with regard to

economic matters and about the criminal code had been rejected.
Lilburne naturally assumed that since this 'Agreement' (unlike the
former one) had been reached by a common understanding with all
the Independents and with Ireton it would at once be presented to
army and Parliament. Deep was his disgust when it was decided
to submit it for further discussion by the army council.

Unhappily for the Levellers' hopes, while they had been indulging in framing paper constitutions, the army chiefs had been acting.
They had been provoked beyond endurance at the way in which
the Parliament in London had continued its interminable negotiations with the King while the King's friends had been fighting and
killing Roundhead soldiers in Essex, South Wales, Yorkshire and
Lancashire. Was not this renewal of the civil war, they protested,
a violation of the specific pledges given by the Cavaliers when they
laid down their arms in 1646?

On 20th November the Southern Roundhead Army, with the
approval of General Fairfax and of Cromwell, presented Parliament with a 'Remonstrance' demanding the rupture of all negotiations with the King and the punishment of Charles I as the 'only
begetter of the civil war.' Parliament had the temerity to ignore
the Remonstrance, whereupon the army took extreme measures.
Officers were sent by Fairfax to the Isle of Wight to take hold of
Charles I and move him to the gloomy castle of Hurst in Hampshire
while his fate was decided. On the next day the army marched from
Windsor to London, dragging in its train the protesting Levellers
who, true to Lilburne's doctrine of the balance of power, did not
wish the Grandees to become too strong. On 6th December Colonel
Pride was ordered to take a company of musketeers and to purge
the House of Commons of its Presbyterian majority. One day later
Cromwell arrived back in London from the north and expressed
his personal approval of Pride's Purge. Thus when Wildman and
Lilburne were drafting their speeches for the new series of constitutional debates, Cromwell and Ireton were more concerned about
how to deal with their royal prisoner. These hard-headed men
were now driven by the force of circumstances to even more
revolutionary projects than the Levellers. Their plan was to use
the purged Parliament as their instrument, put the King finally out
of the way, and cow the Presbyterian party, and by these means
fashion a new English Government. The Levellers, on the other

hand, still said, 'Let us first perfect our paper schemes and constitutional guarantees before we clear away the relics of the old regime.'

Such was the rather unhopeful atmosphere in which these latest constitutional debates in the army council were held. Only a small portion of the reports on these debates—at which Wildman assisted —have survived. The first report, dated 14th December 1648, concerned the reservation in the 'Agreement' about religion. The clause ran as follows:

'We do not now empower our representatives to continue in force or make any laws, oaths or covenants, whereby to compel, by penalties or otherwise, any person or any thing in or about matters of faith, religion or God's worship, or to restrain any person from the professing his faith or exercise of religion, according to his conscience in any house or place (except such as are or shall be set apart for the public worship), nevertheless instruction or directing of the nation in a public way for the matters of faith, worship or discipline (so it be not compulsive or express popery) is referred to their discretion.'

This was simply an elaboration of the first reservation of the 1647 version of 'The Agreement of the People' which Wildman had drawn up. It might have appeared so eminently sensible in view of the religious outlook of that day as to have passed without comment. But it raised a violent controversy.

John Goodwin, a leading Independent preacher who later became Cromwell's chaplain, opened the discussion in the army council in a provocative manner by asserting that they could not lay down the rights of the magistrates in regard to religion until the question had first been argued out by divines. 'I do not apprehend,' he observed, 'that it is a matter proper for you to take notice of or intermeddle in.' Naturally the retort came that every man must decide this problem according to his own conscience. John Wildman then intervened and brought the debate into the realm of practical politics. Was it not true, he asked, that the present state of confusion existed because no one knew where the real source of governing authority in the country lay or what its limits were. Therefore their first duty, he said, was to constitute and define the source of political power and set out the limits of government authority on that most controversial of all issues, religion.

Lilburne supported Wildman's argument. Let the question be simply stated, he urged, 'whether it is necessary to express the magistrate's powers in relation to religion or not?' Ireton, however, insisted that the civil war had not been caused by popular ignorance of the extent of their ruler's powers; it had been brought about by their ruler's violation of his known trust, or, rather, by controversies over where that trust lay. His own opinion was that they should simply determine the seat of the supreme power in the nation and then leave it to that power to settle questions of religion. For once they had handed over the 'power of the sword' to any individual or group of individuals they clearly must confer upon their chosen executive the right to decide religious policy so far as the 'outward man' was concerned. Lilburne and Ireton, however, were in agreement that the subject was unsuited to a general discussion and that a representative sub-committee should be appointed.

Nevertheless the debate ran on. Wildman took up Ireton's point that a supreme ruler must have power over the 'outward man' but could not affect consciences. He denied that the distinction was valid; 'in some cases it can be done. . . . If he hath power over my body, he hath power to keep me at home when I should go abroad to seek God.' He appealed to the gathering and begged those who were present that they, who had overthrown the King, should so reconstitute the government of the country as to ensure the liberty of the individual. 'God has pleased by your means to give us the liberty we have, which we look at as from Himself—I say God hath made you instruments of liberty. In matters of religion that's preferred by us before life. Let's have that or nothing.' Let them lay hold of their unique opportunity to reach an understanding. Otherwise, he concluded, 'I shall never expect freedom while I live.'

After some further debate it was agreed to frame a specific question on which every one might express an opinion for or against. Wildman proposed the question: 'whether the magistrate have any restrictive power in the time or manner of God's worship or [as to] faith or opinion concerning Him,' but Ireton preferred to put the question in the form 'has the magistrate any power to restrain men from the profession of anything good or evil relating to God only?' As often happens, the way in which the question is framed determines the answer. Thus Ireton believed that the magistrate had the right to interfere in religious matters, especially where they impinged upon the civil conduct of the citizen, whereas Wildman maintained that the government had no right to interfere with the individual conscience in any circumstances.

The debate then turned on the issue, which was of such far-reaching importance to the average puritan, whether or not the Old Testament had prescribed the right of civil magistrates to exercise control in religious matters. Ireton insisted that the Jews had such powers; Chaplain Goodwin was convinced that in biblical times the magistrates were divinely inspired; and Chaplain Nye thought that the people in their legislative capacity ought to feed souls as well as bodies. Wildman poured a flood of modern common sense into the debate: to Ireton he replied that if God commanded magistrates to destroy idolatry, He has commanded them to destroy the world; to Nye he said that matters of religion could not be entrusted to officers of State, for those who possessed coercive powers in matters of conscience were but being invited to sin. To the 'light of nature' argument (put forward by Ireton in support of the transcendent validity of the Ten Commandments) he retorted: 'It is not easily determinable by the light of nature what is sin. . . . To frame a right conception or notion of the First Being, wherein all other things have their being, is not [possible] by the light of nature. Indeed if a man consider there is a will of the Supreme Cause, it is a hard thing for [him by] the light of nature to conceive how there can be any sin committed; and therefore the magistrate cannot easily determine what sins are against the light of nature, and what not.' Ireton, confronted by this highly logical line of argument, fell back upon the feebler consideration that the Old Testament Jews had had magistrates to enforce religious principles. 'You say,' replied Wildman in effect, 'what was sin then is sin now. But can you prove it? Cannot it be argued equally well that the Jewish magistrates were empowered to impose certain moral rules because they were Jews and not because they were magistrates?' Chaplain Goodwin chimed in: 'If this power had been destined for all magistrates then every magistrate in the world had been bound to put all his subjects to death.' The debate stood adjourned.

The clause on religion was duly referred to a sub-committee and the other reservations on the powers of Parliament were debated and amended in turn. Finally on 15th January 1649 the council of the army completed an amended 'Agreement of the People,' which was presented to Parliament five days later. Although the army leaders were thus prepared now to meet the Levellers' point of view far more comprehensively than they had done a year before, Lilburne remained dissatisfied; he described the debates as 'a long and tedious tug with the Commissary General Ireton only, yea, sometimes whole nights together principally about liberty of conscience . . . poor fools, we were merely cheated and cozened.' On 15th December, the day after the liberty of conscience debate, Lilburne had published the original unamended 'Agreement of the People,' drawn up by his committee, as an appeal to outside opinion, and left Wildman to fight the rearguard action on its behalf. But, as Cromwell had foreseen, nothing came of it all. The attention of the nation was concentrated on quite another happening at Whitehall, the trial of the King. On the very day when the army council's version of 'The Agreement of the People' had been presented to Parliament, the indictment of Charles I had begun.

On 6th January the 'purged' House of Commons, without the consent of the Lords, had passed an act setting up a high court to try the King and nominated one hundred and thirty-five commissioners to be both judges and jury. The court first met on 20th January and the King was brought before it three times. He refused to recognize the jurisdiction of the court or to plead before it. Evidence was taken that Charles had 'levied war against the people of England' and had tried to import foreign mercenaries for the purpose. On 26th January a warrant was drawn up ordering his execution on the following day, but only twenty-eight of the judges could be persuaded to append their signatures. Cromwell, who had by this time made up his mind that the King must die for his war guilt, spent the week-end collecting further signatures for the death warrant. In the end fifty-nine names were collected and the document altered to bear the date of the execution, 30th January.

On the morning of 30th January the King was brought from St. James's Palace to Whitehall. He previously had taken the sacraments and prayed with Bishop Juxon. At two in the afternoon he was conducted through a middle window on to the scaffold in front of the Whitehall Banqueting Hall. On the platform erected to hold the block there stood only five men besides the King: Juxon, Colonels Hacker and Tomlinson, who guarded him, and the two executioners.

The executioner and his assistant were heavily disguised, no doubt through fear of Cavalier vengeance. They wore thick masks over their heads known as vizards, perruques, and false beards, and were dressed in close-fitting woollen frocks. After uttering a few words affirming that he had always defended the true liberties of the people, Charles I prepared himself to die. He handed his George and Garter, the only jewel he wore, to Juxon to give to his children, and after a word to the executioner he laid his head on the low block. At four minutes past two the blow was struck. The executioner's assistant seized the head and held it up high to the view of a silent and angry people.

The names of the masked executioners who stood upon that scaffold have never been ascertained with utter certainty. The common hangman, Brandon, died six months later, and the Royalists then published an appropriate and improbable story of the thirty pieces of silver which he had received for the deed. A recent writer has claimed the doubtful distinction not for Brandon but for the Reverend Henry Walker, an Independent journalist. Twenty years after the execution a Norwich cordwainer, John Blancher by name, who was awaiting his own execution for murder, in the Norwich gaol, became suspected of the deed because he had been overheard to say that he possessed the gaiters, gloves, and garters worn by Charles I on the scaffold. He further asserted that 'John Wildman had been upon the scaffold and helped him up, and that Wildman knew very well who was the King's executioner.' Questioned more closely by officials only too willing to tell Charles II that they had discovered his father's actual murderer, John Blancher emphatically denied that he 'was the wretch that gave the fatal stroke, but said Wildman was the man.' The officials concluded that it was an unlikely story, and thought that Blancher himself might have been the executioner's assistant.

That Wildman was indeed one of the masked and bearded figures who stood with Charles I upon the scaffold is capable neither of proof nor disproof. The Republicans, although of course anxious for the King's deposition, differed over the need for his execution. Henry Marten was in favour of it, but John Lilburne consistently argued that they must not do away with the King until a democratic system had been accepted and established in place of kingship. When Cromwell hurried on the trial of Charles I before a constituent assembly had been set up or any other arrangement had been made for a golden age of democracy and liberty, Lilburne regarded his action as a deliberate and wanton betrayal of the causes for which they all had been fighting. We may believe that Lilburne's 'bosom friend,' John Wildman, thought likewise.

CHAPTER VI

THE SPECULATOR

There can be slain
No sacrifice to God more acceptable
Than an unjust and wicked king.

Seneca, quoted by MILTON, 1649

THE execution of Charles I was followed at the beginning of
February, 1649, by the abolition of the institution of monarchy
and of the House of Lords. The attenuated House of Commons,
known as the Rump Parliament, appointed a Council of State,
consisting of forty-one members, which was bound by an oath to
concur 'in the settling of the government of this nation for the
future in the way of a republic.'

Although Wildman, Lilburne, and their fellow Levellers had
done effective propaganda work, the establishment of the first
English republic owed comparatively little to the triumph of
political theorists and much to the fact that the King's execution
had made it impossible, or at any rate indecent, for Parliament to
invite any of his children to accept the throne. The Independent
Grandees and their friends in the Commons had perforce to take
over the full government of the country, and they sought their
justification for doing so rather in the Old Testament doctrine that
bad kings must be deposed than in the essential impropriety of the
kingly office. Their self-appointed literary apologist was the poet
John Milton. During the trial of the King he had composed a
pamphlet on 'The Tenure of Kings and Magistrates' in which he
quoted with approval from the Roman, Seneca:

'There can be slain
No sacrifice to God more acceptable
Than an unjust and wicked king.'

He confessed that he would himself have signed the death warrant
of Charles I had he been asked. But Milton was no democrat, and
in later years was to advocate as his ideal government the perpetual
rule of the 'virtuous.'

The reception by the Levellers themselves of Milton's and Cromwell's republic was what was to have been expected. On 26th February Lilburne published *England's New Chains*, the title of the pamphlet describing his opinion of the new rule. In the army Richard Rumbold and six other troopers drew up a protest condemning the new Council of State as being incompatible with parliamentary government and the High Court of Justice as being contrary to trial by jury. 'We were ruled before by King, Lords, and Commons, now by Generals, Court Martial and Commons,' they asserted, 'and we pray you what is the difference?' On 24th March Lilburne published a second part of *England's New Chains*, in which he pleaded for a democratically elected parliament to govern the country in accordance with 'The Agreement of the People.' Oliver Cromwell, first chairman of the Council of State, would have none of this. He was convinced that such propaganda would undermine the loyalty of the army. Lilburne was at once arrested with three of his supporters: Walwyn, Prince, and Richard Overton; and Cromwell told the Council, 'You have no other way to deal with these men but to break them or they will break you.' The early summer of 1649 had to be devoted by Cromwell to the suppression of army mutinies in the cause of those democratic liberties for which many of the soldiers thought they had been fighting. Private Robert Lockyer and Corporal William Thompson were shot dead and became the first martyrs of democratic republicanism under the first English Republic. But Lilburne, in spite of his publication of several more pamphlets, including *An Impeachment of Oliver Cromwell*, was promptly acquitted of treason by a jury of the City of London.

Wildman had not acquiesced in Lilburne's hasty condemnation of the new republic. Perhaps he felt that the world's great age could scarcely begin anew overnight. Whatever his reasons, he separated himself temporarily from his old associates, who abused him roundly as a traitor. In July, 1649, Richard Overton exclaimed in the middle of a pamphlet:

'And where's my old fellow rebel, Johnee Wildman? Mount Atlas, stand on tiptoes, where art thee? And behold a mighty stone fell from the skies into the bottom of the sea, and gave a mighty plump, and great was the fall of that stone, and so farewell, Johnee Wildman. . . .'

In the same month Lilburne, who was then in the Tower awaiting his trial and happily occupied in writing his *Impeachment of
Cromwell*, recalled Wildman's collaboration with him in 1648 and
spoke of him as

'my then bosom friend and zealous and bold asserter of England's
freedom: though now he hath not only lost all his zeal, but I am
afraid his honesty and his principles and is closed with familiarity
and design with Cromwell, although no one knows his knavery
better than he.'

It seems indeed that for a time Wildman did contemplate taking
service under the new Government. A man of his name was ordered
to report to the House of Commons in May, 1649, as one of the new
commissioners for the Roundhead island of Guernsey, and in
August of the same year his name is down in the records as a major
in Sir John Reynolds's Regiment of Horse. But in fact he served
neither in the Channel Islands nor in Ireland. And if he compromised for a while with the oligarchic Republicans he was not
unique in his behaviour, even among the extremists, and Lilburne
had certainly no right to throw stones. 'Wildman and Sexby,'
states Professor Pease, the historian of the Levellers, 'were thought
to have got their price from the Grandees; Lilburne himself by
playing on the fears of the officers obtained the revenues of certain
sequestered Durham estates in part settlement of his claims.' After
his acquittal Lilburne abandoned politics to resume his normal
trade as a soap-boiler. Cromwell left England to fight the Royalist
armies which gathered in dangerous strength in Ireland and
Scotland, and Parliament ordered the taxation of all Cavalier
estates to provide the money for his campaigns.

England's first republic struggled for recognition and survival
in a hostile world. So doubtful was the Council of State of the
community's loyalty that an act was passed to restrict the liberty of
the press; and all members of Parliament, soldiers, sailors, judges,
municipal officials, university officials and graduates, and even the
masters and scholars of Eton, Winchester, and Westminster, were
called upon to take an oath to be faithful to 'the Commonwealth of
England as established without a King or House of Lords.' By 1650
Lilburne had settled down to a comparatively placid, if litigious,
existence in London. In the autumn of the same year, however, he

and Wildman were acting together in a piece of work in defiance of the Government. Thus there is no reason to suppose that Wildman was really unfaithful to the democratic party of which Lilburne was then the leader. For the time being only, while the new republic was fighting for its very existence, he, like Lilburne, dropped his political activities in order to earn his living.

The peculiar economic circumstances that resulted from the English civil war offered extraordinary opportunities to a young and enterprising attorney possessing what business circles are accustomed to call vision. The opportunities were all the more promising if he were able to master the intricacies of the many new acts which had been passed or were being passed by Parliament concerning the sales and taxation of real estate.

In spite of a slow but important growth of commerce the foundation of English economic life in the seventeenth century was still agriculture, and the chief means of investing profits as well as the most conspicuous badge of social standing was landed property. The defeat of the Cavaliers had been followed by one of the most rapid and biggest changes in the ownership of real property in English history, a veritable agricultural revolution. To find funds for the war the Long Parliament had ordered the sale first of the lands belonging to the bishops, then those belonging to deans and chapters of cathedrals, and finally the properties of the King and royal family. In 1646 a tax or forced loan of twenty per cent. was levied upon the real property of all active Royalists, while from a slightly earlier date a fine, known as a 'composition,' which varied between one-tenth and one-half of the capital value of the property, according to the nature of the 'delinquency,' was imposed on all royalist lands. Naturally many property owners were unable to find the cash to meet these vast demands from the victorious party, and in such cases it was ordered that parliamentary commissioners should take over the administration of the lands of those who could not pay their fines and collect rents from them, making the owner an allowance of one-fifth of the income from the property until such time as he could meet his obligations. Such government administration of estates was called 'sequestration.' A number of landlords, however, refused to recognize the right of Parliament to sequestrate their lands and under three acts of 1651 and 1652 a group of estates belonging to such recalcitrants and others declared guilty of treason was seized and sold by trustees.

It is particularly in connexion with this last category of land sales that we learn of the large part played by John Wildman in the real property market during the years 1650-1655. Land naturally became cheap and was frequently sold at less than ten years' purchase, and it has been assumed that Wildman was engaged in bold speculation. This may have been so in the cases where he was buying as a member of a syndicate, but it is known that in some cases he was acting independently as a commission agent. In whatever capacity he acted, he appears to have made a considerable fortune, probably enough to keep him in affluence for the remainder of his life.

His purchases of bishops' lands were small. From the treason trustees, on the other hand, he bought either on his own behalf or for others houses and manorial estates scattered over twenty different counties in England and Wales. The biggest group of houses and estates bought by him were in Lancashire, but that was perhaps mainly because Lancashire was a Royalist and Roman Catholic area and therefore afforded the widest selection. After Lancashire, where he made fifteen purchases, came Yorkshire (seven purchases), Gloucestershire, London, Somerset, and Northumberland. Altogether he completed over fifty separate transactions during these five years.

Wildman's lack of any violent religious convictions enabled him to act, without worrying, in several business deals as an agent for Roman Catholic families. Mrs. Hutchinson, the wife of an enthusiastic puritan colonel, was disgusted to find in 1653 that Lord and Lady (Henry) Howard, who were trying to buy back some land from her husband, were employing 'that cunning person, Major Wildman, who was then a great manager of Papists' interests.' It is likely that in several instances he purchased Royalists' estates in his own name on behalf of the previous owners. Such practices were common.

Among other enterprises undertaken by Wildman during this period was his attempt to acquire the registrarship of the prerogative office belonging to the Archbishop of Canterbury (which would have given him the right to collect fees for wills); he claimed this office as the representative of the only survivor of three patentees to whom the office had been granted ten years earlier. But his claim was opposed on the ground that the abolition of episcopacy had made the grant void, and after counsel had been heard on behalf of both sides before the committee concerned with the claim, the case was settled out of court.

Although Wildman, who was now living in Westminster, was thus doing a profitable business in these years, he did not sever his associations with his old political friends. It is notable that he was chosen by Mrs. Rainsborough, widow of that Colonel Rainsborough who had taken part in the army council debates of 1647 and was later killed, to invest on her behalf £3,000 which she had been allowed by Parliament: Wildman bought for her two manors belonging to the Earl of Derby and another manor in Somerset. He also did not hesitate to act as the spokesman for a policy of democratization in the government of the City of London.

The Levellers had a considerable following in the City of London. After Lilburne had been acquitted of the charge of treason in the Guildhall, he had been elected a member of the Common Council. But when he was required to take the new oath of allegiance he would promise to swear fidelity only to 'all the good and legal people of England' and not to the existing Parliament, Council of State, or Council of the Army; the Lord Mayor and Aldermen were severely shocked and the Commons intervened to quash the election. In spite of this setback, democratic propaganda was spreading, and an agitation was begun against the right of the City aldermen to veto the proceedings of the Common Council and against the right of the Livery companies to take part in the election of the Lord Mayor and sheriffs. Complaints also were heard about the way in which the City's finances were being managed. After the abolition of kingship and the House of Lords, a campaign was started against the Lord Mayor and the Court of Aldermen who were supposed to represent in the City government what the King and Lords had stood for in the English constitution. Several pamphlets were published demanding that the ordinary citizen of London should be given a greater say in its government. The failure of the popular Lord Mayor, Thomas Andrews, to obtain re-election in Michaelmas, 1649, had induced a large number of citizens to petition the Common Council to appoint a committee of inquiry into the existing system of electing the Lord Mayor. In October the court of the Common Council resolved

'That it appeareth to them by the ancient charters of this City that the Lord Mayor and Sheriffs of this City are eligible by the commons and citizens of this City and that the elections of the Lord Mayor and Sheriffs was anciently by the several persons chosen out of the wards joined with the Common Council. And that the same way is the most convenient to be continued.'

The Livery companies hastened to protest against any alteration in the existing method of election. In opposition to the Livery companies John Wildman, together with John Price, another Leveller, was chosen by the freemen to represent before the City authorities their claim to a more direct voting power in these elections. The burden of the argument fell upon Wildman, for Price acknowledged himself 'to be weak in the knowledge of the law.' Wildman came 'without hopes of fees or rewards' to plead the cause of the freemen of London.

The method of electing a Lord Mayor of London in the first half of the seventeenth century was for a Common Hall to be summoned in which sat the Common Council, the Aldermen, and the representatives of the powerful Livery companies—the Grocers, the Goldsmiths, the Mercers, and their like. The Councillors and the Liverymen then nominated two men as candidates for Lord Mayor, from whom the aldermen made the final choice. There seems little doubt that the important part played by the Liverymen in the election dated only from the end of the fifteenth century; and that just as the democratic craft guilds had been superseded by the oligarchic liverymen who had driven out the small masters from the trading privileges of the guilds, so the Livery companies had excluded the ordinary freemen in the wards from nominating delegates to the Common Hall to choose the Lord Mayor. The early constitutional history of the Government of London was checkered. The earliest charter which mentions the mayor, granted to the citizens of London by King John the year before he assented to Magna Carta, confirmed to 'our barons of our City of London' the right 'themselves to elect the mayor every year.' Who these 'barons' of the early Middle Ages were is still a matter of controversy among mediaeval scholars. Writing about the early part of the reign of Henry III (1216–1272), who succeeded King John, the historian Stubbs spoke of the 'cynical contempt with which the King looked upon the ancient claim of the Londoners to the title of barons.' But the citizens of London clung tenaciously to their rights: indeed under the mayor Thomas Fitz Thomas it was said by an unfriendly chronicler that what the common people of London wanted was done 'without consulting the aldermen or chief citizens.' Then for a time the freemen lost their power, but in 1270 their right to elect the Lord Mayor and Sheriffs was restored. Again, in 1319, Edward II by letters patent confined the franchise to members of the craft guilds, but since all freemen belonged to these guilds, this meant that only foreigners were not allowed to share the franchise. Fifty-seven years later, in the reign of Edward III, the right to elect both the Lord Mayor and the Common Council was specifically conferred upon the members of the craft guilds, although by 1384 the wards were again given the right to take part in the elections. Since an Act of Edward IV in 1476, however, the election of mayors and sheriffs had been made entirely by the councillors and liverymen and not by the wards.

Thus the lawyers had a delightful and varied store of mediaeval precedents on which to draw and about which to argue. Wildman opened the 'learned argument of law and reason' before the Lord Mayor, Court of Aldermen and Common Council at Guildhall on 14th December 1650, by explaining that he had been invited by many freemen to appear on their behalf in support of the following petition:

'that by an Act of this honourable Court such a competent number of representatives may be annually chosen by the Freemen of each ward who with the Common Council may elect the mayor and sheriffs.'

Wildman acknowledged the rights of the Aldermen and Common Council to take part in the election but asked that 'our right in electing as we are freemen may be restored to us.' He did not attempt to deny that as the law then stood the Livery companies had the right to take part in the elections. He argued merely that the law was alterable and ought to be altered. He refuted the notion that the present system had prevailed 'time out of mind.' He dilated upon the charter of 1215; he appealed to Magna Carta;

he searched the records of Edward I; he discussed the incidents of Henry VI's reign. He defended the people as the fountain of all political power and added that the Liverymen's right to elect was not made just by the continuance of time unless it were originally just. His legal lore was indeed impressive, and the distinguished opposing lawyer, Sir John Maynard (not to be confused with his namesake who had been released from prison partly through Wildman's efforts), complimented him on his 'very great skill in the very entrance of the business.'

Speaking for the Livery companies Maynard replied that their members were better qualified to elect than the freemen. 'Will any man suppose,' he urged, 'that the education of all the handicraftmen of the Liveries render them so able and discreet that they are fit for government?' Against this argument, which was the same sort of reasoning that Cromwell and Ireton had employed in the army council for refusing a democratic parliamentary franchise, Wildman protested energetically and came back with gusto to the precedents of the early Middle Ages. He added, however, that if the exclusive right to elect the Lord Mayor were conferred upon the Common Council, the freemen would not oppose it. Since the Livery companies as such came into existence only late in the history of London, Wildman's case was historically sound, and ultimately the freemen's point of view triumphed. A year later an Act of Common Council (reaffirming the conclusion reached by its committee in the autumn of 1650) ordered that the elections in the Common Hall were henceforward to be by Aldermen, Common Councillors and 'a like number of honest men out of each ward' and not by the Livery companies. Thus although the democratic views of the Levellers failed to find acceptance in the national franchise, they were triumphant in the revised franchise of the City of London. It seems, however, to have been a barren triumph, for there is no evidence that the Act of 1651 was ever put into effect. Nevertheless Wildman had won. While the London authorities had been unravelling this delicate historical problem, Wildman had been concerned also in another and odder enterprise in company with his friend Lilburne. Although Lilburne had taken no direct part in politics since his acquittal on the charge of treason at Guildhall he had been occupied in several legal disputes which had brought him into conflict with the ruling powers. The quarrel in which he now enlisted Wildman's aid arose out of the draining of the Lincolnshire fens.

In the seventeenth century there were large stretches of England which by reason of the constant overflow of rivers and rivulets and through lack of adequate drainage constituted one vast bog and marshland which was entirely useless for ordinary cultivation. These areas, lying within the boundaries of six counties, were known as the Great Fens and were said to cover some 400,000 acres. Amid the bogs and pools there were a few islands of dry and solid earth on which dwelt an amphibious population who travelled in punts, walked on stilts, and eked out a precarious living by fishing, keeping geese, hunting wild-fowl, and 'swan hopping [upping].' One of these islands, which was surrounded by the accumulated mud and silt brought up by the tides from the Humber into the Trent and deposited in its smaller Lincolnshire tributaries, was named the Isle of Axholme. For many years this island had been the property of the Mowbray family and in the troublesome days of King Henry II it had been turned into an impregnable fortification. In the course of the years the island, together with the neighbouring districts of Dikemarsh and Hatfield Chase, came under the direct overlordship of the King. It seemed a useless enough property. So inundated was the area on account of the silt that boats passed over it in summer as well as in winter. Only the less enterprising cultivators considered it worth their while to live in a district which yielded no crops and was further rendered unfit for cultivation by a chase of red deer which roamed through the greater part of the fenland.

In 1626, however, King Charles I decided to employ a well-known Dutch engineer, Vermuyden, to drain 60,000 acres of this fenland. Whether we should attribute this decision to genuine enlightenment or to an urge for a handsome profit is a matter of doubt. Certainly the King did not offer to pay Vermuyden any ready money for this heavy piece of work. But he promised him and his associates the full possession of one-third of the land which they succeeded in rescuing from the waters, while private owners were to be similarly compensated, and the residue was to pay rent to the royal exchequer. The work was completed in five years at the cost of £55,000. The waters that usually overflowed were conveyed by sluices and sewers back into the Trent. Crops were planted, houses built, and valuable land reclaimed from the watery wastes. The King hastened to sell out his share of the land, a corporation was established to manage and let the property, and outsiders were encouraged to come and settle. Only the wild fenmen whose livelihood was threatened had cause for discontent. For although many of them had lived there from time immemorial, few of them had any legal claim to compensation. Throughout Hatfield Chase indeed the right of the commoners to extract a meagre livelihood from the waters and the waste was unwritten and recognized only as an act of grace. But in the manor of Epworth within the Isle of Axholme the position was different. Here three hundred and seventy freeholders and commoners could point to a grant and confirmation to them by the Mowbray family in the reign of Edward III of their right to the 'common appendant to their several tenements in all manner of cattle levant and couchant at all times of the year in and through all the wastes and commons within the manor of Epworth' had by them 'since time out of mind' was admitted and confirmed. This deed, so they held, should have sufficed to secure to them the whole 13,400 acres which lay adjacent to the royal Hatfield Chase. In 1636 their claim had gone to the arbitration of the Attorney-General, not, in those days, one fancies, a disinterested party, and they obtained only 6,000 acres for themselves, the remaining 7,400 acres going to Vermuyden and company (who had in the meantime bought out the King's shares). Hence when the civil war broke out the Isle of Axholme contained a population consisting, on the one hand, of the three hundred and seventy original and highly dissatisfied inhabitants and their families owning 6,000 acres and, on the other hand, of a group of 'foreigners' enjoying possession of 7,400 acres which they had bought from the draining company.

The civil war, as we have seen, furnished the opportunity for tremendous changes in the distribution of landed property. Moreover the powers of the local and central authorities were relaxed and radical changes at Westminster encouraged a revival of grievances in the countryside. The fenmen grasped their chance. In June, 1642, two months after Charles I had knocked vainly at the gates of Hull, the original inhabitants of the Isle of Axholme rose in revolt against the Vermuyden company and their lessees. Claiming the right of common throughout Epworth manor the fenmen broke down the fences, destroyed crops, and demolished houses:

'And about the beginning of February [1643] they pulled up the floodgates of Snow sewer, which by letting in the tides from the river Trent soon drowned a great part of Hatfield Chase, divers persons standing there with muskets and saying that there they should stay till the whole level was drowned and the inhabitants forced to swim away like ducks; and so [they] continued guarding the said sluices for the space of seven weeks together, letting in the tides at every full water and keeping the sluice shut at an ebb. . . .

And thinking this not enough, the inhabitants of the Isle of Axholme did, about Michaelmas, in the year 1645, tumultuously throw down a great part of the banks and filled up the ditches, putting in cattle into the corn and pastures of those that had been adventurers [responsible] for the draining.'

This was chaos indeed. But with their gradual triumph in the war Parliament began to resume control, and for the next few years many lawsuits followed, the new settlers demanding compensation for the damage. The sheriff of Lincoln was ordered to send a deputy to restore order; a force of a hundred men was sent to put back the banks in the four thousand acres that had been wantonly laid waste. Yet the original inhabitants continued successfully to resist law and order and, after the death of the King, the draining company had once more to appeal to the law courts for assistance.

It was at this point that Wildman and Lilburne entered the scene. A certain Daniel Noddel, described as a 'solicitor,' who was evidently the ringleader of the rioters, decided that they needed outside help to defeat their enemies. Surely Lilburne, the leader of the Levellers, and Wildman, a man skilled in the technicalities of the property laws, were the reinforcements they wanted. Lilburne and Wildman first supplied advice during the hearing of the case before the Court of Exchequer, but when that proved hopeless they went in person to Lincolnshire in the autumn of 1650 and joined with Noddel and his fenmen in a bout of rioting and crop destruction. The company then brought the matter before a local Justice of the Peace, Michael Monckton by name. This move was worse than useless, for not only did Monckton refuse to do anything and exerted his influence to reduce the fines imposed by other magistrates, but he actually joined with Wildman, Lilburne, and Noddel in their terrorist activity. However, in February, 1651, the Court of Exchequer finally published a decree for establishing possession with the company. But what cared the fenmen for the Exchequer, or indeed for Parliament? Lilburne was their man. 'They could make as good a Parliament themselves,' they said. Some of them observed that 'it was a Parliament of clouts; and that if they sent any forces, they would raise men and resist them.' Led by Wildman and Lilburne, they turned to an attack upon the village of Sandtoft, pulled down eighty-two houses, defaced the church, and again ruined the crops. Lilburne, Wildman, Monckton, and Noddel entered into an agreement with the inhabitants of Epworth that in return for a certain number of acres of land (of which 1,000 were to go to Lilburne and 1,000 to Wildman) they would defend them in the possession of the remainder. The portions were straightway measured out and Wildman made a contract with 'several persons for the letting thereof.' For the fenmen's trust in the Leveller leaders was complete. Noddel was willing to bet anyone a pound that as soon as Lilburne returned to London, the Rump Parliament would be turned out and Lilburne himself would become an influential member of a new and more complacent assembly. Wildman and Lilburne do not appear to have depreciated their prospects in the coming Parliament. Meanwhile Lilburne put his servants in possession of the Sandtoft minister's house and instructed them to use the church itself for a barn and stable.

The last date on which Wildman was actively concerned with this curious business arrangement was in October, 1651, when the agreement with the fenmen was signed. For it was only one item among his many activities and other business soon called him elsewhere. In December of the same year we hear of him over at Gloucester negotiating with the mayor and aldermen there for the right to act as their agent in obtaining reparations from Parliament for the losses which the town had suffered during its siege by Royalists in August, 1643. Wildman and his associates in this venture asked one-third of what they obtained for themselves, but the mayor and aldermen considered the terms excessive. Wildman must have regarded the Epworth affair as the least successful of his speculations. Although Lilburne was arrested the following January for another exploit and Wildman became immersed in other business, the dispute between the fenmen and the rioters dragged on for a long time. The rioters were exempted from the Act of General Pardon and Oblivion of 1652 and a parliamentary sub-committee was appointed to investigate the rights and wrongs of the whole affair. Wildman, who was summoned before it, denied 'with great imprecations and invocations and judgments to fall on him' that he was there when the bargain was made or that he had ever been promised a thousand acres for his pains, until he was confronted with witnesses who claimed to have been present at the time and also with the deed itself!

After Parliament had finally decided in favour of the company, one of Cromwell's Majors-General named Whalley was sent down to Lincolnshire to quell the trouble and establish property rights. But since as late as 1656 Whalley was still using his regiment to enforce the rights of the company, it may be presumed that Wildman managed to draw the rents he had been promised from this tricky affair for some five years. Long before that he had turned back from property speculation to the deeper excitements of revolutionary politics again.

CHAPTER VII

THE WILDMAN PLOT

That such a settlement may be made of right and freedom . . . and a peace firmly established, we know no better means under God but a truly free parliament.

JOHN WILDMAN, 1655

THE optimistic belief of the Lincolnshire fenmen that when a new Parliament was summoned their champions, John Lilburne and John Wildman, would be elected to defend their rights and condone their riots was not realized. In 1651 Lilburne had set aside his occupation of soap-boiling to interest himself again in other people's grievances. He had excitedly taken up a claim of his uncle, George Lilburne, to share in the profits of a Durham colliery and had publicly accused Sir Arthur Haselrig, a prominent republican member of Parliament, of having corruptly exerted his influence to resist his uncle's claim. The House of Commons seized the opportunity to show its dislike of this firebrand Leveller who was no respecter of persons or privileges. The House constituted itself a court and for the crime of libel against one of its members imposed the grossly excessive punishment of a fine of £7,000 and banishment for life. Lilburne was ordered never to return to the land of his fathers on penalty of death. This sentence, one of the most scandalous blots on the record of the Long Parliament, obliged Lilburne to retire to Amsterdam, where, in the natural bitterness of his heart, he entered into negotiations with the royalist exiles, hoping no doubt to play off the ambitions of Charles II against those of Cromwell. But in June, 1653, Cromwell, growing tired of the Long Parliament, dissolved it by force, and Lilburne hastened to return to England: for was it not the law that punishments imposed by Parliament came to an end as soon as that Parliament ceased to sit? Cromwell, however, had no intention of pardoning his old adversary. In August the Council of State put Lilburne on trial for his life before a London jury for defying the sentence of perpetual banishment. Although Lilburne did not present his defence on the legal grounds where it was strongest, his appeal in the name of individual freedom against the spite of the ruling powers proved irresistible. Amid the cheers of thousands of spectators, and even of the soldiers who guarded the doors at Guildhall, he was unanimously acquitted. The return and acquittal of this intrepid agitator threatened to arouse a new revolt in London against the tyranny of the army and was too grave a menace to the security of the Grandees for them to abide by the letter of the law. On the order of the Council of State Lilburne was thrust back into prison and later removed to the Channel Islands where the writ of the common law did not run; thence he was to emerge in 1657, a broken man, only to die.

John Wildman came much nearer to achieving entry into the Cromwellian House of Commons. Cromwell had replaced the Rump Parliament by a nominated Parliament of 'Saints,' but at the end of 1653 he decided that he could no longer govern through the 'Saints,' who had shown a tendency both to ignore his advice and to tamper with property rights. He therefore accepted, although with some reluctance, a new republican constitution hurriedly framed by the army leaders with a view to finding a compromise between parliamentary rule and military dictatorship. According to this constitution, known as the 'Instrument of Government,' Oliver Cromwell was to become Lord Protector as well as commander-in-chief, and an elected parliament was to be summoned on 3rd September 1654 to frame or to confirm legislation. It was this parliament, the first to be elected for twelve years, that Wildman tried to enter.

In those days an election was a very different affair from what it was to become in our own time. It lasted for several weeks, candidates could stand for more than one constituency, and the polling which was held in the open air was carried out by show of hands or word of mouth. The 'Instrument' laid it down that the electors must choose members prepared to uphold the new constitution 'as settled in one single person and a parliament,' that all persons elected should be 'of known integrity, fearing God, and of good conversation,' and that the Council of State should have power to decide whether or not persons had been properly elected in accordance with the qualifications prescribed. The electorate was of course far from being democratic. The majority of the constituencies were counties where electors had to be owners of real or personal property worth (in the modern equivalent) about £800: there were relatively few boroughs in the revised list of constituencies, and even in the towns the electorate was, as a rule, narrowly limited. One exception to this rule, however, was the borough of Westminster, the residence of Wildman, and it was reported from London in July, 1654, that 'Major Wildman—a very great Leveller—is or is likely to be chosen for Westminster.' Wildman stood also for another borough, that of Scarborough in Yorkshire. He was rejected at Westminster in favour of government candidates, but was duly elected for Scarborough. But the election of a notorious Leveller leader was one thing; for him to take his seat was less easy. In August a committee of the Council of State had been set up to examine the election returns. It was simple for the defeated candidates to invent reasons why the elections of their opponents had been unlawful and simpler still for the Council to quash the elections of objectionable candidates.

We know, for example, how at this election Samuel Highland, a puritan of extremely advanced and unorthodox views, had been chosen by acclamation; but his opponents brought a whole series of complaints against the manner of his election before the Council of State. He had, they said, 'seduced the electors by a glozing speech of self-praise' (not, one would have thought, a very unusual offence); he was also said to have 'used menaces and violence' and to have induced the sheriff to keep a party of opposing voters and persons of quality out in the rain until they were forced to take shelter in a neighbouring house and then by a clandestine 'Oyez' to have had his own election carried and closed the polling booth. The complaints against Wildman's election were of a different character. His old enemies, the proprietors of the reclaimed fenlands in Lincolnshire, had heard of his election at Scarborough and saw their opportunity for revenge. They hastened to the Council to deliver their protests and expound their long-standing grievances. 'We humbly pray,' they concluded, 'Major Wildman being so great a disturber of the law and peace, one with such guilt upon him may not be suffered to sit in Parliament.' They placed their case against Wildman before the Protector as well as before the Council, and presumably because the rioters in Axholme had been specifically exempted from the Act of Oblivion he was not considered to be a person of 'known integrity' and his election was declared null and void. So he was not in his seat to hear Oliver Cromwell's violent attack on the Leveller party when Parliament was opened on 3rd September. In his speech the Lord Protector pretended that the Levellers were Communists: What 'was the purport of the Leveller principle,' he asked, 'but to make the tenant as liberal a fortune as the landlord?' The motto of these men, he declared, and that of the other extremist puritan sects was 'Overturn, overturn, overturn'; the Protectorate's policy, he said, was to heal the wounds inflicted on the body politic by these dangerous revolutionaries.

Although neither Wildman nor any other Leveller was present in the House to defend his political beliefs against Cromwell's strictures, there was a group of aristocratic Republicans, headed by Sir Arthur Haselrig (who had been responsible for Lilburne's cruel punishment), Thomas Scot, and John Bradshaw, who had presided at the trial of Charles I. Their aim was to amend the 'Instrument of Government' so as to diminish or even abolish the powers of the Protector and correspondingly increase the rights of the Commons. They were not concerned, as the Levellers were, with putting the electorate on a more democratic basis; their sole object was to re-establish the supremacy of the House of Commons and thereby offset the dictatorial tendencies of Cromwell. The Protector naturally refused to let these men call his authority into question. On 12th September, after he had seen that the parliamentary Republicans were likely to block all legislation, he visited the House with his soldiers and required the members to sign a pledge that they would not attempt to alter the 'Instrument,' 'as it is settled in a single person and a parliament.' Since this was the same pledge made on their behalf by the electorate and returning officers, most members did not consider the demand unreasonable. But the pledge effectively excluded all inflexible Republicans from Parliament. About a hundred and sixty members either refused to sign or to attend the House. Those who remained proceeded, to Cromwell's dismay, to tear the other clauses of the 'Instrument' to pieces.

The inevitable consequence of the policy of packing and purging the House of Commons was to drive all Cromwell's opponents into extra-parliamentary agitation. Their usual procedure was to draw up petitions for presentation to parliament. Even before 12th September Major-General Harrison, leader of the Fifth Monarchy men, was arrested for preparing a petition against the 'new tyranny' for which he had hoped to collect the signatures of 20,000 sectarians. At the same time unrest began to develop among a number of army officers at the course that General Cromwell had taken. Colonel Alured, who had already openly used violent language against Cromwell in Ireland and had been recalled, began to discuss with other officers and civilians how they might establish a true republican régime. They invited the assistance of Major Wildman, and in the same month that parliament met, conferences were held at the house of a certain Mr. Allen, who was a London merchant. The first step decided upon was to draw up a petition protesting against the monarchical character of the 'Instrument of Government' and to collect signatures to it. The actual framing of the petition was left to Wildman. But there was a spy in their midst, Colonel Francis Hacker, who subsequently became one of Cromwell's Majors-General. Hacker reported all that he learned to John Thurloe, Cromwell's Secretary of State. The Lord Protector ordered the arrest of Colonel Alured, whose rooms were searched, and the petition was discovered. Only two other signatures, those of Colonels Okey and Saunders, had been added to that of Alured, although the conspirators had certainly expected that many more colonels would sign. Saunders and Okey also were arrested and the three of them brought before a court martial. Some attempt had been made to interest the Republicans expelled from the Commons by Cromwell in the petition, a copy of which had been shown for example to John Bradshaw by Captain Henry Bishop, a crony of Wildman. But no one else was sufficiently implicated to be arrested.

After the three arrests Wildman published the petition as a broadsheet in October, 1654. Its publication caused a sensation in London, for it proved that the republican discontent with Cromwell was not confined to the excluded members of Parliament but was rampant in the army itself. The 'three colonels' petition,' as it was called, was ably drawn up. It began by recalling that they had entered the army not as mercenaries but 'for the liberties of our country.' They had promised to fight the King, whose tyranny had consisted in his resistance to Parliament, his insistence on absolute command of the militia, and his demand for complete control over all the Ministers of State. 'We then declared that we must have constant parliaments freely chosen by the people' and that 'no person should be exempt from punishment by the people's parliament, the principle of the King's unaccountableness being the great root of tyranny.' But after their fighting and their victory, what had happened? Cromwell had stepped into the King's shoes. He had had conferred upon himself a greater power than the King ever possessed—the control of a standing army. This army 'will be mercenary and obey his commands from interest, whereas the ancient militia, having their own arms and officers, were not obliged to obey the King's illegal commands.' Such a commander, so their argument went, will be the master of 'all parliaments, freedoms, and our birthrights.' Equally the 'Instrument' in effect gave all legislative power to a single person, and Parliament could not execute justice on him even if he were guilty of the highest tyranny. The present Parliament was based neither on the people's consent nor their trust nor their control, nor even on the right of conquest. The conclusion was: 'We therefore beg that a full and truly free parliament may consider our fundamental rights and liberties,' in accordance with the terms of 'The Agreement of the People.'

The day before the petition was published, Vice-Admiral John Lawson, who led the Republicans in the navy and had been in close touch with the discontented colonels, also began an agitation. He summoned a council of war on board the Admiral's ship, where it was unanimously resolved to 'tender their grievances by way of petition.' A list of specific complaints was forwarded from the fleet to Whitehall. But Cromwell and Thurloe acted with a mixture of firmness and conciliation. The three colonels were leniently treated by the court martial. Saunders and Okey were merely obliged to give up their commissions and Alured, as ringleader, was cashiered and imprisoned; the seamen were pacified by the payment of their arrears; and the other officers were persuaded— if once their pay and debts were settled—'to live and die with his Highness and the present Government.' So long as the bulk of the armed forces thus remained faithful to Cromwell, the Levellers and Republicans had little hope of achieving their democratic republic; but they continued to plot together. And indeed it was Cromwell's dictatorial tendencies which threw these hitherto antagonistic parties into each other's arms.

While the purged Parliament continued its examination of the 'Instrument of Government,' frequent meetings took place between the Levellers and the excluded parliamentary Republicans at London taverns and private houses. Besides Wildman, at whose house some of these meetings were held, Henry Marten and Lord Grey of Groby took an important part. Captain Bishop seems to have acted as go-between, linking the extremists who followed Wildman with the more orthodox and oligarchic Republicans like Haselrig, Scot, and Bradshaw. Just before the Commons had been purged, Wildman had got into touch with Major-General Overton, whose puritan integrity was the subject of a panegyric by John Milton, and had a talk with him about the existing state of affairs. Overton confessed his dislike of Cromwell's conduct and his belief in the old Leveller views as formulated by Wildman seven years earlier: but no plot was concocted; and Overton left for Scotland to take up a post under General Monk. When he was in Scotland, however, Overton wrote to Wildman to let him know that 'there was a party [in the Scottish army] that would stand right for a commonwealth,' that is to say, for a democratic republic. At the same time Overton's resentment was disclosed by his solemnly copying out some scurrilous verses about the Protector solely, so he said, for his own amusement. Wildman dispatched Lieutenant Brayman, a one-time Agitator, to keep this republican kettle boiling. Discontented officers gathered at Overton's quarters, drew up round robins, and called a meeting at the Green Dragon on New Year's Day. There was some talk, in which Overton was not directly involved, of organizing a mutiny against Monk, and imprisoning him in Edinburgh castle. The next step presumably would have been for the army to advance into England and impose a real republic. Naturally with so many persons in the know and so many officers invited to sign declarations and circulars, the plot was soon reported to Monk. Overton was promptly arrested and dispatched to London at the beginning of January, 1655. There he was to remain in prison without a fair trial until after Cromwell's death.

The failure of the Overton plot, in which the Major-General appears to have been a pawn rather than the chief agent, did not disconcert Wildman. On the contrary, circumstances appeared to be becoming increasingly propitious for an effective republican movement. The parliamentary majority had by resisting the Protector on the religious issue, by limiting its money vote for the army, and by closely circumscribing the right of veto sought by Cromwell, virtually assumed a republican attitude similar to that for which Haselrig, Scot and the rest had been expelled from the House. There was considerable discontent too with the Government among the extreme puritan sects, such as the Fifth Monarchy men and the Quakers, and at the turn of the year a number of Royalists had been arrested in the country under suspicion of plotting a rising. It was at this time of political ferment that Wildman gave birth to his own particular plot.

The details of Wildman's plot were disclosed three years later by a certain Samuel Dyer who had been the servant of Colonel Edward Sexby. Sexby we have already met when he was the leading Agitator to take part along with Wildman in the army council debates of 1647. Subsequently Sexby had been promoted lieutenant-colonel, and in 1651 he had been sent by Cromwell to Bordeaux to spy upon the French Protestants and to stir up trouble against the French Government with whom we were then in a state of war. So convinced was Sexby by the truth of the Leveller creed that he had had 'The Agreement of the People' translated into French and offered to the French Protestants as a constitution that was a cross between the ideas of the Puritan Commonwealth and the French Revolution. He had returned to England in August, 1653, to find the Leveller doctrines were being trampled underfoot by the army Grandees. After the Protectorate had been established he entered into communication with Wildman, Grey of Groby, and others, and numerous meetings were held in different parts of the country whence the conspirators sent out large boxes of declarations and other papers for wide distribution. One centre of activity was the house of Wildman's mother-in-law in Berkshire. Sexby and Wildman met in Sussex and London as well as in Berkshire. According to Dyer, their plans went far beyond mere propaganda. When he was at an inn at Brentford in Middlesex, he heard Wildman say to Sexby: 'Shall such a tyrant live? No; if it be possible to find two Feltons.' Sexby then prepared two buff coats and two saddles for the use of himself and Wildman, whether or not to undertake the desperate deed of which they spoke is obscure. The conspirators counted upon the assistance of various officers and their regiments, and in particular that of Colonel Saunders, who had been restored to his command. Two entire troops out of three regiments and the private soldiers in another were believed to be ripe for rebellion. But, as in the case of the Overton affair, so many soundings had been taken and so many officers approached that it was only a question of time before these plottings were denounced to the ever-watchful Thurloe.

At the beginning of February, 1655, the Government struck. On 10th February Major Butler sent a party of horse from Marlborough to Easton, a near-by village, where in an upper room in his lodgings with the door open Wildman was discovered leaning upon his elbow and dictating to his servant, William Parker, who sat beside him, 'The Declaration of the Free and Well Affected People of England Now in Arms Against Oliver Cromwell.' Probably Wildman had heard the soldiers coming and arranged the scene accordingly, just as Francis Burdett, the radical, was found over one hundred and fifty years later by the police sent to arrest him, reading Magna Carta to his son. Unfortunately for Wildman the people were not in arms. Lord Grey of Groby was arrested by Colonel Hacker; and Colonel Sexby was tracked down to Portland Bill by a party of soldiers but was allowed to escape abroad with the connivance of the local authorities. The new Leveller plot had failed.

Wildman's declaration, unlike the petition of the three colonels, was not published at the time, but it has nevertheless survived. It was an able piece of propaganda calculated to appeal to the widest possible selection of Cromwell's opponents; it was also a frank justification of rebellion. 'Being satisfied,' it began, 'in our judgment and consciences of the present necessity to take up arms for the defence of our native rights and freedoms, which are wholly invaded and swallowed up in the pride and ambition of Oliver Cromwell, who calls himself Lord Protector of England, and hath rendered all Englishmen no better than his vassals, we expect to be branded with the infamous name of rebels and traitors.' They might, continued Wildman, moreover, be stigmatized as Levellers or Royalists or 'under some other odious notion,' but their object was simply to rescue the nation from slavery. If the army itself would do this for them, then of course we 'shall readily lay down our present arms.' The declaration goes on to explain how Cromwell had deceived them with specious promises and alluring pretences. How could they have guessed that a man of 'such mean quality and estate should aspire to make himself absolute Lord and tyrant over three potent nations'? His pretended zeal for God and His people, his professions of godliness, his hypocritical prayers and days of fasting, his 'dissembled humility and meekness and his frequent compassionate tears upon every occasion'—all these things had caused them at first to trust his assurances that he would safeguard the people's liberties and procure for them impartial justice. (Wildman here may have been thinking of his own temporary break with Lilburne in 1649.) Wildman then astutely makes use of some significant sentences in Cromwell's speech of 12th September to his first Protectorate Parliament. In that speech Cromwell had said that after the dissolution of the Long Parliament 'the authority I had in my hand' was boundless, 'for by Act of Parliament I was General of all the forces of the three nations of England, Scotland, and Ireland.' And after the Nominated Parliament was dissolved, Cromwell had said: 'My power again by this resignation was as boundless and unlimited as before; all things being subjected to arbitrariness, and [myself] a single person having power over the three nations boundlessly and unlimited.' 'He hath published,' Wildman could therefore say, 'to the whole world . . . that he had in himself an absolute unlimited arbitrary power without check and control until he put some limit upon himself.' Wildman then turned to one glaring grievance of the well-to-do, namely the heavy taxation which amounted to one-fifth or thereabouts of their estates and urged that it was the duty of every honest man to arm himself in defence of their ancient laws and dearest birthright against the present 'impostor and usurper.' Wildman's declaration in the possibly reduced form in which it comes down to us (although it is some 2,000 words long) concluded with five specific demands at which the rebels should aim:

(1) That all assumed and usurped power and authorities in the country should be abolished.

(2) That the constitution be settled upon a just basis with definite limits set on the powers of the magistrates.

(3) That the ancient liberties, as settled by Magna Carta, the Petition of Right and other laws, be secured.

(4) That free and regular parliaments with all their ancient powers and privileges should be guaranteed.

(5) That the armed forces of the nation 'be so disposed that no man may be master of parliaments and that no parliament shall make itself perpetual and enslave the people.'

'And that such a settlement may be made of right and freedom and these our ends obtained,' concluded Wildman's declaration, 'and a peace firmly established, we know no better means under God but a truly free parliament.'

The declaration was stronger on its destructive than on its constructive sides, as is natural in the case of propaganda. But it was skilfully calculated to appeal to parliamentarians, landowners, democrats, army Republicans, and even possibly to Royalists. Either a few manuscript copies were put into circulation before Wildman's arrest or else it must have freely passed round official circles, for the lawyer Whitelocke, who at that time was a member of Cromwell's immediate circle, tells us that 'any who viewed this declaration knew there was too much of truth in it, and had not the design been nipped in the bud, and timely discovered and prevented, it might have caused some disturbance to the Protector and to the peace of the new Government.'

As it was, Cromwell was plainly upset. Three days after Wildman's arrest he sent all the officers in London to take up commands outside, no doubt through fear of republican disaffection; he recalled in their place forces that had just returned from Ireland; he had the City scoured by parties of cavalry over a radius of four miles, and insisted that all the owners of houses in the City and suburbs gave a good account of their behaviour. Fear of disturbances was heightened by a fire that broke out in the Red Lion Inn in Fleet Street, where crowds of people gathered; and Major-General Skippon was ordered to police the entire City. To obtain the support of the local authorities Cromwell summoned the Lord Mayor, Aldermen, and Common Council and delivered what was described as 'a large and satisfactory speech.' He read them an intercepted letter from Charles II to one of his supporters in England which seemed to prove that there was to be an immediate royalist rising, and also read to them the draft (but surely not the whole draft?) of Wildman's declaration. Although no text of his speech survives, we can be sure that Cromwell told his audience that this was a conspiracy between the Levellers and the Royalists aimed at restoring the King and at nothing else. Whitelocke in his *Memorials* also asserts that many people wondered that 'Wildman and others of his party should now join in this design with those of the King's party' and instanced as proof of this intention the phrase in Wildman's declaration about the need for summoning a free parliament—which could, said Whitelocke (writing, it should be noted, after the Restoration), have had no other result than voting the King's restoration.

The idea, thus deriving from Cromwell and Whitelocke, that Wildman's plot of February, 1655, was planned in concert with the Royalists has been accepted by some later historians. Since the plan for a Leveller rising in the army against Cromwell was detected about the same time as a number of royalist plots, it has been assumed that at this date there was already an unholy alliance between the Levellers and the Royalists and that the two risings were timed to take place simultaneously. It is of course true that when Lilburne was in banishment in Amsterdam he had entered into communication with the Cavaliers, and that as early as 1649 Edward Hyde, Charles II's minister and later Earl of Clarendon, had urged upon the King the advantage of making an agreement with the Levellers. But we possess very full materials on the origin of the two plots. And there is not a single piece of evidence either among the voluminous Thurloe papers or in the comprehensive papers of the exiled Royalists to suggest that the Sexby-Wildman plot of 1654–5 was arranged in collaboration with the Royalist 'Party of Action.' The coincidence of time was no doubt due to the fact that the sudden dissolution of Parliament by Cromwell and the growing discontent with his rule had furnished an ideal opportunity for a rising. If there was any connexion, it was that the royalist exiles, seeing the confusion into which Cromwell's Government had been thrown by Wildman's plot, decided to loose their own long contemplated rising at what appeared to be an appropriate moment. As to the Levellers, it was in fact the failure of the Wildman plot which, as we shall see, drove them *later* into active alliance with the Court of Charles II.

In view of the outspoken character of Wildman's declaration and the discovery of a store of arms at the house where he was arrested, Cromwell must be said to have dealt extremely leniently with the conspirators. Although there was a rumour in London soon after his arrest that Wildman was likely to lose his life, in fact none of the Levellers was heavily punished, possibly because the Government feared that the imposition of severe penalties would have provoked trouble in the army. No such compassion was subsequently shown to the Royalists who were caught.

On 27th February some excitement was caused in London by the news that Wildman's servant, William Parker, to whom he had dictated, or pretended to dictate, his declaration, and who had been put into Chepstow castle with his master, had succeeded in escaping (he ultimately got out of the country); Wildman 'had not been nimble enough to do the like.' For fear of any further escapes Major-General Harrison, the Fifth Monarchy leader, was taken away from the prison in Portland whence Sexby had effected his escape, Lord Grey of Groby was moved from London to Windsor, and on 10th March Wildman was brought to London from Chepstow under a cavalry escort and imprisoned in the Tower. The following day the startling report reached Whitehall that a royalist rising had broken out in Wiltshire and later that the town of Salisbury had been seized in the King's name. The rising was suppressed without difficulty, but Oliver Cromwell took it as an excuse to abandon all further pretence of constitutional government and to introduce a full military dictatorship.

CHAPTER VIII

A TANGLED WEB

He deserves to be hanged.
CROMWELL on Wildman, autumn, 1655

AFTER his escape from the Isle of Portland Edward Sexby had made his way to Amsterdam where he immediately put himself into touch with the group of exiled Royalists. The failure of the Salisbury rising had depressed the spirits of these exiles and consequently they, or at least the more sanguine among them, were inclined to welcome the Leveller into their midst and to listen respectfully to the promises which he made to them. For Sexby assured them that he would be able to stir up a mutiny in Cromwell's army and thereby assist the restoration of Charles II, although he said that he would do this only on condition that he had the King's guarantee that he would accept a democratic constitution.

Sexby was undoubtedly a talented man, gifted with a persuasive tongue and complete self-assurance, and possessing an enormous capacity for intrigue. Edward Hyde has described the impression which he made on the exiled Royalists: 'For an illiterate person he spake very well and properly and used those words very well the true meaning and signification whereof he could not understand. . . . He was very perfect in the history of Cromwell's dissimulation, and would describe his artifices to the life. . . .' Discreditable stories about the Protector would in any case have made him popular in the Cavalier camp. But he had more than these to offer. He produced secret letters from intimates in England to prove that the fall of Cromwell was imminent. He showed Colonel Robert Phelipps at Amsterdam four letters which all agreed on one point, namely that Cromwell would speedily be overthrown by the Levellers. Sexby further informed Phelipps that recently several members of Cromwell's own party had deserted to the Levellers, including many of the judges. Swept away by Sexby's eloquence, Phelipps hastened to notify Charles II's Secretary of State, Sir Edward

Nicholas, that Sexby was the most powerful Leveller out of Cromwell's power, and, despite that, 'was very civil to me and communicative.' The Earl of Norwich, whom Sexby next approached in Bruges, also wrote to Nicholas in his praise. Although he was 'the prime Leveller' and the 'mortal enemy' of Cromwell 'in my presence he drank his Majesty's health with much seeming (at least) affection.' Norwich also believed that Sexby was a devout Roman Catholic.

Although Sexby thus succeeded in conveying the impression that he was a Leveller, a Royalist, and a Catholic all at one and the same time, he did not hide his unwillingness to exert his boasted influence in England on Charles II's behalf without substantial guarantees in return. He demanded the King's promise that parliaments should be called at regular intervals and that he should exercise the executive power only when parliament was not sitting.

The responsible Royalists, though not over-scrupulous, recoiled from entering into negotiations on such a basis. Sexby therefore next tried to enlist the support of the Spanish rulers in the Netherlands for his plans to overthrow the Protector. The real power in the Spanish Netherlands was at this time in the hands of Count Fuensaldaña, and he was inclined to listen to Sexby for several reasons: firstly, because Sexby spoke Spanish, and, secondly, because he knew that Sexby was an old advocate of Spanish friendship as a counterweight to the influence of France. In the third place, the Spaniards may have been inclined to lend their aid to the establishment of a republic in England by the thought that this would weaken their national enemies with perpetual civil wars.

In October, 1655, Don Alonso de Cardenas, formerly Spanish ambassador in England, joined Fuensaldaña in Brussels, which was the capital of the Spanish Netherlands. The dispatch by Cromwell of an expedition to the West Indies, an act of aggression and provocation, had led to war between England and Spain, and Cardenas, after vainly trying to incite the merchant classes against Cromwell, had been forced to leave the country. He came away convinced that the best hope of fomenting trouble against the Protector was by assisting the Levellers and exploiting discontent in the army rather than by means of a royalist rising. For the Royalists had been crushed by the special taxation and restrictions imposed by Cromwell after the latest rising. Cardenas and Fuensaldaña therefore furnished Sexby with a large sum of money and sent him to Madrid to place his plans before the fountain-head of authority, King Philip IV of Spain. But the more level-headed Royalists remained sceptical about Sexby. Sir Marmaduke Langdale, the gaunt Yorkshire commander who had been defeated by Cromwell at Preston, remarked pessimistically on Sexby's journey to Madrid that he hoped the Spaniards would convert him to the King's cause, while Sir Edward Nicholas thought that he was probably an agent of Cromwell.

In order to corroborate the stories that he told the royalist leaders of his tremendous influence among the English Levellers, Sexby had produced on his arrival in the Netherlands a packet of letters which he asserted he had received from prominent men in England. He exhibited letters not only from his fellow conspirators in the abortive February plot, such as Lord Grey of Groby, Vice-Admiral Lawson, and John Wildman, but even from no less a person than Henry Lawrence, the President of Cromwell's Council of State. There is small reason, however, to believe that any of these letters had been genuinely received by Sexby since he left England. It is improbable on the face of it that Lawrence would have had cause to communicate with Sexby at this time, whilst Grey of Groby and Wildman were in prison and could hardly have found the means so promptly to smuggle letters abroad. It is much more likely that Sexby had in his possession some letters from these men written at an earlier date and either forged the signatures to imaginary missives or showed the signatures alone to his hosts and made up the rest. For he was a champion liar.

Yet it was natural enough that Sexby to prove his authority and his immediate power of helping the Royalists or Spaniards should claim to be in contact with Wildman, now since Lilburne's banishment the acknowledged Leveller leader. So as early as June, 1655, Father Peter Talbot, an Irish Jesuit, who acted as intermediary between Sexby and the Spaniards, had reported that Sexby 'had received a letter from Wildman, the great Leveller, this post.' Yet Sexby's claim to have received such a letter can be refuted from out of his own correspondence, for in a letter which he wrote to Wildman in May, 1656, and which has survived, he specifically said, 'it is now about a year and two months since I left England and longer since . . . I received any [news] from thee.' The flourishing before the Royalists of his alleged correspondence with Wildman was simply a small move in Sexby's unscrupulous and grandiose plan for an all-embracing coalition against Cromwell.

The truth was that throughout 1655 John Wildman had languished in the Tower without being able to communicate with his friends outside or being able to obtain any concessions from his gaolers, who had good reason to watch him closely after his attempt to escape from Chepstow. The Majors-General who now ruled England gradually succeeded in locating most of the estates which had been bought by him either for himself or on behalf of others. Major-General Worsley reported to Thurloe in November that he had discovered a large estate of Wildman's in Lancashire and asked for instructions: 'If I hear not from you, I intend to sequester [that is, seize the rents] upon all that belongs to him.' In further letters Worsley announced that he had seized Wildman's Lancashire estates, presumably with Cromwell's approval, and held out hopes of discovering other estates. The Worcestershire commissioners also found some estates nominally belonging to Wildman in 1655 and asked whether they should impound them. The heavy cost of the war against Spain made any odd contributions to the Exchequer doubly welcome. And however lenient Cromwell might have proved himself to be in dealing with other Republicans, he remained adamant against Wildman and the Levellers. In October Colonel Ludlow, a Republican but no Leveller, left Ireland in defiance of his orders and came over to England, hoping apparently to head an opposition to the new dictatorship. He was arrested and imprisoned, but in December Cromwell sent for him and he was given his freedom in return for a promise not to conspire. During the interview Cromwell revealed to Ludlow who it was he considered to be his greatest enemy by complaining 'bitterly against Major Wildman . . . reviling him with unhandsome language and saying he deserved to be hanged.'

But in the spring of the following year Wildman conceived an ingenious plan for getting out of prison and at the same time continuing his campaign to replace Cromwell by a democratic republic. He was not nice as to the means he employed. His scheme was first of all to establish touch with the Royalists abroad through Charles II's agents in England and then offer John Thurloe his services as a spy upon the exiles overseas in exchange for his own freedom. Cromwell's Secretary of State had good reason to be on the look-out for a new agent. In the autumn of the previous year a certain John Manning had been shot by the exiled Cavaliers for betraying their secrets to Thurloe and consequently there was no rush of applicants to fill the vacant position. Wildman's intention was to serve neither Thurloe nor the Royalists but to use any means at his disposal to destroy the military dictatorship and substitute some form of democratic constitution. He experienced no difficulty in making contact with the active Royalists. His bold defiance of the dictator at the height of his power naturally commended him to the exiled Court, quite apart from the testimonials given to him by Sexby. In March, 1656, Mrs. Alice Ross, the wife of an active Royalist who had been obliged to flee the country and who now carried on underground work in her husband's place, had written abroad to suggest that 'a match might be made between the King and Wildman.' Evidently Wildman had suggested that his support for the Royalist cause might be obtained (like Sexby's) on terms. 'I am told,' wrote Mrs. Ross, 'that there is a colonel who is a very [close] friend and allied to the Wildman family which has not [had] the kindness from the King's friends as he did expect; and it is feared if not timely prevented . . . some [people] may make a breach . . . and then there is no hopes for the match to go forward between the King and Wildman. Sir Edward Hyde fully understands, if yourself doth not, the conditions Wildman and his friends require; and it is thought very fit that some that are acquainted with their intentions should speak with this colonel [Wildman] and do what may be done to recover (compensate for) the former neglect.'

On 18th May Sexby himself succeeded in getting through a letter to Wildman in the Tower which is of interest as showing the kind of language in which the conspirators wrote to each other and the hopes held out by Sexby at the time on Wildman's behalf:

'I pity thy condition, but prithee to be of good comfort; all hopes of liberty is not utterly lost and gone; nor do I yet despair but shall I see England again, and thee too before I die, yea before many years pass, I trust many months; neither in this do I feed myself with a fantastic dream, but for what I have good ground as they should understand, if it were possible for this to get to thy hand, and then shouldst send me a cipher, and orders how I should direct mine to you. Your pains would be recompensed by what might possibly be imparted; though I hope thou question not my love; and this I assure you of, I should not say that to any in the world as I would to thee. Oh! what would I give for an hour's discourse; but know that cannot be; let us converse this way, I desire, if possible. I understand thou art much dejected. I cannot but exceedingly blame you for it; you have as little cause so to be as ever had prisoner in thy condition; for though your unrighteous judge [Cromwell] and his janesaires [Christian soldiers] think they sit so sure that there is no condition of falling, yet I tell thee he will not be himself of that opinion long; and then I am sure you would not, if he knows what I can tell thee, and fain would if thou wouldst send me a cipher and thy faithful engagement to keep it secret. That apostate thinks he knows me, but if as he pretends he would not be jealous of me, being in any petty design, I hate foolish businesses; those [serious] undertakings and only such can render him in this falling condition. He is inconsiderable, mark what I say to you; his way within few months will be hedged up by that necessity his own designs will bring upon himself; being frustrated therein his soul (as proud as Lucifer's) will fail within him.

'This will be given to thee if possible by a hand thou knowest; if thou hast it send to me by that person thy character. In my next to you I shall tell thee how and to whom you shall direct thine for me. I shall not further enlarge except to tell thee that I am and for ever shall remain my worthy friend,

'Thine to command till death.'

After his release from prison Wildman answered this letter and sent the cipher as requested, but his reply does not survive.

In any case, however, Wildman experienced no difficulty in finding contacts with the royalist leaders. Two of their regular agents and correspondents were Wildman's fellow-prisoners in the Tower, but both enjoyed milder treatment than he and were therefore able to smuggle information abroad. One of them was William Rumbold, another Leveller soldier who was now in touch with the Royalists. Rumbold told Lord Ormonde, an important Cavalier, who still held the now empty title of Viceroy of Ireland, that Wildman had said that a petition from the army was about to be presented to Cromwell 'which, it is supposed, will greatly displease him.' Wildman hoped, according to Rumbold's information, that 'although the petitioners looked another way' (*i.e.* towards a

republic), 'yet things will turn out to the King's advantage. . . .'
However, so far as we know, no petition was published at this stage.
To Rumbold's communications about Wildman, Charles II
hastened to send a warm reply. Rumbold was told by Ormonde
that 'the King is glad to hear from John Wildman of whom he had
so great a value that he gives full credit to all he says and therefore
desires not only the continuance of his advertisements (information)
and endeavours for his service but his advice when he can afford it
safely and peacefully.' Evidently the King's advisers set greater
store upon establishing a direct contact with Wildman than upon
reaching Wildman through Sexby. Sexby's lie that he had received
letters from Wildman in the Tower clearly failed to convince
Charles's ministers, for Lord Ormonde asked Rumbold to let him
know 'whether there be any correspondence between Wildman
and Sexby' and what Wildman's opinion was of Sexby and his
negotiations.

The other fellow-prisoner and Royalist with whom Wildman
established contact was Sir Robert Shirley. Shirley had been put
upon parole by Cromwell, but his subsequent career shows how
little value the irreconcilable Royalists attached to any promises
they made to the Protector. According to a letter from Shirley to
the King, written on 20th June, 'Wildman was very zealous for the
King's interest, and though he seems to comply with the canting
party, which he had a great interest in and wholly rules, yet he
desires to raise himself by the King's favour.' In this letter Shirley
enclosed the heads of a declaration which Wildman had proposed
that the King should issue, guaranteeing parliamentary, constitutional, and democratic government in the event of his restoration.
Shirley reported that if the King were willing to publish such a
proclamation, Wildman would prove himself to be 'highly
serviceable.' On the other hand, John Weston, another royalist
agent in England, writing through Mrs. Ross to the King, seems to
have reported that Wildman demanded money as well as assurances. His letter was written in cipher and its interpretation must
be largely a matter of guesswork. 'I told you,' said Weston, 'the
ill nerves of your friend Mr. Blackman [Wildman?] being so far
gone in the spleen and the scurvy that his physicians had little hope
if they missed curing him by a course of steel [money?] which
would not be proper till the fall of the leaf [autumn] and this you

were only to know lest his breeding wife [Sexby?] should miscarry with the news.'

Although Wildman had thus established contact with the King across the water and stated his terms through no less than five channels, Dick Pile, a west country surgeon and another Royalist, with a wide reputation for honesty, gave it as his opinion at this time that Wildman's secret negotiations with the King would come to nothing, 'for I am certain that Cromwell knows it.' The Court, of Charles II were thus given the hint from the very beginning, and it was clear that if Wildman were to do any spying for Thurloe he would have to use the utmost circumspection. On the other hand, it is plainly too much of a coincidence to believe that as soon as Wildman succeeded in establishing contact with Charles II from the Tower of London, he should have been set free on bail and all his estates released from confiscation—as now happened—unless he had promised the Protectorate Government some valuable services in return.

Wildman's bargain with Thurloe to spy on the Royalists in return for his release is not susceptible of clear documentary proof. To the ordinary public all that happened was this: during his sixteen months in prison Wildman's numerous business affairs had fallen into a state of utter chaos. His creditors begged Cromwell to release him so that their debts should be settled. On 26th June 1656 a group of them forwarded a petition for his release on the ground that 'many suits at law being commenced against him and since his restraint his estate is likely to be utterly ruined and his right and title cannot be defended without his personal liberty to prosecute the same suits.' Cromwell was asked, out of tenderness to Major Wildman's family and for the preservation of the petitioners' estates, to free the Major if he gave security 'to act nothing prejudicial to the Commonwealth.' The Protector therefore acceded to the request, and on 1st July Wildman was granted three months' liberty on the substantial bail of £10,000, a measure of his wealth or his dangerous character, or both. But in view of the violent attacks made by Wildman on Cromwell in his notorious declaration, of the cruel punishment inflicted upon his fellow-Leveller, Lilburne, and of the anger expressed by Cromwell against him only a few months earlier, it is impossible to believe that Wildman would have been released except on the understanding that having already obtained valuable contacts while in the Tower, he would now spy on the Royalists on Thurloe's behalf. Certain subsequent events showed plainly that such a bargain must have been made. At the same time there is every reason to suppose that Wildman had no real intention after his release of doing anything other than using his improved position to crush the Cromwellian dictatorship and obtain a democratic constitution in its stead.

After his release Wildman returned to his London house and his office at St. Martin's le Grand, and he also laid the foundations for becoming a country gentleman. About the time of his arrest he had completed negotiations for the purchase of a house and estate at Shrivenham in Berkshire, some seventeen miles from Oxford. This estate, known as Becket, was at least as old as Domesday Book, when it belonged to the Earl of Evreux. Later it became a royal property and was used as a country seat by King John. In 1637 Sir Henry Marten, the Judge Advocate, bought Becket together with two other Shrivenham estates; but in 1652 his son, the first of the Republicans, who spent money like water, sold all these manors to Sir George Pratt, who, however, conveyed them three years later to Wildman's trustees. The Becket estate thus became the real home of Major Wildman and his family. His son adopted John Shute, a kinsman by marriage, later first Earl of Barrington, as his heir, and the Becket estate remained with the Barrington family until 1936, when it was sold to the War Department.

One other purchase was made by Wildman soon after his release. He bought a tavern, known as Nonsuch House, in Bow Street, Covent Garden, and there installed William Parker and his wife as innkeepers. Parker was Wildman's servant who, after his successful escape from prison, had fled overseas and then returned to England with letters from Sexby. Wildman appears to have made this investment partly as a reward to Parker for his faithfulness and partly to secure a convenient meeting-place for himself and his friends. Nonsuch House was to become a principal centre for republican plotters and thinkers between 1658 and 1661.

Having thus settled his family affairs, Wildman plunged into an extraordinary Spanish-Royalist-Leveller manoeuvre to blow Cromwell sky-high, hoping out of the resulting confusion to fashion a democratic utopia.

CHAPTER IX

WILDMAN'S POWDER PLOT

We have been led, cheated, cozened, and betrayed . . . by that sink
of sin . . . who now calls himself the Protector.
WILDMAN's 'humble address' to Charles II, 1656

JUST before Wildman's release the Spanish Government had
decided to sign a treaty with Charles II in the rather tenuous
hope that the Royalists would be of some assistance to them in their
war against Cromwell. The Spanish King undertook to provide
Charles with a force of four thousand foot soldiers and two thousand
cavalry, all fully equipped, together with ships to transport them
and funds to maintain them, to invade England and restore him to
his throne. But to this undertaking was attached a very difficult
condition. The troops were not to be made available until
Charles's supporters in England had secured a port suitable for the
disembarkation of the Spanish forces. The same treaty permitted
Charles to move his Court to Bruges and granted him a small
pension. It was signed on 12th April 1656.

The terms of the treaty explain why it was that the Royalists
were anxious to obtain the active aid of the Levellers. Their own
sympathizers in England were so closely watched that their chances
of seizing a port were negligible. But the Levellers asserted, or
pretended, that they would have no difficulty whatever in placing
a port at Charles's disposal. In May Wildman sent a message
through Rumbold saying that his party had 'some seaport towns
and several garrisons in their power, and he named particularly
Deal castle.' Since by now Sexby's boasts had been somewhat
exposed, his letters intercepted, and his republican predilections
and intrigues with Spain had alienated the leading royalist
ministers, they turned hopefully towards Wildman as a man
sufficiently powerful to deliver them a port and paid attention to
all his professions and promises. Wildman appeared willing to
meet them more than half-way.

Directly after his release he had hastened to sign, together with
William Howard, a younger son of Lord Howard of Esrick, and

eight obscure Anabaptists and Levellers, a 'humble address' to
Charles II. The address opened with a dirge sounded over the
present state of the nation and a lamentation for past sins: 'We have
been led, cheated, cozened and betrayed by that grand impostor,
that loathsome hypocrite, that detestable traitor, that prodigy of
nature, that opprobrium of mankind, that landscape of iniquity,
that sink of sin, and that compendium of baseness, who now calls
himself the Protector.' Such was the man they had exchanged for
the late King, who was 'a gentleman of the most strong and perfect
intellectuals, so of the best and purest morals of any prince that ever
swayed the English sceptre.' And unhappily and confessedly the
fault was entirely their own. For had not they trampled underfoot
all authorities, laid violent hands on their sovereign, ravished their
parliaments, and deflowered the virgin liberties of the nation?
Now for their sins they had been chastened with scorpions and fly
'like partridges hunted from hill to hill and from mountain to
mountain but can find no rest. . . .' At last they began to whisper
among themselves: 'Why should we not return to our first husband?'
So for the common good and prosperity they turned to King
Charles II and promised to hazard their lives and all that was dear
to them 'to re-establish your Majesty on the throne of your fathers.'
Not, however, without conditions. For the petition asked for the
restoration of the Long Parliament, the stringent terms of parliamentary supremacy offered to Charles I when he was a prisoner in
the Isle of Wight, complete freedom of worship, the abolition of
tithes, and an act of full amnesty and oblivion. The humble
address was dispatched to Charles by a certain Captain Titus with
a covering letter from Howard in which he suggested that the King
might send £2,000 to defray the necessary costs of this royalist
group of Levellers. Charles II did not have £2,000 to spare and
instead sent an invitation to Howard to come to see him at Bruges.

Howard's father had been created a peer by Charles I, but joined
the Roundheads, and in 1650 was a member of the Council of State.
He was, however, soon discovered to be taking bribes from the
Royalists and was dismissed from all his offices and imprisoned in
the Tower. His son was a man of pleasant conversation and few
principles. When he saw Charles II at Bruges, he openly mocked at
the extravagances of his fellow conspirators and observed that once
they were 'engaged in blood' they would recede from their

'republican' demands. Charles was delighted with him and he with Charles, who in due course sent him back to England with a personal letter for Wildman. Howard was to tell Wildman how welcome his messages had been and how glad the King was to see his name subscribed to the address; he desired to be informed 'of a particular transaction' (presumably the seizure of a port), for without that information he could not decide many points. Unfortunately, Charles II added, he could not send any money but he promised to repay everything that might be laid out on his behalf.

Want of money was the insuperable obstacle to all these schemes. After all, Wildman had been obliged to find £10,000 for his bail and his lands had been only just released from sequestration. He had already sent a message through Sir Robert Shirley that 'when the King says what sum he will give, on what security, etc.,' he (Wildman) 'will treat with the deputy Governor of Portsmouth, a man sufficiently necessitous.' Later the Levellers notified Charles that he might have Portsmouth for £15,000 and asked the King to send someone to take command of the port, as they would not surrender it to the Royalists in the neighbourhood.

Charles had plenty of agents to send, but, probably wisely, he had no intention of parting with cash for so dubious a project. All his available funds were being spent on raising four regiments of mercenaries who were to co-operate with the Spaniards when the time was ripe for the invasion of England. Yet without money the Levellers frankly confessed that they had no real hopes of over-throwing the Protectorate. In June, 1656, Sexby had paid a flying visit home, where of course he did not see Wildman, who was still in the Tower, and on his return he wrote to him, thanking him for his cipher and explaining that English liberties could only be restored by the judicious distribution of gold in the army and hinting that he might be able to get his hands on some shortly. 'In my judgment,' he continued, 'they are mad men, if not worse, if worse can be, that think either paper politics or great words can free us from our miseries. No, it's that must free us from it [that] hath brought it upon us; the sword it is that now enslaves us and it's that must deliver us; that which keeps it sharp and the users of it seemingly united it's not love nor fear but money for the present livelihood among the common sort . . . the sword hath gained the power to enslave us, and it's that they will keep the power to entail it upon us, and that money is the only thing that ties up with this entrust. They begin at the wrong end who think to untie this knot without this key or bodkin. . . .' Sexby therefore asked Wildman to exert his influence to win adherents to their cause in the army. 'If the soldiers were to declare for liberty and hold out for a month I doubt not,' he said, 'that through God's blessing we may be able to fire our country.' If Wildman would set about this propaganda in the army, Sexby promised to send him money and asked him whether he should send it 'by bill or ship.' Sexby believed that once a rising were started others at present too cautious or cowardly would join them. But 'as the proverb is of Yarmouth herrings, smoking will make them good if anything will.'

Meanwhile both Republicans and Cavaliers had fastened their hopes upon confusion arising after the meeting of Cromwell's new Parliament. Cromwell, like Charles, was short of money and had therefore been obliged to hold an election. The expensive Spanish war was not particularly popular and the rule of the Majors-General was widely disliked, so that there seemed good reason for Cromwell's enemies to expect that he would soon find himself in difficulties. Certainly there were stirrings. The old oligarchic Republicans like Ludlow and Sir Henry Vane raised their heads and the extreme sects, like the Fifth Monarchy men, published manifestoes. But the Protector took every precaution. Early in September thirty Royalists were arrested; a hundred of the elected M.P.'s, many of them Republicans, were forcibly excluded from the House of Commons. Moreover Sir Richard Willis, a member of the inner circle of English Royalists, betrayed their plans to Thurloe,* whilst Wildman was not behindhand in supplying vague warnings about the royalist plans by way of payment for his release from the Tower.

It was a complicated web of treachery which Wildman now proceeded to weave. On the one hand, he conveyed the impression to the Cavaliers that he was a far more valuable link with the Levellers than was Sexby, for not only was he a more ardent Royalist (he said) than Sexby but he would reach a 'more advanced point' with his schemes. No less a person than Chancellor Hyde

* Miss Marjory Hollings, in the *English Historical Review*, January, 1928, wrote an ingenious but not entirely convincing defence of Willis.

endorsed Wildman's assertions. For in a paper of instructions for the Earl of Bristol (the chief royalist go-between with the Spaniards) he wrote that the Spaniards were to be informed 'that there is a close correspondence [between the King] and Wildman, who does not trust Sexby with the knowledge of his plans.' Wildman was contrasted favourably with Sexby whose 'immediate trust was for those absolutely engaged for establishing a republic.' Yet at the same time Wildman was in active correspondence with Sexby. Together they concocted the plan for the seizure of Portsmouth; together they played with the idea, which they had envisaged two years earlier, of assassinating Cromwell.

In the same lengthy letter of Sexby's, from which we have already quoted, Sexby observed that he had been 'much tossed up and down in his spirits for fear of you, for I heard the rumour of the enlargement [your release] and of some jealousies that you were gained from the old cause.' He added his hope that 'you will have no cause to complain or regret the renewing our old correspondence, the great and only end of my desiring it with you is . . . to serve my poor enslaved country.' However, he outlined details of his plans to Wildman and assured him that once money 'which will not only gain the bodies of men but their souls also' were distributed he would be revealed as possessing 'jackals in the forest amongst the lions and some cubs who hath seasoned claws and teeth . . . which I warrant will help to beat their own kind out of the den.' He suggested that Wildman should prepare the path for these 'jackals and cubs' to move against Cromwell in September and October, and said that he himself would remain in Holland for the next eight or ten weeks in readiness for any opportunity.

The 'jackals and cubs' employed by Wildman and Sexby consisted of three seedy old soldiers, headed by ex-quartermaster Miles Sindercombe, who were bribed to try their hand at shooting the Protector. Their efforts were consistently unsuccessful. They intended first to let fly their blunderbusses at Cromwell on his way to open parliament on 17th September, but 'finding so many people standing on both sides of the way as the Protector came by and as he passed, they darest not do anything, for fear of being observed before they shot.' They made other attempts, they said, near Hampton Court, at Kensington, Hyde Park, and at Turnham Green. But somehow on each occasion something turned up to prevent them. Either Cromwell failed to come their way or arrived at the wrong time. Finally they took the decision to abandon their project until the spring and in the meantime to set fire to Whitehall Palace. Wildman, Sexby and a Major Wood were all privy to the new scheme. Sexby and Major Wood were inclined to think that the plan, which was to dump a box of gunpowder or of fireworks in Whitehall Palace to be burnt with a slow match, would require too much time and too many persons and was subject to too many accidents to be carried out with any prospect of success. Wildman thought otherwise, for he asserted that even if the fire failed to destroy Cromwell, the burning of Whitehall would prove the signal for a rising. He was so fervent in his opinion that his authority prevailed. The box of gunpowder was smuggled into Whitehall chapel with the connivance of one of the sentries, Toop by name, on the evening of Thursday, 8th January. But at the last moment Toop's nerve failed him and he informed the Protector of the plot. As soon as the would-be incendiaries had dumped their infernal machine, the officer of the guard put out the slow matches and next morning Sindercombe and his fellows were arrested. One of them confessed, and Sindercombe escaped execution by taking poison which had been smuggled into prison by his sister.

Wildman was deeply disappointed, for he was convinced that the preparations had been so perfect that but for Toop's betrayal Cromwell could not have survived that night. It is important to notice that although Wildman was well aware of the plot, he gave no hint of it to Thurloe. Moreover, even after the plot was discovered he refrained from informing against Sexby or Wood, whom the witnesses against Sindercombe did not know were involved. This is decisive evidence that Wildman never betrayed anything of value to Cromwell's ministers or did anything likely to endanger his fellow Levellers. If, as has been suggested, he was the author of the anonymous letters among the Thurloe papers informing against Howard, it is obvious that Howard was not a man who was likely to be of value to the democratic cause and indeed was more likely to betray it.

The discovery of the Powder Plot strengthened the hands of those lawyers, Presbyterians, and other members of Cromwell's last Parliament who believed that the only security for the future of England lay in making Cromwell king. Consequently the first four months of 1657 were filled with negotiations between the parliamentary majority and Cromwell about the exact terms on which he would consent to accept the Crown. This proposal was not received with universal pleasure. The army leaders, who hoped one day to inherit the supreme power from Cromwell, looked askance at the idea of an hereditary monarchy; the Independent soldiers who had fought to attain a puritan republic were perplexed and dismayed; and all Cromwell's unflinching enemies, from the expelled Republican oligarchs to the Fifth Monarchy men and Levellers, hoped to draw profit from the dissensions which the proposals engendered.

Meanwhile, Wildman and Sexby took the discovery of Sindercombe and his box of fireworks with philosophic calm. Sexby told Captain Titus that he was still resolved to press on with the business of assassinating the Protector, and in March he announced his intention of returning to England 'resolved on either Cromwell's death or his own.' The Royalists, for their part, now decided that all hopes of an invasion or a rising must be set aside for the time being. Above all, they had not the least intention of devoting their hardly collected troops, raised and paid at so heavy a sacrifice, to a purely democratic and republican adventure. For Sexby had told them that no mention must be made of King Charles's name until after Cromwell had been overthrown, and that any Cavaliers who took up arms in alliance with the Levellers must 'speak of nothing but the liberty of their country.' Thus although the Spaniards were still inclined to favour Sexby's plans for a Leveller-Royalist invasion and uprising, Edward Hyde blew cold upon them, and Sexby was obliged instead to prepare simply for the assassination of Cromwell in the hope that it would encourage an internal Leveller rebellion. The Royalists, young and old, grave and gay, gave their unanimous approval to the idea of killing the usurper.

But Sexby and Wildman delayed the execution of their schemes until too late. In March Titus reported that Vice-Admiral Lawson was 'totally governed by Sexby and Wildman,' but as Lawson had resigned his command the previous year, their influence was of negligible value. On 9th April the Fifth Monarchy men, indignant with the notion that Cromwell might accept a temporal crown, attempted a rising in Mile End, but so meagre was their following that the outbreak was scarcely noticed even in the House of Commons. At about the same time (April, 1657) Wildman wrote from England to Major Wood in Flanders, saying:

'I would give anything I had in this world if you were at present here, but cannot yet advise you to come, though I shall do so shortly. We are as active as ever, and upon a business that Sexby will communicate to you. . . .'

But all Sexby did was to show Wood and Titus another letter, which he had perhaps received from Wildman, that 'said in general that either Cromwell must fall or thousands of us have proceeded too far to make any retreat.' A little later, however, Sexby, commenting on the suppression of the Fifth Monarchy rising, told the Royalists abroad not to be discouraged: 'So long as I live there is no danger but [that] Cromwell shall have his hands full, and I hope his heart ere long; for I have more irons in the fire for Cromwell than one . . . believe it, his own people in the army are upon the wing.' But on 8th May Cromwell confounded his friends and enemies alike by finally refusing the crown.

Sexby, with the aid of Titus, had been mainly employed that spring in writing a pamphlet entitled *Killing No Murder*, in order to justify and to stimulate Cromwell's assassination. Fully documented with quotations from the Old Testament and from the highest authorities among the Greek and Roman philosophers, the pamphlet set out to prove how entirely proper it was to kill a tyrant; but at the same time it was not lacking in wit and it was audaciously dedicated to the Protector himself:

'to your Highness justly belongs the honour of dying for the people, and it cannot choose but be an unspeakable consolation to you in the last moments of your life to consider with how much benefit to the world you are like to leave it.'

The pamphlet reached England too late, for Cromwell's refusal of the crown proved that, even although he might have betrayed the true Republicans, he was at least not technically a usurper of the throne.

Sexby himself ventured into England in the train of his pamphlet. He came in disguise to consult Wildman and to spy out the land. On his way back to Holland he was caught by Cromwell's officers

and sent to the Tower. Here his nerve cracked, but he refused
to betray his associates, although clearly one of them must have
betrayed him. Was Wildman the traitor? Naturally, in view of
his peculiar relations with Thurloe, suspicion must rest upon
him; but as there is a complete absence of evidence and as there is
no proof that Wildman ever betrayed a fellow-Leveller, he has
the right to be acquitted. Yet on the basis of *cui bono* alone Wildman could be deemed guilty. For when six months later Sexby
died in the Tower, Wildman stepped into his place not only as
plotter-in-chief but as the link between the English Levellers and
the Spanish authorities.

Don John of Austria, an illegitimate son of Philip of Spain by
an actress, had succeeded the Count of Fuensaldaña as Governor
of the Spanish Netherlands in 1656. Like Fuensaldaña, he and
Don Alonso de Cardenas, who acted as his chief minister, never
set much store upon the royalist plans of invading England and
gave more credit to Sexby's promises of engineering a rising in
Cromwell's army. Now that Sexby was in prison, Wildman
entered into negotiations with the Spaniards. In the summer and
early autumn he paid several visits to Flanders, where he tried to
throw dust into everybody's eyes in the hope of strengthening the
influence of the English Republicans. Don John seems to have
told Wildman that he would not provide troops for the invasion
of England unless the Levellers came to terms with the Royalists.
On the other hand, Wildman told the Royalists, no doubt to dis-
courage them from undue dependence upon Spain, that 'the
King of Spain had no affection for the King of England and was
in communication with Cromwell.' Wildman therefore represented to King Charles II that he must rely less upon the Spaniards
and more upon the Levellers and upon his [Wildman's] own
ability to kill the Protector; he asked for money for this enterprise
and for the King's promise to 'govern according to the ancient
laws of the land.' To strengthen his own position further Wildman
also assured Sir Edward Nicholas that Sexby was 'a knave.' But
Wildman's lies were scarcely convincing, and the Royalists had
good grounds for suspecting his sincerity. In October, 1657,
Hyde received a report of the way in which Wildman had got out
of England to come to Flanders. According to this report, Wildman was at Gravesend and was stopped by the port authorities

although he had a passport in the name of John Jones, signed with Cromwell's signet. The port officer, who happened to recognize the Major, properly committed him to the blockhouse and sent word to Cromwell. But Cromwell not only ordered his release but sent instructions to the captain of the boat 'not to question his journey but to carry him wherever he should direct.' This story, however, is circumstantial rather than plausible, and Hyde's reports on Wildman were varied and contradictory. The royalist Weston, for example, remained of the opinion that Wildman was 'an honest man,' and Captain Titus thought that the safe arrival of Major Wood back from England in November was 'no small argument' for Wildman's integrity, since Wood had frequent meetings with Wildman when he was in England. Nevertheless it was typical of Wildman's caution that when he was in Flanders he interviewed only the Spaniards and carefully refused a pressing invitation from the Irish priest, Peter Talbot, to present himself to Charles II or his ministers on the ostensible ground that any delay might cost him his life.

The negotiations between Wildman and the royalist chiefs over the plan to kill Cromwell were therefore carried on by post. As early as August Ormonde told Hyde of rumours from England about Wildman 'and the approaching commotions,' but it was not until the end of November that the question of Wildman taking Sexby's place in the murder plot was fully studied. The intermediaries were Father Talbot and Captain Titus, part author of *Killing No Murder*. On 3rd November Ormonde wrote from Bruges to Talbot as follows:

'I am commanded by his Majesty [King Charles II] to return you his sense [opinion] upon yours of the 27th which is that he finds Captain Titus hath rightly related to you the discourse his Majesty had with him, and that you may confidently assure Wildman that the sum proposed shall be deposited in such a manner, and that it shall be evident to any reasonable person that the work [of assassination] being done, the reward is sure; but his Majesty holds it not prudent or reasonable for him to put it into the hands of any merchant at London, from whence he cannot hope to draw it, in case the thing should not be as much as attempted; much less will he consent that it shall be distributed under pretence of gaining persons to effect the business [of murder], unless such distribution be made appear to be rational either to himself here or to someone in England trusted by him, and such a person the King says Wildman knows how and where to find. In fine, nobody can doubt his Majesty's willingness to make the bargain, and the undertaker [assassin] may satisfy himself in his ability to perform his promise; nor can it be reasonably suspected that whatever the event be, the King will leave a real attempt of the nature unrewarded, unless he at the same time means to tell the world he never means to look more after the recovery of his right.'

It appears from this letter that John Wildman had been trying to induce the King to deposit in London a sum of money as a reward for the murder of Cromwell—as Sexby had tried a year earlier. The impecunious Charles naturally refused to do anything so rash. Wildman also seems to have inquired whether Charles's own army of 1500–2000 foot would be available to support a rising in England. Here again the King answered warily. He would, replied Ormonde, 'be glad to know for what particular end the question was made.' 'On the whole matter,' concluded Ormonde, 'he conceives it were best if Wildman himself cannot come over safely or without prejudice to his negotiation where he is, that he should send over someone with credentials and instructions from him.'

Peter Talbot, as intermediary, acknowledged this letter on 3rd December: 'I . . . will to-morrow write all that his Majesty is pleased to command, which cannot but seem very rational to Wildman himself, though I offered him so much in the Spaniard's behalf and he then would not hear of it. He bids me put them in mind of desiring the King to give under his hand and seal an engagement to govern according to the ancient law of the land. . . .'

Fortunately we are for once not dependent upon other people for Wildman's views. In three letters of November and December, 1657, to Talbot he set out his attitude to the scheme for assassinating Cromwell and for invading England. The letters are written in commercial jargon, as was the habit of conspirators in those days, but the names of the persons concerned are deciphered in the transcripts—in the originals they would be hidden under the names of merchants. Wildman's object was to find out how soon the Spaniards and Royalists would be ready to move.

Wildman to Talbot, 23rd November 1657:

'I wish I knew whether the Spaniards will supply the King with money and men for the time approacheth and his corre-spondents [supporters] here are in great expectation, and if I knew certainly I could better resolve. In my opinion your endeavours will be to no purpose if something be not done speedily, yet the King shall not by my consent send men without further advice. 'Tis to be feared his correspondents [the Cavaliers] will forestall a good market.'

Wildman to Talbot, 3rd December 1657:

'I perceive the Spaniards deal very uncertainly with the King, or he with himself and his correspondents. It is high time that the soldiers were here where they have been expected by their friends these three weeks, and I doubt will . . . lose their market and custom by their uncertain dependence, they telling their customers [supporters in England] so often that this time and that time they should have them, and all in vain. Cromwell had a factor [agent] lately with the King who brought him all his Majesty's pacquet [post] and I believe Cromwell is to settle, and undermine the King's trade, which I like not unless he corresponds with some surer traders [plotters], trade [plots] having been long dead here, but we believe there will be a sudden reviving of it. It is very hard to speak with Cromwell and Fairfax is ill-used by him.'

Wildman to Talbot, 24th December 1657:

'. . . I find the King and my lord of Ormonde's desire to dis-course with me in person about the garrisons and other things, and I wish heartily it had been sooner moved both in regard of the opportunity of my going and of the market, for now the Cavaliers have so filled the town with the noise of the great quantity of horse and foot that he [Charles II] hath ready, that Cromwell doth attempt to engross [arrest] as many as he can to spoil the others' market [plans], which is so strangely spoiled for the garrisons that I fear some mischief and that his friends will be arrested, so that upon the whole I am afraid if it should be possible for me to speak with Ormonde or the Chancellor or the King himself, the market [opportunity] will be spoiled before my return, that the goods [money] which I should bring over will not be of that use which they would have been formerly, yet I will consider of going or sending if it is possible. But I doubt the King's factors [agents] here will be all attacked, and it may be in my absence it would be worst [worse].

'Sir, you may perceive that I insist much upon what I told you as to the time when the market [opportunity] was to be expected, and I fear the King hath slipt it [let it slip] if he be now thinking that he hath time enough to let me come to him, and return before anything be done. . . .'

Wildman's demand that Charles should promise to govern according to the ancient laws, by which he meant according to the Leveller conception of constitutional monarchy, was side-stepped by Hyde's drafting of a proclamation referring all disputed questions to a free parliament; but Charles in any case possessed neither the money nor the men to carry out an invasion in December, as Wildman wanted. The best that the King could do was to write to his sister Mary, Princess Royal of the United Netherlands, begging her to send him a jewel that he could pawn. Mary did what he asked and Charles at once sent Ormonde to Don John to tell him that the time was ripe. But the Spaniards would do nothing until Ormonde himself had gone to England to investigate the chances of an internal rising in support of the invasion. This, it proved, was a useless delay. The only hope for the Spaniards to transport their troops to England in the teeth of Cromwell's navy was to get them across in mid-winter. Indeed by December the chance was already lost. The French had warned the English Government that the Spaniards were contemplating an attack and this warning caused Cromwell to strengthen his defences. In December the forces around London had been doubled, and in January the garrisons in Southern England had been reinforced and a coast-watching system completed. Several more Royalists were arrested on suspicion, and Titus had to confess his fear that 'Cromwell clapping up so many at present may abate for a time the courage of our friends.'

The paradoxical truth was, as Ormonde discovered during the dangerous mission to England which he undertook at Charles II's request in February, 1658, that the Royalists and Levellers would not rise at home without support from abroad, while the Spaniards would not assist an invasion until they were convinced that an internal rising was imminent. Moreover, the position was complicated by the existence of a sharp division of opinion among the Royalists in England. On the one hand, there was the 'Sealed Knot' or group of older Royalists, including the traitor, Sir Richard Willis, who were cautious and pessimistic; their chief hopes rested in being able to find an ally in the Presbyterian party which was becoming increasingly dissatisfied with Cromwell. On the other side, there was a group of younger men banded together by Dr. John Hewitt, who had been allowed to continue holding his living at St. Gregory's, St. Paul's Churchyard, and was the author of a little volume called *Prayer of Intercession for their use who mourn in secret for the Public Calamities of the Nation*. This group was fecund in promises to raise troops of horse, seize ports, and the like. The depth of their squabbles and the hollowness of their pretensions were not hidden from the King's envoy.

Ormonde managed to land in Essex in the middle of January, 1658, and, 'a green case over his hat, and a night-cap on his head,' he reached London and interviewed a number of important Royalists. Although Cromwell was aware of his presence in England, he succeeded in getting away safely and presenting his eagerly awaited report. His final analysis of the situation was that whilst there was no probability of a successful rising and no reliance ought to be placed on the promises of the younger Cavaliers, yet if the King could but land a force and supply of munitions near Yarmouth, the general discontent might be crystallized into a big insurrection against Cromwell. Edward Hyde, the chief royal adviser, agreed with Ormonde's report and said that unless his scheme were put into action their sympathizers in England would never stir.

Ormonde's report, however, persuaded the Spaniards that a diversion in England could be engineered and might help to disrupt the preparations which were then being made by the French and English armies for attacks on the ports of Mardyke and Dunkirk. The Spanish decision came too late, as Wildman had foreseen. On 4th February, just as Ormonde reached England, Cromwell had suddenly dissolved Parliament, which had become the focus for sectarian and republican agitation. Ludlow grumbled that 'His Highness walks from Parliament to Parliament to find one fit to plague the people.' The Protector also purged his army

of untrustworthy elements and enlisted the assistance of the City
of London to maintain order and suppress plots. By the time the
Spaniards had made up their minds to prepare a combined
operation against our shores, the English fleet had blockaded
Ostend, and Willis and others had betrayed the chief conspirators
in England. So the whole elaborate scheme fell to pieces. Ormonde had to confess that 'nothing will be begun in England
unless some accident give rise to it,' and Hyde admitted that no
invasion expedition could start unless Cromwell was obliged to
recall his fleet. In May a plot was detected in the City of London;
Hewitt and another Royalist were put to death; three others were
executed and many imprisoned.

Wildman had at one time been connected with Dr. John Hewitt's
side of the conspiracies, but how much he knew it is hard to say.
Thurloe's main source of information about Hewitt had been the
Reverend Francis Corker, who since the middle of 1657 had been
giving Cromwell's Government a generous measure of intelligence
about his fellow Anglicans' plottings for £100 cash down. Hewitt
had aimed at organizing a revolt in the City and also planned
for a number of risings throughout the country, especially in
Sussex and Yorkshire. In the winter of 1657 Corker wrote to
Thurloe:

'I have been with Dr. Hewitt who . . . tells me that the business
will be begun by a party of Levellers, a great distance from London
[this was probably at Chichester in Sussex]; and at the same time
they intend to rise here [in London] and that with such desperate
fury that (to use his own words) he fears the City will be fired in
many places. He tells me that one Wildman is the chief instrument
to raise that party of the army and Levellers abroad; yet withall
they have some suspicion of Wildman because Mr. Seymour repeats
from Colonel Overton in the Tower that Wildman holds some
correspondence with the Protector.'

In another letter written late in 1657 or early in 1658 Corker says
that Hewitt told him that he was writing to his friends to have
nothing to do with Wildman. The Gravesend incident had now
been widely reported among the Royalists on both sides of the
Channel, and this report, together with Overton's information,
had made many Royalists—trusting though they so often were—
suspicious about Wildman's fidelity.

Nevertheless Wildman remained in close touch with the Sussex section of the plot through his friend Henry Bishop. Bishop, who lived at Parham in Sussex, had a considerable reputation with the exiled Court as a thoroughly dependable person. He was also on the closest terms with Wildman—with whom he had been associated during Overton's plot of 1654—and knew all about the grandiose plan for a Leveller-Royalist insurrection. When he went up to London he was accustomed to stay at Nonsuch House, the coffee-house kept by Wildman's old servant, William Parker. Through him Wildman probably learnt of the Sussex branch of the plot—of how young John Stapley, a nephew of Lord Goring, had been persuaded by Hewitt to lead and organize an armed rising and had promised captains' commissions to his brother Anthony and to Thomas Woodcock, besides enlisting Bishop himself and the older men. Wildman may also in this way have heard of the activities of Major William Smith, who had been engaged in distributing blank commissions throughout the Sussex inns and had established relations with the Royalists of Hampshire.

When he had acquired sufficient evidence, Thurloe struck. In March, 1658, John Stapley was arrested. Full information about the Sussex end of the plot was obtained from Major Smith and other gentlemen who all accused each other. The whole plot was a complete fiasco.

What share had Wildman in the betrayal of the plot to Thurloe? The Royalists were angry and scattered accusations of betrayal far and wide, and their suspicion centred on Wildman and Bishop rather than on Willis and Corker. William Howard, who about a year after he had signed the 1656 petition to Charles I had been put into the Fleet prison, wrote to Edward Hyde directly after Hewitt's execution that he was sure that none but Wildman and Bishop 'were the first discoverers of Stapley's design.' Howard, however, innocently added that he thought the reason why Sir Richard Willis was not kept in prison was 'so that Wildman may not be discovered to be the traitor'—though Willis was almost certainly Thurloe's chief informant. Thomas Woodcock also reached the conclusion that he had been betrayed by Wildman and Bishop, while Major Smith, who when he was arrested vainly tried to implicate Wildman and the Levellers, 'solemnly protested on his death-bed and left it under his hand in writing that those words which Cromwell accused him of (by which he found he was betrayed) he never spoke to any flesh but Bishop.' He was, however, mistaken, for the evidence of his examination and trial, which exists among Thurloe's papers, shows that he had spoken to many people, including the Reverend Corker.

Now it is of course possible that Wildman did tell Thurloe what he knew, since he had every reason to wish this purely Cavalier plot to fail. But there is no concrete evidence among the voluminous Thurloe papers, which deal extensively with this plot, that Wildman had acted as stool-pigeon. Moreover, there was very little that he could tell. He may have pumped Bishop, but Hewitt, as we have seen, was specifically warned against him. Nor had Wildman any longer any contacts with Charles II's exiled Court. Since the New Year Father Peter Talbot and the other Royalists in Flanders had ceased to communicate with him. In answering Howard's letter about Wildman in September, 1658, Hyde stated that Wildman 'holds no correspondence with us.' But he continued to command some influence among the Spaniards, and there were also Royalists who were convinced that he was not responsible for the betrayal of any of the conspirators and deemed him still to be an 'honest man.'

CHAPTER X

A LABYRINTHINE INTRIGUE

They [the parliamentary republicans] have much the odds in speaking,
but it is to be hoped that our justice, our affection and our number
which is at least two-thirds, will wear them out at the long run.

ANDREW MARVELL, 1659

OLIVER CROMWELL, who had scourged the democratic Republicans as he had the unyielding Royalists, died on 3rd
September 1658, and his son, Richard, nominated by him as his
successor on his death-bed, succeeded to the Protectoral throne
without incident. Richard was a mild and reluctant recipient of
power and, being far less of a puritan than his father and not a
soldier, did not appeal to the ruling classes. Sir Henry Vane
unkindly described him as 'an idiot without courage or sense.'

Nothing in the events of this period is more remarkable than
the failure of either the Royalists or the Republicans to take
advantage of the opportunity of Richard's succession to undertake an invasion or stage a rising. But the exiled Court was at the
lowest ebb of its fortunes. Poverty stalked the lodgings of Bruges.
The King was indulging in a bout of promiscuous love-making.
The threadbare Cavaliers quarrelled among themselves and
fought duels. The royalist regiments, which had been raised
with so much difficulty and at so severe a monetary sacrifice,
were waging war for Spain against France and could not be withdrawn for service against Richard Cromwell. The Spanish
authorities were far too busy with their campaign in Flanders
and too suspicious of King Charles's supposedly French leanings
to furnish any assistance at this point of time. As for the Republicans, they wisely held their hands in the correct expectation
that there would soon be a quarrel between Richard Cromwell
and the Roundhead army leaders who considered that they had a
better claim than this idle country gentleman to inherit supreme
political power.

The army Grandees who, on account of their meetings at the
house of Charles Fleetwood, Richard Cromwell's brother-in-law,

were now known as the Wallingford House party, began to draw up a series of demands. They asked that Fleetwood should be made General of the Forces, with the power to confer commissions on all except field officers, that others of Cromwell's Majors-General, including Desborough and Whalley, should be given high well-paid positions in the army, and that no soldiers should be cashiered except by court martial. In effect they wanted to make the army a State within the State. General Monk, faithful to the memory of the dead Oliver, from his secure and independent position in Scotland, advised Richard to halve the size of the army and thereby squeeze out the malcontents and at the same time diminish his heavy expenses. Richard Cromwell foolishly preferred to take a middle course. He refused to grant Fleetwood a higher rank than that of Lieutenant-General, and by a couple of disarming speeches he induced the English army to proclaim its loyalty to him—at least for the time being. In return he refrained from reducing or purging the army, and trusted to the summoning of two newly elected Houses of Parliament, which were to meet in January, 1659, to enlist civilian support on his side. For his advisers he depended mainly upon the group known as the 'New Courtiers'—civilians like John Thurloe, Bulstrode Whitelocke and Lord Broghill, who had thrown in their lot with Oliver—while he tried to borrow money from the French King to put his finances straight.

The general election, which took place around Christmas, 1658, was on the whole favourable to Richard, whose supporters were estimated to number about two-thirds of the new House of Commons and were chiefly Presbyterians. The other one-third consisted largely of Republicans, but they were divided between the old oligarchic Republicans like Arthur Haselrig and Henry Vane, and the democrats headed by Wildman's friend, Henry Nevile. Wildman himself was not a member. This combined republican opposition devoted its first efforts to amending the Bill under which Richard had been recognized as Protector in such a way that he would become little more than a puppet ruler or a 'Venetian Doge,' to use the expression of that day.

To achieve their ends they adopted every form of obstruction known to House of Commons tacticians. Some light is thrown on their methods in a letter written by the poet Andrew Marvell, who at that date was an under-secretary of John Thurloe and therefore a member of the Court Party:

'Upon Monday [7th February] the bill for recognition of His Highness was read the second time. Thereupon the House entered into that debate and all hath been said against it which could be by Sir Arthur Haselrig, Sir Henry Vane, Mr. Weaver, Mr. Scot, Mr. St. Nicholas, Mr. Reynolds, Sir Anthony Ashley Cooper, Major Packer, Mr. Henry Nevile, my Lord Lambert and many more. Their doctrine hath moved most upon their maxim that all power is in the people, that it is reverted to this House by the death of his [late] Highness, that Mr. Speaker is Protector in possession and it will not be his wisdom to part with it easily, that this House is all England. Yet they pretend that they are for a single person but without negative voice [the right of veto], without militia, not upon the "Petition and Advice" [the Cromwellian constitution], but by adoption and donation of this House and that all the rights of the people should be specified and endorsed upon that donation. But we know well enough what they mean. A petition from some thousands in the City to their purpose hath been brought in (and they say they are trying to promote another in the army) but laid by to be at the end of this debate in which nothing is to intervene. They have held us to it all this week and yet [we are] little nearer [the end]. It was propounded on our side, seeing the whole bill stuck so, that before the commitment of it it should be voted in the House as part of it that His Highness is Protector, etc.; and not to pass but with the whole bill. But all we could gain hitherto is that there shall be a previous vote before the commitment but that that should be it is yet as far off as ever. For they speak eternally to the question, to the orders of the House, and in all the tricks of Parliament. They have much the odds in speaking, but it is to be hoped that our justice, our affection and our number which is at least two-thirds will wear them out at the long run.'

While the small group of democratic Republicans in the House of Commons were thus putting up an excellent if losing fight in alliance with the oligarchs and the disgruntled army chiefs, Wildman was trying to exploit his contacts abroad to promote the cause of republicanism with a far more remarkable combination of allies. He had by now completely broken his connexions with Hyde and the serious statesmen of Charles II's Court. Hyde had been told and was convinced that Wildman was false to the King's cause, although he noted that Wildman still had the confidence of 'some honest men.' Wildman could therefore use his influence in royalist circles to persuade the royalist members of the House of Commons (of whom there were several) to vote with the republican Opposition; and he schemed to interest the Spaniards in a new plan—'a fine spun scheme,' as William Howard called it—for invading England by suggesting that Charles's younger brother, James, should be substituted for Charles as the figure-head in a movement for re-establishing the English monarchy on a narrowly circumscribed constitutional basis.

Although in the light of James's later history as James II, the bigot Catholic King, such a plan seems both fantastic and wrong-headed, in fact at that date James might easily have seemed a much more suitable monarch for Wildman's purposes than was Charles II. James might well have appeared to be not only an abler figure, but more attractive to the citizens and soldiers of puritan England. James was now twenty-five years old, and whilst since the battle of Worcester in 1651 Charles had been idling and intriguing, James had become a fully qualified professional soldier. He had joined the French army and under the leadership of the military genius, Turenne, had fought against the rebel Prince Condé in 1654–5. After Charles II had at Oliver Cromwell's insti-gation been expelled from France, he had refused to allow his brother to remain in French service, but in 1657 James had joined the Spanish army in Flanders where he had fought against his old commander Turenne. There is no evidence that James at this date had leanings towards Roman Catholicism, but he was estranged from his brother and distrusted Hyde and the other advisers of the King.

Wildman's principal fellow conspirator in England was George Villiers, second Duke of Buckingham. Buckingham's father, the first Duke, had been the self-made favourite of James I and Charles I. After his father's murder by Felton, Charles I had adopted the young Duke and brought up him and his brother together just as if they had been princes of the blood. George Villiers had been educated at Cambridge and after the first civil war had his large estates restored to him by Parliament, as it was argued that although he had supported the King he was too young to know what he had been doing. However he soon entered into the plot which was to bring about the second civil war; in 1651 his estates were confiscated and sold; many of them were purchased by the former Roundhead commander-in-chief, Fairfax, including Buckingham's London residence, York House in the Strand. Buckingham then became a member of Charles II's Privy Council, where he advocated an understanding with the Presbyterians. He went with Charles to Scotland where, according to Hyde, he offered to take over command of the Scottish army in place of the experienced David Leslie. This self-reliant young gentleman of twenty-two 'was confident that what he proposed was so evidently for his service that David Leslie himself would willingly consent to it.' His suggestion was declined, as was later his hand in marriage when he offered it to the King's widowed sister, the Princess of Orange. He gradually lost favour with Charles, and Hyde considered him to be a man of inferior calibre to his father. Despairing of carving out a career for himself abroad, Buckingham tried to make his peace with Cromwell; when this plan failed he came back to England without permission and brought off the remarkable coup of marrying Fairfax's daughter and only child, although she was engaged to another man. Thus he regained by marriage most of the estates he had lost by treason. By Oliver Cromwell's orders Buckingham was confined to York House, and when he evaded these restrictions he was put in the Tower, from which he was released, together with a number of Cromwell's other victims, in February, 1659. Essentially an adventurer, Buckingham was a dabbler in alchemy, poetry, and politics. In 1652 he had discussed with Lilburne the terms upon which the monarchy could be restored, and four years later Wildman had tried to persuade King Charles II to take him back into his favour. But at that time Charles had told Wildman that Buckingham 'had not the interest to compass what he proposes . . . the King will not be averse from any course conceived necessary, but he has no mind at present, for many reasons, to employ him.'

The other chief agent in Wildman's new plot was Father Peter Talbot, the Irish Jesuit, who had an urge to be a king-maker and was therefore ready and anxious to try to substitute James, Duke of York, for his brother. Talbot and Wildman exerted their influence with Don Alonso de Cardenas to interest the Spaniards in the scheme; Buckingham was to enlist the Royalists and presumably approach the Duke of York himself; and Wildman was to be responsible for the backing of the Levellers, Anabaptists, and other extreme sectarians. Finally, a couple of noble ladies contributed their help to the plot. According to one of Hyde's informants, Lady Herbert 'belched out devilish and damnable slanders' about the king as her daily practice, whilst Lady Newport was 'another of these jewels,' both 'great trumpeters of the Duke of York' who 'think they cannot do it emphatically enough but by railing at his Majesty.' Although the Duke denied that he was a Roman Catholic, Colonel Samuel Tuke tried to persuade the Roman Catholics that James was already a co-religionist, while Dr. Fraser spread a rumour that Charles II was a consumptive. 'Nothing,' it was said, 'was neglected to defame the King and cry up the Duke of York.' So far as the Levellers were concerned, the ultimate objective of the movement to make James into an all-party monarch was to create a constitutional system of government and establish complete religious toleration. Needless to say, a plan so full of holes and so inadequate in anything but paper resources never awoke into the realm of action. But it developed far enough to interest and even worry Hyde. At the time when Richard Cromwell's Parliament was meeting, Hyde told Rumbold that 'Wildman has an intrigue with Don Alonso by some Jesuits' and he thought that he would 'cozen [deceive] the Spaniards as he has done others.' Later he told another Royalist that many Roman Catholics were 'guided, I believe, principally by the Jesuits and by the Duke of Buckingham, who are steered by Wildman and will join with the republic.' He was sufficiently concerned about Wildman's activities to seek information about his character and motives and learned, to his surprise, that some thought him both able and honest. In April some of Hyde's friends offered 'to search out into the bottom of the business of Wildman.'

Among others the Presbyterian Captain Titus, who had worked with Wildman and Sexby in earlier plots, devoted himself to spying on Hyde's behalf. And Hyde was delighted with Titus's assistance; for he wrote in May, 1659: 'Though I am very far from having confidence in Wildman or that he hath not heretofore betrayed some of our friends, yet I am very secure he cannot corrupt or outwit Titus.' But Titus was quite unable to penetrate Wildman's designs and indeed was satisfied as to his bona fides. Yet in general Wildman and Buckingham were unable to make any impression on the Presbyterians. For these puritans did not want, and never had wanted, a republic. They were content to obey either Cromwell or Charles so long as their religion was fully protected by law. Indeed in the end the Presbyterian-Royalist combination was to defeat the Republicans and sectarians. Meanwhile, although Titus discovered nothing, Hyde was fully informed about what was on foot. He wrote to Howard at the end of May, 1659, that he had heard all about Buckingham's intrigues, 'which no doubt have good countenance from abroad, yet I think do rather receive countenance from Father Talbot and four persons that we have here [in Flanders].' But he could not fathom Wildman's motives; for although he had long ceased to expect him to help the royalist cause, he thought that he was wiser 'than to entangle himself in such a labyrinth.' But in the end nothing whatever came of these complicated intrigues; for when in May, 1659, the army Grandees overthrew Richard Cromwell—who vanished from history without a protest and with scarcely a trace—Wildman abandoned his labyrinthine combinations and instead tried to impose his democratic ideals directly upon the new republic.

CHAPTER XI

THE SECOND ENGLISH REPUBLIC

The government of England ought to be by laws and not by men.
WILDMAN in *The Leveller* (1659)

THE three months which constituted the span of life of Richard Cromwell's Parliament were devoted by the House of Commons largely to criticism and amendment of the Bill reaffirming the Cromwellian Protectorate in its entirety. The members in opposition to the Court did all they could to limit or abolish the powers of the Protectorate which, in their view, had lost all reason for its existence. Forty or fifty members followed Sir Arthur Haselrig, whose goal was the restoration of the Rump Parliament as it had been when Oliver had dissolved it in 1653; eight or ten members formed a group around Henry Nevile, who sought a new democratic constitution; and General Lambert with a considerable following represented the interests of the army.

But the most dangerous opponents of Richard Cromwell were outside the House of Commons. The army Grandees did not abandon their claim for virtual independence from the Government and for the placing of supreme military power in the hands of General Charles Fleetwood. The junior officers and other ranks had grievances against both the Protectorate and the parliamentary majority. The Commons had failed to provide financial resources for either their current pay or arrears; and Richard was without influence in the army. Many of the soldiers who had been ardent Republicans in 1647—for whom Wildman had acted as spokesman—had acquiesced in the Protectorate because of the personal magnetism and puritan implacability of Oliver Cromwell. They owed no such allegiance to his son, and whilst Parliament was slowly confirming Richard's position, the old Roundhead soldiers began to recall among themselves the 'Good Old Cause' of the puritan republic for which they had fought their fellow citizens and executed their King a decade before. So, as the spring of 1659 began, not only did the army officers hopefully resume their meetings at Wallingford House, but the ordinary soldiers independently pressed their point of view upon the attention of their generals and of Parliament.

The tardiness of the Commons in making provision for the army, the frequent denunciations of all forms of military rule by the M.P.'s, and the impeachment of one of Cromwell's Majors-General by Parliament combined to reduce the patience of both officers and men with the Protectoral Government. So restless were they at the beginning of April, 1659, that Fleetwood had to ask Richard Cromwell for permission to summon a General Council to examine their grievances and the Protector had to consent. Five hundred officers therefore met at Wallingford House on 2nd April. Richard Cromwell's friends were among those present and they vainly tried to persuade the meeting that the soldiers' best plan was to accept the Protector as their commander-in-chief and to trust him to put matters right. The majority resolved, however, to draw up a petition detailing their complaints. Three days later the petition was drafted: it pointed out that want of pay might compel soldiers to live at 'free quarter,' that lawsuits had started against officers who were merely obeying orders, and that the Cavaliers were being encouraged. The Army concluded by demanding that its arrears of pay should be found and that freedom of worship (which had been threatened by the Presbyterian majority in the Commons) should be reaffirmed, and by way of a hint offered to 'pluck down the wicked from their places wherever they might be.'

Fleetwood presented this petition to Richard on 6th April. It was graciously received and forwarded to Parliament on the eighth. For ten days the House of Commons ignored the petition. Meanwhile the officers continued to meet. On 13th April they assembled in prayer, and next day, although reaffirming their loyalty to the Protector and their enmity to Charles II, they resolved that the command of the army must be entrusted to someone in whom they had confidence. These further meetings, together with the arrival of other petitions from different regiments, induced the Commons to take the original petition into consideration. On 18th April the House met behind locked doors in secret session. The result of the debate was that the majority decided that while they would attempt to solve the financial problem, no further army councils must be held without the permission of the Protector and both Houses, and no officer should be allowed to retain his post unless he promised not to interfere with Parliament. That afternoon Richard conveyed these uncompromising resolutions to Fleetwood. The challenge was accepted. Three days later, after Richard had measured his forces against those of Fleetwood and decided that resistance was hopeless, he consented to the dissolution of Parliament. The Cromwellian Protectorate was at an end.

What part did the Republicans play in the destruction of the Protectorate? It seems certain that some of the junior officers in the army and the old Roundhead rank-and-file had pressed the Wallingford House Grandees to act. The leaders of the republican section of the army were Colonel Ashfield and Colonel Robert Lilburne, a brother of Freeborn John. They in turn were probably egged on by the oligarchic Republicans in the House of Commons. Edmund Ludlow, M.P., had been a link between the various republican groups and the army chiefs (although Haselrig and Vane had been too cautious to meet the Grandees directly). Colonel Nehemiah Bourne, who claimed that he was familiar with the inner councils of the army, asserted in a private letter that the Republicans outside the army urged the Republicans inside the army to move against the Protectorate, and that the army Republicans in turn 'came up to the superior officers and began to work upon them also to revive the good old cause.' This statement is virtually confirmed from the other side by Bulstrode Whitelocke, who was a confidant of the Protector. Finally, in the crucial debate of 18th April Haselrig, Scot, Vane, Alured, Baynes and other Republicans had urged that the Commons ought not to suppress the meetings of the army council, since to do so would be held to imply that Richard Cromwell was commander-in-chief as well as Protector and therefore that he was as much a military dictator as his father had been. Thus although the Army was their instrument, it was the English Republicans who destroyed the Cromwellian Protectorate.

When Richard had been deposed, Fleetwood and the army Grandees found themselves obliged hurriedly to call Vane, Haselrig and Ludlow into consultation about what form of government should replace the Protectorate. Important meetings were held in Vane's house at Charing Cross. The outcome of the discussions was a decision not to have a general election and try to set up a republican government directly responsible to the people, but to recall the Rump Parliament, whose patently oligarchic character had partly justified its dissolution by Cromwell. Thus the more conservative section of the English republican party had carried the day which had been won through the efforts of all Republicans alike. Yet an alternative and more democratic scheme of government had been available for the consideration of the new rulers. The author of this scheme was James Harrington and its supporters included John Wildman and the Levellers.

If John Lilburne and Wildman may claim to be the first authors of a conception of democratic republicanism and Henry Vane and John Milton were the earliest advocates of oligarchic republican rule, James Harrington was the first Englishman to try to reconcile the democratic notion of sovereignty with the idea that experts were needed as legislators as well as with the economic facts of the time. His political thought was so brilliant, so novel, so convincing to many of his contemporaries, and so plainly compatible with the needs of a distracted country, that his fellow Republicans were content and indeed anxious to graft on to their own political schemes either the whole or a large part of his concrete proposals. It is not too much to say that for the next thirty years after 1656, when Harrington published his great book, *The Commonwealth of Oceana*, his political ideas dominated English republican thought. Wildman had the wit to recognize the somewhat negative character of the old Leveller ideas and became one of Harrington's earliest disciples. It is therefore necessary to understand Harrington's main proposals and to have some idea of their author.

Harrington was born of a respectable county family near Northampton and was a commoner of Trinity College, Oxford. He travelled on the Continent, where he studied the republican institutions of the United Netherlands, of Switzerland and, especially, of Venice. In 1647 he was chosen to be a groom of Charles I's bedchamber when the King was a prisoner at Holmby. Charles and Harrington got along well enough together. 'The

King,' wrote Aubrey, the seventeenth-century historian of Oxford worthies, 'loved his company; only he could not endure to hear of a Commonwealth; and Mr. Harrington passionately loved his Majesty.' After Charles's removal to Windsor, Harrington was dismissed from his post for refusing to swear not to assist the King's escape. A brief period of imprisonment followed, but Harrington was allowed to be with Charles at the time of his execution. The death of the monarch, who had gained his personal devotion, now released Harrington to pursue those political studies to which he had been inspired by his wide reading and by his foreign travels. He had at first thought of specializing in poetry, but his friend, Henry Nevile, who also had pretensions as a poet, persuaded him to abandon work for which it appears he was ill fitted in order, as Aubrey says, 'to improve his proper talent, political reflections.' Nevile himself was also a thinker of first-rate ability and came of the same sort of county set, was at Oxford at about the same time as Harrington, and also had travelled in France and Italy. Nevile was elected a member of the Long Parliament and became very friendly with Marten and other early Republicans. Although in 1651 he was a member of the Council of State, he abandoned active political life when Cromwell betrayed the republic. Nevile was described as being of a 'factious and turbulent spirit,' whereas his friend Harrington was good-humoured, tolerant, even-tempered and hospitable. Since the two men were able to build the foundations of friendship in a common interest in poetry and political speculation, their differences of character tended to stimulate rather than to check the development of original political ideas. While Nevile claimed no credit for it, there can be little doubt that he contributed in a large measure to the production of Harrington's great work.

Harrington is said to have spent twenty years of his life in the collection of materials for *Oceana* and to have taken six years in writing it. According to his biographer, John Toland, who had access to many of his papers not long after his death, Wildman became acquainted with Harrington at an early stage of his studies. It is possible that Wildman met Harrington through Nevile, for both came from Berkshire. Toland relates that Harrington lent some of his unpublished work to either Wildman or

JAMES HARRINGTON
A portrait attributed to A. van der Venne

Nevile, one of whom published an essay entitled *A Letter from an Officer of the Army in Ireland*. As no copy of this pamphlet appears to have survived, it is impossible to tell whether Wildman, Nevile or someone else was the author, or how far its conclusions anticipated those of *Oceana*. It may, however, be pointed out that Wildman was once posted as an officer for service in Ireland, although it is unlikely that he went there. In any case Harrington was not in the least upset by this theft of his ideas, and (says Toland) 'notwithstanding the provocation, so true was he to the friendship of Nevile and Wildman that he avoided all harsh expressions or public censures on this occasion, contenting himself with the justice, which the world was soon obliged to yield to him by reason of his other writings, where no such clubbing of brains could be reasonably expected.'

To publish a substantial republican work during Oliver Cromwell's Protectorate had been no easy problem. Indeed, except for Henry Vane's *Healing Question* (an attack on Cromwell by an old personal friend of his in 1654) no other republican writings appeared during that period. *Oceana* was reported to have been seized whilst in the press, and to obtain its publication Harrington, writes Toland, had to enlist Oliver's favourite daughter, Elizabeth Claypole, as an intermediary. Cromwell looked at the book and observed that 'the gentleman had like to trepan him out of his power, but that what he had got by the sword he would not quit for a little paper shot.' The second half of this story sounds apocryphal, for Harrington was careful to argue in his book not for the immediate suppression of the Protectorate but that Cromwell should prepare the way for an ideal republican constitution, a task which he estimated would take sixty years and would not have required Cromwell to retire from action during his lifetime.

Partly in the hope of getting his book past a strict censorship and partly in order to cover the powder of political theory with the jam of 'romance,' Harrington cast his work in a Utopian form; the discussion of his ideas was entrusted to a number of thinly disguised political figures seated around a council table.

In Harrington's view a Commonwealth must be a Government of Laws and not of the Sword. Therefore, like the Levellers and

the army Grandees, he favoured a written and unchangeable constitution as a starting-point. One fundamental and novel law
which he advocated was an agrarian law aiming at the distribution of property more in accordance with that of political power.
The Greek philosopher, Aristotle, had pointed out that a democratic form of government could not survive unless landed property
was evenly distributed among citizens—for example in a community of smallholders or shepherds. Henry Ireton in the army
council debates of 1647 had argued, on the other hand, that
democracy was undesirable because the propertyless would at
once attack property-owners and anarchy would follow. Harrington agreed with Aristotle that the form of a national government will be determined by the economic conditions of the community, but, in sharp contrast to Ireton, he thought that if
democracy could not be reconciled with the existing distribution
of property, then that distribution and not democracy should be
abandoned. Harrington's agrarian law therefore would have
provided that no one in England or Ireland should possess land
above the value of £2,000, or above £300 in Scotland; that no
one owning property worth £2,000 should be allowed to buy
more; that marriage portions should be restricted to £1,500,
and that fathers should be permitted to divide their property
equally among their children instead of entailing it by primo-
geniture. Harrington believed that by so dividing property he
would be cutting with the grain, since property had already
become more widely diffused. The exact details of Harrington's
proposals are not on the long view significant—and he seems to
have overlooked the importance of other forms of property than
land—but in his grasp of the direct relationship between the distribution of property and political power he made a new and
valuable contribution to English political science; his ideas
were later to be pushed much further by Karl Marx in his
theory of the class war. Harrington indeed indicated the theory
of the class war when he explained how the alienation of
estates by Henry VII and Henry VIII had imperilled the absolutism
of the Crown because it ceased to be able to manage on its
own revenues. Thus, in his view, economic power had been
divorced from political power, the old and new landed classes
had come into conflict, and a civil war become unavoidable.

It is remarkable that this scientific believer in the inevitable triumph of the English republic should have thrown in his lot with Charles I.

Harrington, although undoubtedly a democrat, was not as extreme in his views as Wildman and Lilburne had been in the Leveller heyday. Harrington's land policy, wrote Russell-Smith, 'was meant to achieve two objects. By his socialistic division of property he hoped to make republican institutions possible. By keeping power in the hands of the steadier section of the community, which engaged in agriculture, he hoped to avoid the extreme form of democracy.' For Harrington agreed with Vane, Milton, and other advocates of oligarchic republicanism that there were in the State a few men peculiarly fitted to govern—an intellectual aristocracy. He tried to resolve the age-old problem of how to make universal suffrage compatible with expert government by inventing methods whereby experts should be chosen with full powers to decide any question on its merits. A Senate of mature property-owners was to have the power to debate laws or to propose alternatives to laws submitted by the executive. A popular assembly was also to be elected to listen to the debates and to vote upon the Bills laid before it, but with no right to put forward its own motions. The reason for this division of functions was, in Harrington's words, because 'a Popular Assembly without a Senate cannot be wise and a Senate without a Popular Assembly will not be honest.' Both the Senate and the Assembly were to be chosen by an elaborate system of indirect election based ultimately on manhood suffrage. A ballot, an entirely new expedient in parliamentary elections, was to be employed both in the elections and in the parliamentary votes. The Senate was to be a permanent institution, and its vigour was to be preserved by a law of 'rotation' which provided that one-third of the Senate must withdraw from office every year and could not be immediately re-elected. None of these devices—the ballot, rotation, indirect election or the differentiation of function between the two Chambers—was wholly original. But by combining them all in one constitutional system Harrington intended to accept the triumph of democracy while maintaining the advantages of aristocratic government. Harrington's system, like the United States constitution of 1787, sought to make a world safe from democracy by acquiescing in the principles of democracy while limiting their application.

Nevertheless from the democratic point of view *Oceana* was an immense advance upon any of the other republican schemes put forward during the Interregnum. Much of its economic analysis was bold and sound. And Harrington, by also approving absolute liberty of conscience and the establishment of a volunteer instead of a standing army, showed himself to be one of the most liberal thinkers of his day. Although so long as landed property was widely diffused Harrington regarded the existence of an English republic as unavoidable, he did not see why his political theories should not be welcomed by the Royalists. He said that 'the Cavaliers ought of all people to be pleased with him, since if his model succeeded, they were sure to enjoy equal privileges with others and so be delivered from their present oppression.' Moreover, because in his system the executive power might remain in the hands of one man, his 'magistrate,' who proposed and carried out laws, his constitution could be put into force either by Cromwell or Charles II. Whilst this opportunity was first offered to Cromwell, if King Charles II were restored, Harrington thought that he could, by accepting the teaching of *Oceana*, avoid all Charles I's mistakes, 'since all that is said of this doctrine may as well be accommodated to a monarchy regulated by laws as to a democracy or more popular form of Commonwealth.'

It thus fell out that during the reign of Richard Cromwell there were Harringtonians alike among the Royalists, Cromwellians, oligarchic Republicans, and Levellers. We may probably date Wildman's final conversion to this creed from the time of the publication of *Oceana* (autumn, 1656). Three years later the Leveller party had largely adopted its teaching. In February, 1659, an anonymous Leveller pamphlet was published which embodied many of Harrington's ideas. As Wildman was at this time the leader of the Levellers, an old and close acquaintance of Harrington, and an experienced pamphleteer, it is reasonable to assume that he concocted this pamphlet or had a big hand in its composition. Its full title was *The Leveller: Or the Principles and Maxims concerning Government and Religion, which are assented to by those commonly called Levellers*. After refuting the 'childish fear' that the Levellers' object was 'to make all men's estates equal and to

decide laws by telling noses,' the pamphlet lays down four basic
political principles:

(1) That the government of England ought to be by 'laws and
     not by men.'
(2) That legislation, taxation, and the right to declare war and
     peace ought to lie with the people's deputies in parliament.
(3) That all men must be equally subject to the laws.
(4) That the people should be masters of their own arms (*i.e.* a
     militia is preferable to a standing army).

The character of parliament was explained on Harrington's principles: 'They [the Levellers] conceive it would be of much greater
good to our country if our parliaments were moulded into a better
form and some deputies were chosen by the people only to give
their consent and dissent unto laws proposed and other deputies
were chosen for senators that consult and debate.' The Levellers
thus accepted a two-chamber parliament, whereas ten years before
they had definitely favoured one chamber. The pamphlet went
on to discuss religion. Since no man can compel another to be
religious or by force and terror constrain people to be of the 'true
religion,' there ought (it said) to be no penalties for unbelief.
Moreover, since 'true religion' consists of revealed truths and works
of righteousness and mercy, it cannot be compatible with oppression or the shedding of blood. These religious views were of course
the same as those put forward by Wildman before the council of
the army in 1647 and 1648. Finally, it was said to be the Levellers'
doctrine that 'every authority ought to be of small continuance'
(presumably a reiteration of the idea of annual parliaments from
the 'Agreement of the People') 'and the several authorities ought
to be so balanced each by the other that people cannot suffer
common injury.'

Harrington's doctrines were advocated in Richard Cromwell's
Parliament by Henry Nevile and Captain Baynes, an official who
had been in charge of the sale of royalist lands, and by eight or
nine others. There were several debates bearing on the agrarian
law and Baynes expounded Harrington's interpretation of history
on more than one occasion. But the pure Harringtonians were a
very small, if active, minority and were unable to put their case
as such before Parliament. Nevertheless they were able to place

their programme before the ruling powers on 2nd May, ten days
after the dissolution of Parliament, when the army officers and
Republicans were meeting to decide what form of government
should replace the Protectorate.

Harrington himself then entered the fray with a pamphlet
entitled *Pour Enclouer le Canon* ('To Spike the Guns'), while six of
his disciples, John Wildman, Henry Nevile, John Lawson, John
Jones, Samuel Moyer, and Henry Marten—the last of whom
was now to emerge from the obscurity of a debtors' prison to
the republican front line—wrote two joint letters to Fleetwood
expounding 'the Army's Duty.'

'We appeal to your conscience,' said the first of these letters,
'whether your father [in-law, Oliver Cromwell] was more safe
with a footboy only following him in the streets when he was
believed to intend that good which your lordship may, if you
please, effect [*i.e.* the establishment of a democratic republic]
than when he was afterwards surrounded with guards and enclosed with locks and bolts without number.' Fleetwood, the
writers went on to point out, had a stewardship to defend the
rights of the people and it would be equally a mistake only to
advance 'good men' to power or to create merely one sovereign
prince. What was needed was a carefully thought-out and well-
balanced republican system. Had not God formed the people of
Israel into a Commonwealth?—they asked. Was not England 'an
unnatural soil for a monarch' and had not Richard proved 'a
surgeon unfit to cure'? 'Your only business, then, my lord,' they
concluded, 'is to give the order for the continual successive
assemblies of the people to make their own laws and magistrates.'
But the same assembly, they argued, should never have the right
both to debate and to make the final decisions on policy, for otherwise it would degenerate into an oligarchy or tyranny, as the Long
Parliament had done. If, on the other hand, he was to set up an
assembly of the people to make final decisions, a senate to debate
them, a Council of State to make peace and war and control the
armed forces, and a magistracy to administer laws impartially,
he would create a form of government which would combine the
relative advantages of democracy, aristocracy, and monarchy.
Fleetwood was begged to follow their advice and thereby to
establish 'eternal liberty' with his 'shining sword.'

The views of the Harringtonians and Levellers were ignored alike by Fleetwood and by the House of Commons leaders like Haselrig. Five days after these letters were published, forty-two members of the Rump Parliament were collected with some difficulty and gathered at Westminster, no doubt rubbing their eyes to find themselves after so many weary months again the rulers of the fair realm of England. Henry Marten and Lord Monson, who also had been imprisoned for debt, were hastily released and dispatched to Westminster to form a quorum. The army officers forcibly prevented the former Presbyterian members of the Long Parliament (who had been excluded in 1648) from resuming their seats, and eventually some hundred and thirty Independent members of the old Long Parliament, chosen by the electorate about fifteen years earlier, were whipped together to govern.

The army Grandees, who had acquiesced in the recall of the Rump Parliament with reluctance, had been outmanoeuvred. What they had intended by their *coup d'état* of 21st April had been to dissolve Richard Cromwell's Parliament and to use Richard as their own puppet, a dictator to whom they should dictate. But the republican movement among the junior officers and other ranks of the army had gone so far that this plan had to be laid aside, and since Fleetwood and Lambert had no alternative scheme of government they were obliged to recall the Rump. So completely had they been outwitted that they were not able even to make good terms for the army with the leaders of the Rump; on 12th May an army petition was presented to the Rump asking for an act of oblivion for all acts committed during the previous six years, for the payment of debts, for the establishment of a senate equal in power with the Commons, for a speedy general election, for the setting up of a Council of State, for a settlement on Richard Cromwell, and for the appointment of Fleetwood as commander-in-chief. But once the Republicans had laid their hands upon the reins of government they refused to be rushed into sharing or abandoning their power or into making hasty concessions to the army. They set up a Council of State, but the members of the Rump had a two-to-one majority, so that the influence of the army Grandees was negligible; and although Fleetwood was at last created commander-in-chief in name, the

Commons appointed select committees of their own members to nominate his officers and to control the Navy. No Senate was set up, no immediate arrangement was made for a dissolution, and the Act of Indemnity was entirely unsatisfactory to the army. What the Commons deliberately set out to do was to make its own position supreme by governing through its own committees and by enlisting republican support in the country. The House inspired and welcomed over thirty addresses of republican support from its friends throughout the nation. It hoped to neutralize the growing antagonism of the army leaders by transforming the machinery of government into that of an aristocratic republic where virtue would triumph over self-interest. But the Rump made the mistake of formulating their plans on too narrow a basis. The only way in which a republic might have been firmly established in England in the summer of 1659 was by a joint agreement between all the republican groups, whatever their shade of opinion and whatever their background. The French ambassador in England wrote at that time: 'It seems to me that if a perfect Commonwealth were established, it would appease a great many malcontents.' Instead of this, the Republicans and Roundhead officers quarrelled interminably among themselves. Fleetwood was at loggerheads with Haselrig; Lambert intrigued against Fleetwood; Haselrig quarrelled with Vane, Vane with Nevile, and Ludlow with Algernon Sidney. The constitutional discussions to which the Commons turned in July did nothing to produce an agreed plan for a permanent republican settlement. Every one had a different scheme. Never in the history of England have so many books and pamphlets been written on the republican cause and means of realizing it as in the year 1659. Republican tracts poured from the presses; appeals to the 'Good Old Cause' and pleas for liberty, for aristocracy, and for the rule of the Saints filled the book market. Edmund Ludlow has a famous passage in his *Memoirs* which describes the state of affairs:

'At this time the opinions of men were much divided concerning a form of government to be established amongst us. The great officers of the army ... were for a select standing senate to be joined to the representation of the people. Others laboured to have the supreme authority to consist of an assembly chosen by the people and a council of state to be chosen by the assembly to be invested with executive power, and accountable to that which should next succeed, at which time the power of the said council should determine. Some were desirous to have a representative of the people constantly sitting, but changed by perpetual rotation. Others proposed there might be joined to the popular assembly a select number of men in the nature of the Lacedemonian Ephori, who should have a negative in things, wherein the essentials of the government should be concerned. . . . Some were of opinion that it would be most conducive to public happiness if there might be two councils chosen by the people. . . .'

This last proposal, part of the scheme put forward in *Oceana*, was presented by Henry Nevile to the Commons on 6th July under the title of the 'Humble Petition of Divers Well-Affected Persons.' Wildman was concerned in drawing up this new Harringtonian petition, as he had been in writing the letters to Fleetwood. On 1st July it was reported to the Royalists that Mr. Wildman and others 'though they are not at all satisfied with Vane and the rest that are for oligarchy, yet they will hardly be reconciled to monarchy till they are quite out of hopes of their Commonwealth,' and that 'Wildman hath set on foot a petition that will breed bad blood.' It seems from this report that the Harringtonians were optimistic about winning support in the army for their point of view—presumably from those regiments which had been receptive to Leveller ideas in earlier days. Edward Hyde, in commenting on this report from the Royalist headquarters overseas, said he hoped to hear that 'Wildman's petition had stirred the army to dissolve Parliament with some outrage.' The petition, although it asserted that single-chamber government was dangerous, was received by the single-chamber without rancour and thanks were returned. But the Harringtonians made no more headway with the leaders of the House of Commons in July than they had with the chiefs of the army two months before. Speaking about this episode, the French historian Guizot observed a little gratuitously that 'the supporters of the tottering Commonwealth had something else to do than to discuss and make a trial of systems.' Certainly the Rump Parliament had the army's grievances still to meet, a peace with Spain to conclude, and a fresh royalist rising to put down. And it had by that date become common knowledge that any form of election, especially the type of free election envisaged by Harrington, would mean a victory for the Cavaliers.

This last Harringtonian petition appears to have been drawn up at a club of which Wildman was the chairman. The following report was received by Hyde:

'On Wednesday was presented to the Parliament a Commonwealth's model framed at a club held in Covent Garden by well-wishers to a republic; the chairman, if you please, or the penner, appears not much unlike a Wild Man. . . .'

This Commonwealth club met at Nonsuch House in Bow Street— the tavern which had been bought by Wildman and was managed by his old servant, William Parker. Nonsuch House had been a republican meeting-place even before the death of Oliver Cromwell and afterwards it became a well-known resort for intellectuals in the left-wing republican party. The Commonwealth Club had over eighty members, including Henry Marten, Francis Hacker, Thomas Okey, and even at one stage Arthur Haselrig. This club was evidently the predecessor of a more famous republican club, the Rota Club, which held its first meeting in the autumn of 1659. And after the Rota Club dissolved, Nonsuch House was again to become a great republican centre in the first two years of King Charles II's reign.

CHAPTER XII

COFFEE-HOUSE PHILOSOPHERS

I admire Harrington's model and am ready to cry out as if it were
the pattern of the Mount.

HENRY STUBBE, 1659

THE state of tension which prevailed in the summer of 1659
between the Rump and the army inspired the exiled Royalists
to plan another rising. The more cautious and conservative
Cavaliers in England, who belonged to the Sealed Knot, tended to
hesitate before moving, and asserted that at that time of year the
farm workers would prefer to bring in the harvest at half a crown
a day rather than fight for the King for nothing. A more optimistic and younger group headed by Lord John Mordaunt, who
had a year before escaped execution by a casting vote in the
High Court, refused to be discouraged. Contacts were established
with a number of Presbyterians, including two Majors-General,
Massey and Browne, who were incensed at their exclusion from
the government of their country.

The plot followed a very similar course to the unsuccessful rising
of 1655. Sir Richard Willis of the Sealed Knot again betrayed
his English associates; Browne ratted, Massey was arrested, and
in London the Rump took adequate precautions. As in 1655
the insurrection was virtually confined to Wiltshire and the
seizure of Salisbury, so in August, 1659, the only outbreak was in
Cheshire where Sir George Booth, a Presbyterian and a Royalist,
occupied Chester. General Lambert was sent from London to
deal with Booth. As the royalist force failed to fortify Chester,
and when it marched out to meet the enemy left most of its am-
munition behind, Lambert had no difficulty in crushing the
isolated outbreak. At sea Edward Montague, the admiral of the
republican navy, who had listened to the persuasions of royalist
agents, brought back his fleet from the Baltic as if to support the
rising. But he arrived too late and was immediately replaced by
Wildman's friend, John Lawson, who had resigned from his
position as vice-admiral three years earlier precisely because he

was too sincere a Republican to stomach the dictatorship of Oliver Cromwell.

For the moment therefore it looked as if the new English Republic was securely in the saddle. 'Never,' wrote Guizot, 'had the position of the republican Parliament appeared more prosperous.' But the army leaders, who had watched the Rump's proceedings throughout the summer with sullen resentment, now perceived their opportunity. The regiments under Lambert, returned from their victory over Booth, dispatched a petition from Derby on 22nd September recalling that the demands put forward in the army petition of 12th May still remained unfulfilled and requesting that Fleetwood should be made commander-in-chief with complete powers, Lambert his second-in-command, and Desborough and Monk commanders of horse and foot respectively. The House of Commons remained adamant, retorted that to have any more generals would be 'needless, chargeable, and dangerous to the Commonwealth,' and ordered Fleetwood to reprove the officers for daring to petition. Fleetwood, who had his own reasons for dissatisfaction, ignored the order. Instead of submitting, two hundred and thirty officers signed a new petition, in which, while they affirmed that they were faithful to 'a well-regulated Commonwealth,' they insisted on their right to petition Parliament and again asked that no officer or other rank should be dismissed from the army except by court martial. The Commons, discovering that Lambert had inspired the new petition, dismissed him and eight other officers. On the following day (13th October) Lambert retorted by dismissing the Rump. The building at Westminster was surrounded with his troops and the Speaker was turned away. The weak and vain Fleetwood betrayed his trust and threw in his lot with the mutineers. For the time being the civilian Republicans were defenceless. Unlike Oliver Cromwell, Lambert did not even trouble to make a speech to the members of the Parliament whom he now thrust from their seats. For the second time the Rump had been destroyed by the army.

In place of the Rump, a Committee of Safety was now nominated by the army chiefs to govern the country. It consisted mainly of soldiers, but Sir Henry Vane accepted a place on the Committee because he was rightly afraid that a conflict between the army and the republican leaders would only open the way to the return of Charles II. Whitelocke, the complacent and somewhat opportunist lawyer who had served under Oliver Cromwell, was also on the Committee; but Haselrig, Scot, and the rest bided their time and planned a revenge which did not look as if it would long be delayed. Once again the triumphant military party had no permanent constitutional solution to offer. Moreover the army itself was divided. General Monk, with a well-trained and disciplined force in Scotland that was personally loyal to him, had no intention of allowing Lambert and Fleetwood to govern the country. The army in Ireland was indifferent to Lambert, and so were the republican Admiral Lawson and the Navy. Resistance to the payment of taxes was widespread throughout the country and particularly in the City of London which was always antagonistic to the Roundhead army. Soldiers had to be employed as tax collectors.

Thus the autumn of 1659 was filled with political and military intrigues and general confusion. The entire absence of any prospect of stable government stimulated the hopes of the Royalists and at the same time promoted the sales of republican literature of all sorts.

Such was the anarchic condition of England when the Harringtonian republican club, the Rota Club, was first formed. The club's sole avowed purpose was to discuss the theoretical problems of government and of political science, but it is easy to guess that the strong desire which then prevailed for some permanent form of republican rule lent point to its meetings. Wildman was a prominent and regular member, and the club may well have been the successor to the earlier Nonsuch House Club, of which he had acted as chairman.

The new club began to function in the Michaelmas term of 1659 (29th September is Michaelmas Day) and its meetings were held at Miles's coffee-house, Westminster. The members sat round a large oval table which had a 'passage in the middle for Miles to deliver his coffee.' Although Harrington was in effect the president and guiding spirit, the chair was taken by Cyriac Skinner, who was described as 'an ingenious young gentleman, scholar, and friend of John Milton.' Besides Major Wildman, the regular members included Henry Nevile and Roger Coke, grandson to the great lawyer, Sir Edward Coke, and himself to become a well-known Restoration pamphleteer; other members were Francis Cradocke, a merchant and inventor of land banks; Sir William Petty, economist and statistician; Sir Charles Wolseley, former member of Oliver Cromwell's Council of State; and many other of the most intelligent Londoners of the day whose names were to be associated with the foundation of the Royal Society. The club was open to everybody, and aristocrats and Cavaliers like the Earl of Tyrconnel and Samuel Pepys used to drop in as listeners.

John Aubrey, sponger, gossip and man about town, who was himself a member, has left a brief description of the club:

'The discourses were the most ingenious and smart that I ever heard or expect to hear and bandied with great eagerness; the arguments in Parliament were but flat to it. Here we had (very formally) a balloting box and balloted how things should be carried by way of tentamens [experiments]. The room was every evening as full as it could be crammed.'

The method of procedure at the club was for some member to bring forward a constitutional proposal or to open a discussion upon the merits of some historical constitution. The question would then be debated and voted upon by ballot. Harrington himself kept the minutes and took a prominent part in the discussions. Pepys recounts how at one meeting Harrington brought forward the argument that the Roman republic was not a 'settled' government because property and political power were not in the same hands. But the verdict was carried against Harrington on a vote by ballot, and the next day the members who had disagreed with Harrington undertook to prove the contrary proposition.

Indeed it is plain from what we know that many persons who did not wholly agree with Harrington's scheme for a republic haunted the club:

'Scot, Nevil and Vane
With the rest of the train
Are into Oceana fled
Sir Arthur the brave
That's as arrant a knave
Has Harrington's Rota in's head.'

The jokes and parodies that were made about the Rota Club were facile and numerous. Samuel Butler, the Restoration poet, suggested that Harrington should be allowed to go to Jamaica and establish his Commonwealth there. The Royalists were beginning to feel that soon the ripe fruit of government patronage was going to fall into their laps and could afford to laugh, while not a few 'practical men' (as is always the case where advanced thinkers make their opinions public) joined in with cheap jibes at this group of earnest and disinterested intellectuals. After the meeting it was the usual custom of the club to adjourn from the coffee-house to a Rhenish wine-house near by. On one occasion a gang of drunks came in and began jeering at the Rota members, their leader tearing up the club's papers and minutes. But the soldiers who were present speedily interfered and offered to kick the drunks downstairs, and refrained from doing so only at the persuasion of the mild Harrington himself.

Harrington's doctrines spread widely. The republican pamphleteers of the day were obliged either to accept or repudiate his theories. John Milton in his *Ready and Easy Way to Establish a Free Commonwealth*, published early in 1660, even went so far as to admit the principle of rotation for offices in his grand aristocratic council. Henry Stubbe, an Oxford don and prolific and intelligent republican writer of the time, said, 'I admire Harrington's model and am ready to cry out as if it were the pattern of the Mount,' but added that he did not consider that the nation was then to be entrusted with liberty, since if a free general election took place— in which votes would be given out of a sense of revenge, ignorance, or personal interest—the results might well be prejudicial to the establishment of an egalitarian Commonwealth. Harrington himself waited philosophically for some soldier to emerge who was willing to prepare the way for the Commonwealth of Oceana. Like Marx in later years, he was inclined to think that the shift in the distribution of property would sooner or later make inevitable the establishment of a republic in which political power in the nation corresponded with the division of property.

Almost alone of Harrington's disciples John Wildman was unwilling to devote himself entirely to academic debates and do nothing else until another and greater Oliver Cromwell should see the light of political truth and reason, or until the materialistic interpretation of history should work itself out according to the accepted rules.

While the philosophers of Miles's coffee-house were talking, the army Grandees, who now ruled a restless realm, were more urgently seeking to discover some practical and permanent basis for government. On the whole, they inclined to return to a written constitution like Ireton's 'Heads of the Proposals' of 1647; and a plan was proposed for seven fundamentals and twenty-one 'conservators of liberty' to assure that these fundamentals were not violated. But the civilian Republicans, who had associated themselves with the generals, were against any plan that should limit the rights of the House of Commons—even although the House now stood empty. At length General Fleetwood invited a committee to draw up a fresh constitution. The two most active members of this committee were Bulstrode Whitelocke and John Wildman. At first thought it seems astonishing, in view of Wildman's record, that he should have been asked by the army Grandees—his opponents of old—to undertake such work. But we must remember that he now had acquired a considerable reputation as a drafter of constitutions and might be reckoned sobered by his association with Harrington and the pundits of Covent Garden. It was not Wildman's nature to refuse so congenial a task, but it was equally contrary to his habits to avoid exploiting his opportunities in favour of the fuller and freer republican movement in which he believed. Thus while he was solemnly considering 'a form of government of a free State' in conjunction with Whitelocke, he was at the same time preparing to overthrow his task-masters, Lambert and the Grandees, who were now confident that they had finally destroyed the Rump Parliament.

In reality the position of the military Committee of Safety, which claimed to be the executive organ of government in the autumn of 1659, was exceedingly precarious. Lambert and Fleetwood had omitted from their calculations the feelings of General George Monk, the commander of the Scottish Army, who had promptly announced his intention of disregarding the *coup d'état* and lending his moral and material support to the deposed parliamentary Council of State. Monk was a remarkable man, whose character and motives have not yet been convincingly disentangled by his biographers. Originally he fought on the royalist side in the civil wars. In 1644 he was imprisoned in the Tower, where he took his laundress for his mistress. Later Oliver Cromwell, who detected his outstanding ability as a soldier, pardoned him and found him employment in the parliamentary armies in Ireland and Scotland. When Cromwell finally returned to England after the battle of Worcester, he left Monk as Lieutenant-General in military control of Scotland. Monk was not ungrateful for the old Protector's trust. He would have saved his son Richard from being black-mailed by the Grandees if Richard had displayed the slightest wish to save himself. 'Richard Cromwell forsook himself,' said Monk, 'Else I had never failed my promise to his father in regard for his memory.' So devoted were Monk's soldiers to him that at that time they observed openly, 'If there must be a Protector, why not old George? . . . He would be fitter for it than Dick Crom-well.' Gradually Monk built up a virtually independent political group centred on Edinburgh. He gave his soldiers a measure of freedom in discussing political and religious problems, but his own views seem to have been remarkably devoid of personal ambition. He was of the opinion that the army should be subordinate to the civil power, so long as that power was stable and reasonably representative of the people. Thus he saw no virtue in either of the ambitious and unpopular Lambert's armed interferences with Parliament. He 'told Lambert in so many words that what he was prepared to tolerate in Oliver Cromwell he could not stomach in a lesser man.'

As soon as they learned Monk's views Haselrig and the deposed parliamentary Council of State sent Monk their commission as commander-in-chief of all the forces in England and Scotland and empowered him to negotiate with Lambert on their behalf. Meanwhile they enlisted the republican Admiral Lawson and the fleet on their side and also induced the Governor of Portsmouth to side with them and declare for Parliament. In Ireland Dublin castle was seized by republican officers. Various English garri-sons began to turn against Lambert. Wildman told Lord White-locke, who was Constable of Windsor castle, that he would put three thousand men at his disposal if he would secure the castle and declare for a Commonwealth. Whitelocke refused; so Wild-man took matters into his own hands. He went to two other officers, Colonel Henry Ingoldsby and Major Huntington, and made his proposal to them. These officers collected three hundred volunteers, marched to Windsor castle and invited the Governor, Colonel Whitchcoat, to surrender it to them on behalf of the English Commonwealth, which he did. The trend of events was accepted by the Grandees. The weak-minded Fleetwood confessed that 'God had spat in their faces' and hastened to offer his submission to Haselrig and the Council of State. Lambert's army showed that it was less faithful to him than Monk's army was to Monk; for his soldiers declared that they would not fight in quarrels among their officers. On the day after Christmas the pertinacious members of the Rump Parliament, that solid phalanx of well-meaning oligarchs who for a full ten years had clung to their divine right to govern England, once more met at Westminster. Monk, learning the news, prepared to move south from Scotland, apparently in order to give the Rump the backing of his unsullied sword.

Two days after the members of the Rump had met they conveyed their thanks to Wildman and Ingoldsby for securing Windsor castle, whose strategic and symbolic importance was recognized. They resolved that the House 'doth approve of the action of the forces in securing of Windsor castle for the Parliament' and voted that the thanks of the House be given them for their affection and service therein. And the House doth declare that they will take into consideration their good service in time.' The royalist exiles, who had optimistically believed that the castle had been seized in their interests, were mystified and disappointed by the course of events, and it was reported to them that Wildman was to be made governor of the castle as his reward. In fact Whitchcoat was confirmed in his governorship, and Whitelocke sighed with relief when he learned that Wildman had refrained from betraying his refusal to declare for the Rump. It seems that in recognition of his service Wildman was promoted from his somewhat honorary rank of major to an equally honorary rank of colonel. He then went into his home county of Berkshire to organize the defence of those parts against the enemies of the Republic; and on 24th January 1660 the Council of State wrote to the militia commissioners for Berkshire thanking the officers under the command of Colonel Wildman for suppressing seditious meetings. At the same time the Rump proceeded to purge the army of the officers responsible for the recent *coup d'état* and to punish the generals who had commanded it. It also offered to fill up the vacancies in the House of Commons to the number of four hundred and to arrange a general election within a year. It was high time that all Republicans of whatever shade should come together. As Monk pursued his march from Coldstream to Westminster many royalist petitions began to pour in upon him asking either for a 'free parliament' or for the readmission of the excluded Presbyterian members into the House of Commons, either of which steps, they believed, would promote the restoration of Charles II. Considerable pressure had for some time been brought to bear on Monk both by the Presbyterians and the Cavaliers. Mrs. Monk, the former laundress whom Monk had made an honest woman seven years before, was said not to have concealed the family opinions. 'Mr. Monk,' she said, 'is a Presbyterian, but,' she added, 'my son Kit is for the Long Parliament and the Good Old Cause.' Several of Monk's staff leaned towards a restoration. One Captain Poole told Monk that there would never be a quick or lasting settlement in these nations so long as there was a parish priest or steeple-house left. 'Fair and softly, Captain Poole,' retorted Monk, 'if you and your party once came to pluck these I will pluck with you.' Nevertheless in his bloodless contest with Lambert, Monk had invited the co-operation of the retired Presbyterian general, Sir Thomas Fairfax, and although he resisted the blandishments of his brother, a Cornish vicar, and of other royalist agents, he did not send them away altogether without hopes of his ultimate conversion. When he reached London in February he frankly told the House of Commons that the people everywhere seemed to be unanimous for a free parliament and that he thought that the excluded Presbyterians ought to be readmitted without any conditions. The Commons concealed their anger and replied by ordering Monk to dissolve the Common Council of the City of London and to destroy the City gates because the City had refused to pay taxes on the ground that they would lend their money only to a free parliament. Monk, however, threw in his lot with the City and permitted the Presbyterian members to resume their seats in the Commons by the simple process of withdrawing the guards round the House. In April, Charles II published his Declaration

JOHN WILDMAN

of Breda promising an act of indemnity and general toleration, subject to the approval of parliament. A general election was held under the direction of Monk; a royalist majority was returned; and Charles was invited back to the throne of England.

Thus the English Republic was destroyed by the army which had created it. Towards the end of February the Rota Club closed its doors. Pepys visited the club in its last days and heard Harrington discussing with Lord Dorset and another peer the possibility of finding an alternative meeting-place at the Cockpit near Whitehall. About the same time John Milton optimistically published his *Ready and Easy Way to Establish a Free Commonwealth*, in which he offered to make concessions to Harrington's principles. Henry Marten, that 'indomitable little Roman pagan,' as Carlyle called him, wrote a pamphlet defending the execution of Charles I. Sir Henry Vane reprinted the *Healing Question*, the republican tract that had originally been aimed at the dictatorship of Oliver Cromwell. In February too Harrington published his *Ways and Means whereby an Equal and Lasting Commonwealth may be Suddenly Introduced*. It is ironical that these great republican figures, who had never agreed with each other, should still be putting forward independent and mutually incompatible schemes of government as all their golden hopes were changing to dust. That was the tragedy of the seventeenth-century republican movement. It was too rich in ideas and its adherents were too proud. There were many able and sincere Englishmen, perhaps the best men of their age, who honestly believed that monarchy in a literal and actual sense was an evil thing: there were republican officers and other ranks in the army who had consistently and with religious fervour maintained their belief in the 'Good Old Cause'; higher officers like Edmund Ludlow; intellectuals like Vane and Algernon Sidney, ready to die gladly for their principles; politicians like Marten, Scot, and Haselrig; men of letters and philosophers like Harrington, Milton, and Henry Stubbe; Independent and Baptist preachers and Fifth Monarchy men—all convinced Republicans. But just as the breakdown of the Catholic Church had produced not merely Protestant dissenters but Protestant dissent, so the destruction of the monarchy had produced both a republic and republican dissension.

John Wildman was indeed the typical Republican, alike in his

opposition to the two Cromwells, his initial distrust of the oligarchic leaders of the Rump, and his tardy and final conciliation
with them in 1659. Evidently he was one of the last to acquiesce
in the royalist restoration. In March, 1660, there was a highly
premature report that he was dead, and on 15th April 1660, three
weeks before the new Convention declared Charles King, Major-
General Massey reported to Edward Hyde that 'Wildman cannot
be reduced as yet.' Finally, like all the rest, he gave his nominal
allegiance to the Restoration which he had plotted should never
take place except on his own stringent constitutional terms. During
the next twenty-eight years he was not going to admit his defeat,
but he was to pay a stiff price for his and the other Republicans'
failure to unite during the Interregnum.

CHAPTER XIII

REPUBLICANS AND THE RESTORATION

> I grant all courses are in vain
> Unless we can get in again . . .
> We know the arts we us'd before
> In peace and war, and something more . . .
> To keep the Good Old Cause on foot
> And present power from taking root;
> Inflame them both with false alarms
> Of plots and parties taking arms.
>
> BUTLER *Hudibras*

IN the second half of May, 1660, King Charles II boarded the *Naseby*, renamed the *Royal Charles*, and accompanied by his dogs and the faithful band that had shared his exile, but preceded by his mistress, set sail for England. He owed his 'unconditional' restoration largely to the statesmanship of Sir Edward Hyde, later Earl of Clarendon, his Lord Chancellor, and to the clever manoeuvre whereby the thankless tasks of punishing Charles I's 'murderers,' of distributing sold or confiscated royalist estates, and of disbanding the army, were left to the decisions of a 'freely elected' parliament. Nevertheless the magnificent reception accorded to the royal party on the Dover road, the daily bells, bonfires, and firing of cannon, and the fountains of wine that flowed in the capital did not entirely conceal from the royal advisers the delicate readjustments that lay ahead of them. Many leading Royalists were of course in favour of a policy of wholesale revenge on Republicans and Cromwellians alike and wished to re-enter without hesitation or scruple into the inheritance for which they had patiently waited. But vested interests were soon found to be so intricate and the persons who, at least since the death of Oliver, had stretched out a helping hand towards the exiled King were so numerous that these simple aims could not be realized. Unconditional or not, the Restoration was perforce a compromise in which naked royalist ambitions were tempered by political expediency and therefore by mercy.

Nothing is more curious in Wildman's career than the manner in which, whatever the blows of fate might be, he soon emerged smiling (that is, if he ever smiled) in a place of profit, interest, or importance. Although to the last moment he had struggled against the Restoration, within some six months of the King's return we find him a dominant figure in the reconstituted royal post office. On the other hand, such was his incorrigible gift for intrigue that no one can have expected that he would keep his position for long.

The father of the post office in its modern form was Thomas Witherings, who in 1637 combined for a brief space the older offices of Master of the Inland and Master of the Foreign Posts. Under his reorganization scheme every one had the right on payment of the appropriate fee (known as a port, not postage) to have his letters carried by the royal mail, whereas previously they had been carried only as an act of grace. A regular post set out on horse along the main roads from London to Edinburgh and Chester, to Plymouth and Dover, dropping bags at the large towns as it went. From the large towns bags would be carried in their turn to the neighbouring towns and villages, each of which had their postmaster, who would send out postmen blowing their horns to deliver the letters. At the same time letters for the post would be collected and carried back to the main road in time for the return delivery to London. The drawback to this system was that, unless the towns or villages between which letters passed happened to lie on the same post road, the letters had to go through London, this causing much delay and adding to the expense. Hence London dominated the post office and a large proportion of all letters written passed through the Central Post or General Letter Office, as it was then called, in Lombard Street.

Until Witherings' time the post office had not been self-supporting. But by cheapening the rates (he directed that a letter could be sent eighty miles for twopence) and thereby increasing the demand the service now became profitable to all concerned. The local postmasters were paid a wage, together with the right to make what profit they could out of the hire to travellers of post-horses when they were not required for the mail, and the Post-master-General was no longer given a salary as an officer of the Crown, but himself paid a substantial sum for the right to farm the postal services. Edward Pridaux, the Postmaster-General approved by the Long Parliament, paid £5,000 a year for his office; in 1653 the office was sold to Captain John Manley for £10,000; in 1655 John Thurloe paid £10,000 for the office (which he sublet at a profit to himself); and in 1660 the office was knocked down to Colonel Henry Bishop at more than double that figure—for £21,000.

Bishop, whom we have already met as an intimate of Wildman and concerned with him in the plots of 1654 and 1658, was apparently now reckoned a Sussex gentleman of unimpeachable political sympathies, and it was at first assumed that he would appoint reliable Royalists as postmasters. In 1644 many of the local postmasters had been dismissed; the dangers of letters being tampered with and information disclosed to the enemy during the civil war were too obvious to be neglected. But when in 1660 James Hickes, who had helped Charles I with his communications at Oxford, was appointed to inquire into the employment situation, he reported that many of the old postmasters were dead and many who were now applying for jobs were in reality enemies of the King. Consequently for the time being most of the officials who had been employed by Thurloe (and therefore had republican sympathies) were retained in office.

How did Wildman become so influential? Two possible explanations present themselves. The first is that he provided Bishop with part or all of his capital. (A definite statement to this effect was made by one of the post office clerks.) Wildman, because of his wise investments during the Interregnum, was undoubtedly a wealthy man, and Bishop was a friend of his who three years earlier had indeed been said to be completely under his influence. Secondly, there is evidence that Wildman furnished the Restoration Government with valuable hints on how the post office might be used as an instrument of police, and he was possibly installed there to give shape to his ideas.

The opening of letters by officials for the purpose of obtaining intelligence is a practice nearly as old as the post office. It was intensified and systematized under Cromwell. In 1655 Thurloe as Secretary of State had taken over control of the post office, specifically in order to have 'the best means of discovering and preventing many dangerous and wicked designs which have been and are daily contrived against the peace and welfare of this

Commonwealth the intelligence whereof cannot well be communicated but by letter.' Wildman, as one of Thurloe's agents, was well informed about the methods of intercepting correspondence that were then used with such success.

The King's Government did not hesitate to avail itself of this instrument of intelligence. For a letter to be a 'virgin unviolated' was in the reign of Charles II a matter for surprised and delighted comment. In the Restoration Act establishing the post office a general power was reserved to the Secretaries of State to 'have the survey and inspection of letters.' Wildman came forward with information on how they might most profitably exercise their rights. He could do this with impunity since in all his days of plotting he rarely put anything in writing himself and, even when he did so, he was careful to ensure either that his letters were destroyed by his correspondents or that they were written in somebody else's handwriting.

In a remarkable document (undated and penned by a clerk), entitled 'A brief discourse concerning the business of intelligence and how it may be managed to the best advantage,' Wildman outlined for the benefit of the Restoration Government the methods employed by Secretary Thurloe to detect the machinations of Royalists and other then enemies of his master. 'There is now no Cromwell, no Thurloe, to manage the intelligence,' wrote Wildman, 'but so long as the King's enemies remain so numerous and so industrious in plotting against the public peace neither his royal person nor Government can be at all secure without a well settled intelligence.' The proposals that Wildman put forward for this purpose were four: first, that the Government should secure spies in each of the 'reigning factions' to give them regular information about what was being planned against them. The second proposal was that a close watch should be kept upon the General Letter Office, 'for through this office are conveyed all the poisonous distempers of the City into the whole kingdom.' Even the letters of ambassadors should not, he considered, be exempt from a thorough system of search; for are not 'all ambassadors and public ministers for the most part but great spies?' Thirdly, he suggested that a commission should be given to some fit person (possibly Wildman had himself in mind) to treat in private with all ordinary messengers and footposts about the City of London and by selling them licences and administering to them an oath of loyalty to cut the direct communications of plotters within the city itself. Cromwell's method of merely arresting an occasional messenger was, he thought, 'but to shoot at rovers.' Finally, a few spies and agents disguised as messengers to follow any strange messengers seen about the town would, he thought, be a useful precaution. In general, Wildman advised that when useful intelligence was discovered, it should not be taken direct to the Secretaries of State but should be carried by night to some secret rendezvous where it could be examined at leisure without the victims of discovery being made aware of the intelligence methods which were being employed against them.

Whether Wildman obtained his influential but unofficial position in the Restoration post office as an intelligence officer or as the financial backer of the Postmaster-General (or in both capacities), he certainly manoeuvred his way rapidly into a place from which he had unique means not of spying upon the discontented elements but of plotting against the monarchy, should promising opportunities arise.

Apart from the post office, the other main potential source of disaffection against the new Government was the army. Inevitably many of the soldiers, who even under the Cromwellian dictatorship had remained so faithful to the republican cause that Cromwell had been prevented from accepting a crown, bitterly resented their betrayal by Monk. Clarendon dared not keep in being, even if he could afford to do so, a weapon so powerful and so liable to be turned against the Government. 'The King well knew,' he wrote, 'the ill constitution of the army, the distemper and murmuring that was in it, and how many diseases and convulsions their infant loyalty was subject to.' One of the first steps of the Court party therefore was to remove from their commands all officers whom they viewed with suspicion. Monk purged the army thoroughly and replaced many of his old officers with Cavaliers who were naturally unpopular with the men. The House of Commons was induced to vote taxes amounting to nearly a million pounds, the bulk of which was used to pay off the Roundhead army. An extra week's pay was allotted to non-commissioned officers and soldiers, and their entry into civilian life was facilitated by an act which absolved them from the requirements of the apprenticeship laws.

Only Monk's own regiments—including the Coldstream Guards—were maintained to protect the person of the King, and trust was rather imposed in the nation-wide expressions of goodwill manifested at the Restoration for keeping order and stifling plots.

Indeed the more one reads of the history of the Restoration the more conscious one must be of the skill with which its initial stages were carried through. Although for the time being the policy of gradually dismissing the army was painful, it was managed with extraordinary care, and proved in the long run to be the soundest way of eliminating one of the principal centres of unrest. It is true that there were some exceptional Presbyterians who realized the danger to their cause of the disbandment of the army, and a tract aimed at preventing it, entitled *The Valley of Baca*, was actually published. But apart from one or two indiscreet remarks heard in the London taverns and in a few provincial towns, there were astonishingly few signs of political discontent in the first months of the Restoration. Wildman and his friends in the post office and the dismissed republican officers and soldiers formed groups around whom anti-Government agitation might crystallize, but the general feeling among the former Roundheads was that they ought to wait to see how Charles's promises of pacification, outlined in the Declaration of Breda, were fulfilled before desperate measures were taken.

The Convention Parliament was responsible for only one piece of legislation which was calculated to provoke unrest. Its settlement of the land question, whereby it permitted all estates not previously belonging to the Crown or Church or directly confiscated for treason to remain in the hands of their new owners, was more irritating to the old Cavaliers than to the old Roundheads: indeed it has been described by a learned historian as Charles II's 'first great act of ingratitude.' The financial arrangements for the disbandment of the army were carried out cleverly and were unsatisfactory rather to the King than to Cromwellians. But in its Act of General Pardon, Indemnity and Oblivion, which dealt with political offences committed during the Interregnum, Parliament was, or tried to be, more royalist than the King.

In his Declaration of Breda, Charles had promised 'a free and general pardon . . . to all our subjects . . . excepting only such persons as shall hereafter be excepted by Parliament.' The King's own view was that only regicides, that is to say, those who had signed the death warrant of Charles I, should be punished. The Commons, which contained a substantial Presbyterian element, was inclined to accept this view but defined regicides to include all Charles I's judges, whether they had signed the death warrant or not; they also selected twelve men specifically to be executed, and added the names of other Republicans, such as Henry Vane and John Lambert, to those who were not to be pardoned. The House of Lords, outspokenly revengeful, would have been more merciless than the Commons and wanted to put all the former King's judges to death. To the credit of Charles II and Clarendon they resisted such extreme measures of vengeance, and in its final form the Act of Indemnity completely exempted only nineteen regicides from pardon, and while four non-regicides, Hacker, Axtel, Lambert, and Vane, were also completely exempted, there was an informal undertaking that the lives of the last two should be spared.

Of those named in the Act who stood their trial before a special commission in October, 1660, ten were condemned to death, nineteen suffered all the penalties of the law except death, and three escaped to Holland to be arrested there in March, 1662, and brought back to England to be executed. The ten, like the Royalists of the French Revolution, knew how to die well: Hugh Peters, 'the mad chaplain of Cromwell,' alone showed fear at the last. At their trials their defence, made without counsel and with frequent interruptions, was that they had acted with the authority of Parliament which was the supreme court. As the time drew near for their executions (which the gentle John Evelyn and Royalists generally hailed as an example of the miraculous providence of God) they all gladly acknowledged as righteous the cause for which they were to die. What was that cause? For Daniel Axtel and Francis Hacker it was 'against the surplice and Common Prayer Book which shall not stand long in England,' and for all of them the desire for freedom of worship was closely bound up with their political opinions. It was for that reason that most of them believed that the execution of Charles I had been, and still was, hallowed by the approval of the Almighty. It was 'a cause not to be repented of' to Thomas Scot in his prayer on the day of his death. The sledge which was to draw them to the scaffold was to Colonel John Jones the fiery chariot of Elijah. 'Let not our enemies think to break the spirit by putting us to death,' said John Carew, 'for I am confident that God will give His spirit sevenfold unto them that are left.' And thus these brave men went proudly to their death, not the first nor yet the last martyrs of English republicanism.

Some of the other Republicans may well have come to regard their end with envy—Henry Marten, the first Republican of all, for example, was to drag on twenty years of wretched life as a prisoner in Chepstow and other castles; and John Milton, who, through the exertions of his friends, was to escape all penalties, lived to write:

> Now blind, disheartened, shamed, dishonoured, quelled,
> To what can I be useful, wherein serve
> My nation and the work from Heaven imposed?

To others the blood of the martyrs served as an inspiration to over-throw the Stuarts as soon as a suitable opportunity arose.

With the disbandment of the army and the execution of the regicides, whose speeches on the scaffold, to the Government's indignation, had been secretly published and widely read, the authorities were in a nervous mood and prepared for trouble. They regarded the assassination of General Monk, now Lord Albemarle, as an extremely likely event and thought that although Lambert lay safely in prison, his followers would exact their revenge. Unfortunately the profession of spy, turncoat, or stool-pigeon, though poorly paid, was already so firmly established under Thurloe and so well maintained under Charles II, and the Government so readily swallowed any stories of plots, that it is hard at this distance of time to tell how far they were genuine. Clarendon himself wrote in his autobiography that 'spies were employed who for the most part had the same affections which they were to discover in others, and received money on both sides to do, and not to do, the work they were appointed to do.' This atmosphere clung particularly to the first plot of the reign, known as 'White's plot.'

A certain Major Thomas White, whose regiment had been disbanded, was indiscreet enough to talk a trifle too loudly one

December evening in the 'Rose' tavern in Tower Street. The major had been invited by a friend of his in the same regiment, Captain Greenway, to act as intermediary in the matter of some money owed to him by Robert Rose, purser of the *Foresight* frigate. Rose was under the impression that White was a serjeant or bailiff and promptly paid up six pounds to avoid trouble. Afterwards the three of them drank wine amicably together and discussed the political outlook, and Major White also had a few private words with the tavern porter. It is likely enough that White spoke resentfully of the changes which had resulted in the disbandment of his regiment. One John Hall, who was also present, overheard a portion of the conversation and reported to the authorities that White had said he would have General Monk's blood before Christmas—indeed he would have killed him when Monk first came to London and burned the city if only his colonel had given him the order—and would make the city a second Jerusalem by burning it and pull the King off his throne. Hall also asserted, by way of additional evidence, that White had pulled a piece of parchment out of his pocket, on which were written the names of persons who had promised to join with him in his plot, and had offered to include Hall as a captain. Thus Hall; but Robert Rose, the purser, stated that he had heard nothing of a plot, nor had Captain Greenway, while another independent witness who also had been in the tavern that night swore, in direct contradiction to Hall, that White had said the King had treated him nobly in paying his arrears, that he would 'lie still' all the winter, and seek civil employment in the spring. With such a conflict of testimony, dealing with what a disbanded officer had said in his cups, one might have thought that White would have been safe. On the contrary, not only was he arrested, but so also were a number of other officers, including Captain William Rainsborough, brother of the Thomas Rainsborough who had been killed by the Royalists during the civil war, Major-General Robert Overton, who had been mixed up with Wildman in the plots of 1654, and Major-General Desborough, Cromwell's brother-in-law. Altogether about forty men were arrested on suspicion and lodged in the Tower.

Rumour soon had it that a 'great conspiracy' had been detected against His Majesty's person. Overton was accused of smuggling arms into London, and a story was circulated that a plot had been deliberately allowed to ripen 'so that the King will have an opportunity of cutting off by present justice that obstinate irreconcilable sort of men.' The official tale, as told by Clarendon himself, was that the plot was aimed chiefly against General Monk and that the disbanded officers planned to be revenged upon him because of his betrayal of the army to the King. The surviving evidence does not suggest that any such plan was anywhere near realization. Samuel Pepys was 'surprised' to hear of such a plot, and the exiled republican leader, Ludlow, denied that it ever existed. The most probable explanation is that the authorities seized the excuse of the tales told by the informer Hall to lock up all those officers who might have become a rallying point for a real plot. As a further precaution spies were sent across to Amsterdam to watch over the Republicans and Cromwellians there, and a few free lances penetrated to Switzerland to try to murder Edmund Ludlow, who had exiled himself at Vevey. White's arrest in the middle of December certainly stirred up nervousness. On 30th December a woman was arrested in Great St. Bartholomew's for saying the King was to be poisoned; ten days later came the report from the North: 'most of the disbanded forces lie about Newcastle and would join the fanatics to raise a new war. The pulpit blows sparks, and it is a common discourse that the Government will not last a year. Fears hellish designs in embryo.'

By 29th December Sir Edward Nicholas, the Secretary of State, was able to boast that 'White's plot' had been completely crushed; and the trained bands were (unwisely, as it proved) sent home. This was the very day on which the Convention Parliament was dissolved and preparations were set in motion for a general election to secure a parliament properly summoned by writs from the new King. That the new House of Commons would be largely royalist and Anglican was as certain as such things can be. But nothing was better calculated to assist in the election of the required Government majority than the creation of an impression that the old Republicans were already planning to overthrow the Restoration settlement. 'White's plot' was a circumstance of which any good campaign manager was sure to make full use.

If the Government indeed had this object in view, it might be considered fortunate that in January, 1661, there took place a rising about the reality of which there could be no question. Provoked by the execution of their leader, Major-General Harrison, who had been the first to die for the 'Good Old Cause' in October, the Fifth Monarchy men staged a rising in the City of London. Relying upon passages in the Book of Daniel, members of this small sect were convinced that it was their duty to take up arms for King Jesus against the Powers of the Earth. In a manifesto entitled *The Door of Hope* it was stated that 'they would not make any league with monarchists but would rise up against the carnal, to possess the Gate, or the world, to bind their kings in chains and their nobles in fetters of iron.' Only fifty persons actually marched out from their meeting-place into Coleman Street crying, 'The King Jesus and the heads upon the gates!' But they were indifferent about numbers, for they believed that 'one should chase a thousand and two put ten thousand to flight.' They caused infinite commotion in St. Paul's churchyard and elsewhere. After they had killed several men in the City, most of them went out to Ken Wood, where Monk had to send a party of horse to round them up. Three days later they rose again under their leader, Thomas Venner, a wine-bottler, and sought to sacrifice the Lord Mayor to their cause. For a time they held out against the trained bands who had now been raised, and ultimately, after two had been killed, Venner and nine others were arrested. On 19th January, the day of Venner's execution, they rose once again, but this time the revolt was summarily put down and many of their number hanged.

Of all the seventeenth-century religious sects the Fifth Monarchy men were most nearly committed to republicanism; for their intention was to make ready the way for the coming reign of Christ by their own rule during the transitional period. Hence such government as tended in the direction of saintly rule had their approval. The original establishment of the English republic received their hearty commendation, and when Cromwell defied the European monarchs they were delighted. Disillusionment followed. They soon recognized that Cromwell himself aimed at monarchy and they wanted 'no King but Jesus.' The restoration of the Stuarts upset them still more, and for the ten years after 1660 rumours of their activities abounded and hundreds remained true to the cause of the only King.

The genuine Republicans, however, repudiated all association with these half-witted millenarians. In a pamphlet called *A Judgment and Condemnation of Fifth Monarchy Men*, published on 17th January 1661, a 'modest' (and anonymous) gentleman, speaking for the devotees of the Good Old Cause, expressed their abhorrence of the risings. But the risings provided an excellent excuse for the Government to imprison any whom they regarded as potential enemies. The fifty fanatics were magnified tenfold even by an informed Cavalier like Pepys. Thousands of harmless Quakers were thrust into prison. In every chapel meeting the local magistrates detected plots against the Government. And, according to Dr. Burnet, only the fierce expostulations of the Lord Treasurer prevented the reconstitution of a standing army to deal with similar disorders.

While exaggerated reports about Venner's rising and 'White's plot' roused the fears of the electorate against dissenters in general and the Presbyterians in particular, the coronation of King Charles II, which was celebrated in April, stoked up the fires of loyalty. Never again perhaps until modern times was such a magnificent display beheld. It was on St. George's Day that the King went in procession to the Abbey to be crowned and returned thence by gilded barge to Whitehall and left the City to drink itself to distraction. Yet while Charles II rode the waters in triumph, the republican martyrs were not altogether forgotten. Ten days earlier prayers had been said in Bristol for Axtel and Harrison, and someone was heard talking about a dagger factory in London and a 'coming change.' As a safety measure all the cashiered officers were ordered out of London until 20th May, lest discontented voices should mar the national rejoicings.

In this atmosphere the general election resulted in a splendid royalist triumph. Throwing off the puritan restraints, the electors drank so deeply that even the King expressed his disapproval. The 'Cavalier Parliament,' which met on 8th May, contained only about sixty Presbyterians out of over five hundred members. Only the City of London remained sufficiently Puritan to return two Independent and two Presbyterian members—a triumph described by the Court as an 'ill and malicious election.' The King greeted the new members of Parliament graciously—'I know most of your names and faces and can never hope to find better men in your places'—and is reported to have observed in private that their youth was no disadvantage, as he would keep them until they grew beards. In fact he kept this House of Commons for seventeen years.

Among the first acts which were now passed was one 'to preserve the person of the King'; it defined high treason to include 'any compassing, imagining, inventing, devising or intending' death, harm or restraint to the King, whether by word of mouth or by writing, and imposed severe penalties on anyone who expressed the political opinions which were fashionable between 1642 and 1660. A later Act (of 1662) introduced, or, more accurately, put on a legal basis, a system of censorship applicable to both books and newspapers. Printers had to be licensed by the Archbishop of Canterbury and the Bishop of London, and no book could be published without passing the censor. The sectarian literature published in 1661—little or none of it was republican—furnished the excuse for licensing. Even before the Act was passed, the circulation of anti-Government literature, which was being smuggled from hand to hand, was stopped as far as possible: 'Booksellers and printers, their wives, their apprentices and helpers were arrested, houses searched, carriers' carts overhauled, tracts and books and unbound sheets seized and burnt by the thousand.' The third big repressive measure, or rather series of measures, passed in the early sessions of the Cavalier Parliament was even more radical, for it denied Presbyterians or other Puritans comprehension within the restored Church of England and strove—vainly, as it proved—to extirpate nonconformity from the soil of England.

Politically, the attempt to destroy Puritanism proved to be the unwisest action taken by the Restoration Parliament. Neither Charles ii nor his minister, Clarendon—although the repressive measures are known to history as the Clarendon Code—was responsible. In the Declaration of Breda, Charles had promised 'liberty to tender consciences,' and on 4th November 1660 he had published a declaration which envisaged a modified form of episcopal government, in which the bishops would be advised by Presbyterian synods. A meeting between representative Anglicans and Presbyterians to work out details was arranged at Savoy Palace, residence of the Bishop of London, one of the most powerful men in the Church. But the Bishop did not want to make concessions to the Presbyterian point of view and got the better of his opponents by inducing them to put forward what appeared to be excessive demands and even to quarrel among themselves. In any case, differences over doctrine were fundamental. Thus the negotiations, of which the country squires now dominating the House of Commons would certainly not have approved, broke down, and the opportunity was awaited by the enemies of Puritanism to overbear Charles II's amiable leanings towards toleration and crush the Presbyterians entirely. Just as the early plots or alleged plots of Charles II's reign helped in the electoral triumph of the Royalists over the Presbyterians, so too the later plots of the next decade were to provide the excuse for the imposition of the complete structure of intolerant legislation known as the Clarendon Code. Because of this code the more courageous nonconformists were directly driven into the arms of political plotters who, like Wildman, were indifferent to specific creeds. And if the Government officials believed, or pretended to believe, that every chapel meeting was a republican conspiracy, finally they were to cry wolf when the wolf came. When a big plot ultimately did take effect, it was not a republican plot, but it obtained liberty for nonconformity and spelt exile for the Stuart dynasty.

In those days when the letter was the only national form of communication, the post office was better placed than any other organization to reach conclusions about the political state of mind of the country. Its officials could learn most quickly whether disaffection was brewing in Bristol, say, or whether the discontent in Yorkshire was serious or just the eternal grumbling of Englishmen in taverns. Hence Sir Edward Nicholas must have been concerned to hear during the course of 1661 that all was by no means well with the post office. The first report to this effect arrived in December, 1660, from Humphrey Cantell, the postmaster at Newbury. His information was

that there are several members belonging to the Post Office being ill affected to the Government and that none of the Post Office have taken the oath of allegiance; the persons named were Major Wildman, who puts in and out whom he pleases, and there is one Thompson and Oxenbridge Anabaptists who are employed as [his] agents to put in and out whom they please to the Office.

Cantell asserted further that some plot was on foot and particularly that one Baxter, who was an instrument of Cornet Joyce (himself Oliver Cromwell's underling in 1647) 'did say how now the army was disbanded we shall see good sport as ever was, swords drawn again.' At the same time Captain Henry Leicester stated that when Colonel Birch, another Republican, disbanded his regiment, he had said that he hoped his men would serve him again if he had occasion. This alleged evidence of a connexion between discontented officers and the post office was really too slight for credibility, and no doubt the arrests made that December satisfied the authorities for the time being. But complaints against the management of the post office accumulated in the Secretary of State's office in the course of 1661. For example, it was said that the master of the Dover packet boats made use of his office for smuggling purposes and delayed the dispatch of letters to suit his own interests. A petition was also received by the Secretary of State, which purported to come from no less than three hundred of the postmasters of England, Wales, and Ireland, complaining about Bishop's administration and contrasting it unfavourably with that under Cromwell. They asserted that Bishop had exploited his unhampered control over the under-postmasters by threatening them with the loss of their jobs and thereby forcing them to work for him on worse terms than those for which they had worked before the Restoration. These three hundred postmasters were men who had been employed alike under Charles I and under Cromwell, but there were also numerous petitions from the 'several honest suffering postmasters who were turned out for their loyalty to the late King and desired to be restored.' In regard to the case of the ex-royalist postmasters Bishop was able to refer to Hickes's impartial report that they were not as numerous or as loyal as they pretended to be, and he was also able to state that appointments in the counties had been approved by the Secretary of State himself.

In August, 1661, however, the allegations about Bishop's mismanagement of his office came before the Secretaries of State and the Privy Council in a more specific form; in particular, the statements of Thomas Ibson, a clerk in the London office, whom Bishop had discharged for fraud and negligence, threw a curious light on the state of affairs there:

Upon strict examination (said Ibson) there will be found [in the Post Office] four or five persons solely employed, if not entrusted, who formerly have been eminently active for Cromwell and served in all the revolutions of the late Government.

The chief of them, he said, was Major Wildman, whose character he described as follows:

'A great Leveller by profession, formerly an Agitator in the Army, after a great solicitor in that horrid cause and at this day but an indifferent royalist if not more inclinable to anti-monarchy. As subtle a person as any of his quality perhaps in England. A great confident in, if not a faithful correspondent with, many of the adverse party, suspected for a Papist or an Independent, Socinian [*i.e.* a Unitarian] at the least. This man hath the greatest share in the present post farm, solely rules, directs and governs all in it, and the Postmaster (an honest gentleman) [is] little better than the other's pupil.'

Ibson then went on to discuss in equally critical terms Clement Oxenbridge, who had actually held a position in the post office under Charles I but, according to Ibson, betrayed many of his party to the later usurper; Dorislaus, the son of 'the wicked person' Dr. Isaac Dorislaus 'who pleaded and urged the King's death so vigorously' that he was murdered by royalist exiles in Holland in 1650; and Mynheer Vanderheyden, who was 'an agent of that unworthy person, Monsieur Nieuport,' Dutch Ambassador in London to Cromwell. 'This Vanderheyden with Oxenbridge,' said Ibson, were at that time engaged on a treaty 'by order and the underhand connivance of Major Wildman for settling the new post by way of Amsterdam' so as to obtain complete and unauthorized control over the foreign as well as the domestic posts. Finally, said Ibson,

'Colonel Bishop himself, though he [may] have appeared active and very affectionate for the King and no question may be a very just and worthy person yet having formerly been a Papist (if yet he be of any other opinion) is so absolutely under the dominion of Wildman (as well for purse as conduct) that he cannot be accounted Master himself, much less of his office and that great trust thereby reposed in him, which sufficiently appears by Major Wildman's over-acting and directing all things in that office and that the good colonel does little, or rather can do nothing by himself without the other.'

By way of circumstantial evidence Ibson added 'some observations on that treaty which the Postmaster-General of England and his Governor Major Wildman' had made through Vanderheyden with the postmaster at Amsterdam. The facts, he claimed, 'were taken out of the instructions to Oxenbridge sent to Holland by the postmaster and Wildman and returned but a few days since for England.' Major Wildman's objectives were, he asserted, to get a good sum of money for himself, to monopolize the Anglo-Dutch packet boat trade and to export bullion abroad contrary to the law. The Dutch side of the bargain was the right to smuggle in prohibited goods and to make themselves 'masters of intelligence.'

It is obvious that the Privy Council was not impressed with these stories and made full allowance for the fact that Ibson was a man with a grievance. Colonel Bishop, however, was sufficiently concerned to rebut the allegations: he was not content to dismiss them as the distorted imaginings of a discharged official but also retorted on him in kind. He averred that Ibson had himself in fact been one of Thurloe's own particular jackals and had been ordered by Thurloe to examine what letters he pleased; he added that Ibson had continued this practice in an entirely unauthorized manner after the Restoration, and named specific letters that had been improperly opened by him. Ibson's reply when he was examined by Sir Henry Bennet (afterwards Lord Arlington, who succeeded Sir Edward Nicholas as chief Secretary of State in 1662) was that Wildman had 'framed' him. 'It was,' he then swore, 'an old practice of Wildman's when he [was] minded to call the reputation of any of the clerks in question to take letters out of one road and dispose of them into another,' and added that he could prove that Wildman had often done this.

By the time that Ibson put forward his second series of accusations, Wildman was already in prison for treason. But in August, 1661, Sir Edward Nicholas was content simply to take note of all the allegations and to accept for the time being Bishop's explanations of their falsity. Yet there is no reason to question the broad accuracy of the statements about Wildman's position or to doubt that he was in fact, if not in name, the first Restoration Postmaster-General. Information obtained by the Government later in the same year convinced the authorities that he had indeed made use of his position to keep the republican movement on foot after the execution of the regicides and had employed the post office as a republican plotting centre in the heart of London, under the very nose of the new King.

CHAPTER XIV

THE CAVALIERS' REVENGE

Thus inborn broils the factions would engage
Or wars of exil'd heirs, or foreign rage,
Till halting vengeance overtook our age:
And our wild labours wearied into rest
Reclin'd us on a rightful monarch's breast.

DRYDEN *The Medal*

THE first session of the Cavalier Parliament ended at the close of July, 1661, just before the series of accusations against the administration of the post office came to their culmination. A little earlier the Savoy conference finally broke down. The decisions reached by the Church of England Convocation on the revision of the prayer book and the attitude of Parliament now made it clear that there was no likelihood of the Presbyterians being included in a united Church and no willingness to tolerate them outside it. It therefore suited the mood of the ruling powers to have proofs that the dissenters were not only theologically wrong-headed but politically obnoxious. Reports of plots against the Government grew in volume. Sir Charles Lyttleton wrote from his country seat in Worcestershire in August that 'we have been mightily alarmed here with reports of plots from London' and that orders were being given to keep a strict eye on the 'fanatics,' to disarm many of them, and to call out the militia. In November, as a convenient bolt from the blue, news reached Whitehall that, in spite of the precautions mentioned by Lyttleton, a veritable Presbyterian plot, centred in Worcestershire but covering no less than sixteen other counties, had been accidentally discovered.

The details of the 'plot' deserve close study because they illustrate clearly the flimsy foundations upon which contemporary politicians and some later historians were content to build and the nervous and cunning temper of the Cavalier Parliament in 1661.

On Sunday, 10th November, a certain Richard Churme appeared before Sir John Packington, the High Anglican M.P. for Worcestershire and a Justice of the Peace, with two letters in his hand. He told the following story. He had been walking along a country lane when he saw a yellow-haired, broad-faced man, wearing a grey coat and with a green carpet wrapped around his shoulders, lying on the ground sorting letters. After the man had gone—according to one version of Churme's story the man was a Scottish tramp who had stopped to cut a stick from a hedge—he had dropped two of his letters. On seeing their contents Churme, as a public-spirited citizen, hurried with them to the proper authorities. The letters were written by a woman who signed herself 'Ann Ba' or A. b.' and they were addressed respectively to Ambrose Sparry, the puritan minister of the neighbouring village of Martley, and to Captain Andrew Yarranton, an enlightened local engineer and iron expert, who was one of the earliest advocates of a modern canal system. In Sparry's letter the lady spoke of 'a company' that 'had been increased to 300,' of hopes to 'see merry days and business suddenly done' and signed herself and her husband 'yours to the last drop of blood.' In the letter to Yarranton there was talk of an oath taken on 1st November, of the need to acquaint men with a time and place, while it urged him to pray for the Gospel and 'a fatal blow to adversaries.' Packington and his fellow magistrates read these letters as implying a widespread plot against the Government, although on the face of them they sound like an excitable way of describing a nonconformist meeting. The magistrates at once started inquiries and unearthed two witnesses, whose names have not survived, who were ready to swear that Captain Yarranton had been given a mysterious commission 'to cure people of the simples' and that a rendezvous had been arranged at Edgehill—site of the first battle of the civil war—where Lambert's old soldiers would gather and meet the plotters of Worcestershire. The interrogations took place on 12th November, and their results, together with copies of the letters, were sent to London. Sir Edward Nicholas ordered all those implicated to be arrested, but even before his instructions arrived Packington had acted and had seized Yarranton, Sparry and two other ministers and two officers. No further confirmatory evidence was ever discovered either by the Worcestershire magistrates or by a Joint Committee of the two Houses of Parliament. Sparry and Yarranton denied everything, and after Yarranton had escaped from custody, had been rearrested and had several other adventures, he was ultimately acquitted at the assizes.

Twenty years afterwards Yarranton wrote a pamphlet in which he said that the whole alleged plot was a sham. Packington, he asserted, had written the letters himself and arranged for their discovery. This fact, he stated, had been disclosed to his wife by the brother of one of Packington's accomplices while he himself had still been in prison. So desperate had the authorities been to find evidence that when an old man ventured to inquire what had happened to the nonconformist ministers, he was arrested and, as he refused to confess what he knew, lighted matches were put between his fingers. They were equally unsuccessful in trying to prove the existence of a plot in Oxford. One significant point raised by Yarranton about the genuineness of the Worcestershire plot concerned the alleged implication of Richard Baxter, the saintly Presbyterian minister of Kidderminster, who had been present at the Savoy Conference and had been offered a bishopric by Charles II. The letter from 'Ann Ba' to Sparry made mention of Baxter as a man he 'must be sure to speak to'; according to Yarranton, it was also alleged that Baxter had promised to provide a considerable body of well-armed men for a rising. Now it is significant that, although two other men referred to in the letter who were also dissenting ministers were arrested, Baxter was carefully left alone. His reputation was such that no one would have believed that he was engaged in armed conspiracy. Moreover, he was not in Worcestershire at the time, having settled in London, and could no doubt have produced a conclusive alibi.

Edmund Calamy, whose account of the misadventures of Presbyterian ministers in the reign of Charles II has generally been deemed pretty reliable, has a different story. Ambrose Sparry, whom he describes as 'a sober learned minister who had never espoused Parliament's cause and was for moderate episcopacy,' had, he says, a 'wicked neighbour' who bore a grudge against Sparry because he reproved him for adultery. By way of revenge this neighbour framed the letter 'as from a nameless person and deliberately involved all the local Presbyterians in a scheme for a rising. Sparry was long kept in prison, and even when the forgery was detected they had much difficulty in obtaining his release.'

Baxter, adds Calamy, escaped arrest, but in 'distant centres' it was called 'Baxter's plot.'

To sum up, both Calamy and Yarranton assert that the letters were proved to be forgeries, they read like forgeries—especially the reference to Baxter (unless they were harmless)—and no evidence of any value was ever found even after the most searching inquiries to confirm Packington's intelligence. On the other hand, Packington, who was an exuberant Anglican, was the very man most likely to swallow, if not to concoct, any story that would clear Worcestershire of nonconformists.

The Yarranton or Baxter plot was magnified out of all proportion by the Cavalier Parliament and by the Anglicans. The local clergy hastened to provide a force of foot soldiers who were known as the 'clergy band.' When Parliament reassembled on 20th November, the King devoted much of his opening speech to the 'Presbyterian plot' and its 'wicked instruments.' Next day, after Packington had told his story from the floor of the House, the junior Secretary of State, William Morrice, delivered a message from the Commons to the Lords urging that once again the King should issue a proclamation banning all cashiered soldiers from the City of London, since they had full intelligence of 'some design amongst them tending to a breach of the peace.' Delighted at the excuse, the House of Commons also prepared to pass the Corporation Bill, which, among other things, obliged all mayors and officials to take the sacrament according to the rites of the Church of England and to declare themselves against the Solemn League and Covenant, the charter of Presbyterianism to which Charles II himself had sworn fidelity in 1649. Thus this dubious plot enabled the Cavalier Parliament virtually to exclude all Presbyterians henceforward from civic life and to undermine the pledges made by the King to them as a reward for the active part which they had played in his restoration.

Once again the Government was fortunate that just as the excitement over one alleged plot began to die, intelligence of another was discovered. Sir Edward Nicholas had not been slow in following up the evidence against Wildman and the officials of the post office put forward by Thomas Ibson, the clerk. As we have seen, Wildman in 1656 had established his old servant, William

Parker, and his wife in a victualling and coffee house, called Non-such House, in Bow Street, Covent Garden, where meetings of a republican club were held in the last years of the Interregnum. Nicholas set inquiries on foot in Bow Street and accumulated evidence from Parker's neighbours about the kind of things that were going on in Nonsuch House. The results went to show that Nonsuch House was still a republican meeting-place and moreover that the post office clerks and Bishop, the Postmaster-General himself, frequently went there for their dinner. The neighbours, headed by a gentleman named Joseph Bilcliffe, had few good words to say for Parker or for his guests. 'The fellow that keeps this house,' they averred, 'was a dangerous person and one well known to be ever ill affected to His Majesty and his interests.' More direct evidence was obtained from Mary Ellis, who was servant to the Parkers. She stated that Wildman, Harrington, Praisegod 'Barebones,' Major Haynes, Colonel Salmon, Colonel Bishop, Henry Nevile and Sir John Lenthall often met at Nonsuch House and that it was the weekly meeting-place of the post office clerks. The girl was evidently frightened and one need not question the substantial accuracy of her testimony as far as it went. Moreover Wildman's connexions with Nonsuch House were disclosed to the Government by an intercepted note from Mrs. Wildman to one William Godolphin, instructing him to use Non-such House as an accommodation address. But the mere fact that the most distinguished of the old Republicans were accustomed to use Nonsuch House as a place at which to meet and eat was not good enough evidence for the Government to act upon.

However, in the meantime the Chancellor, the Earl of Clarendon, also had found an informer against the Republicans. Who this informer was is not known; he told Clarendon that some of his associates had been planning to murder the King and, as his conscience would not permit him to go as far as that, he preferred to confess but also to remain anonymous. He related a circum-stantial story of what was being plotted at Bow Street and in the other taverns where the old soldiers gathered. He asserted that a great meeting was being planned for 10th and 11th December where the details were to be settled about a rising to take place during January or February in Shrewsbury, Bristol, Coventry and several other places simultaneously; he added that the conspirators optimistically thought that even if they were only successful in disturbing the peace of the nation a little they would be advertising to foreign Powers that all was not well in England and thus lay the train for international confusion which would be helpful to their ultimate designs against monarchy. In view of this story three of the alleged conspirators, Packer, Haynes and Kenrick, the first two Cromwellian officers and the third a prominent City merchant, were arrested.

At this point the revengeful figure of Widow Smith appeared on the scene to offer her contribution to evidence of a widespread republican conspiracy. Mrs. Smith was the widow of Major William Smith, who had figured in the Sussex plot of 1658, and had died some time after his arrest, convinced (quite wrongly) that he had been betrayed by Henry Bishop, now the Postmaster-General and his friend Wildman. The widow lived on, determined to punish Bishop and Wildman for their imaginary betrayal of her husband. After the Restoration she retired to take charge of an inn named 'The Sign of the Catherine Wheel' at Hounslow and bided her opportunity for revenge. It duly came. On the night of Sunday, 24th November, two of the clerks of the post office rode out post haste to Hounslow and intercepted the western mails. They took them into a private room at the inn and examined their contents for two hours and afterwards charged the postboy that he was to mention this to no one but to carry the mails on to London as if nothing had happened. Widow Smith at once reported the news of this secret and unauthorized interference with the direct delivery of the royal mail by clerks appointed by Bishop and Wildman. Bishop's reputation as a sound Royalist stood him in good stead, but next day Nicholas, who had been accumulating evidence against Wildman, gave orders that the rest of the Nonsuch House clientele was to be rounded up. On 25th November Praisegod 'Barebones' and Samuel Moyer, a republican merchant, were arrested, and the next day Wildman, James Harrington and John Ireton, brother of the late Henry Ireton, Wildman's old opponent, were put in the Tower. By the middle of December all the alleged ringleaders of the conspiracy had been arrested.

Interrogations were undertaken by members of the Privy Council. Wildman's and Harrington's examinations have survived and we can follow from them the line of the Government's investigations. Here are the questions put to Wildman on 26th November 1661, together with his non-committal answers:

'Do you know of no present design to disturb the peace of the nation or to alter the Government?'

'I know of no design tending to disturbance at all.'

'When were you last in Mr. Harrington's company? Where was it? And what company was present?'

'I have not seen Mr. Harrington this twelvemonth but in passing.'

'Did you consult about members choosing to serve in this Parliament for the City—those very persons that were chosen? Who were present there? Was Alderman Love there? Alderman Fowke? Alderman Ireton? [It is to be remembered that two Independents and two Presbyterians had been chosen to represent the City of London in the Commons, a disconcerting result for the Administration.] Were you never at an alehouse in Covent Garden with Mr. Harrington about last March?'

'I know nothing of a meeting in Covent Garden about choosing the burgesses of the City to be in Parliament. I do not know Mr. Love.'

'Do you know Mr. Barebone, Henry Nevile, Major Haynes, Samuel Moyer, John Portman? Have you never had any conference with the latter about setting up the Long Parliament? Did you not meet these people at a meeting at St. Martin's the Grand? Was an Oath of Secrecy taken?'

'I know Mr. Barebone, but I was never at any meeting with him and was not present about him except in his shop. I have not seen Mr. Nevile [for] a long time but in Colonel Bishop's company. I have not seen Mr. Moyer this twelvemonth but in passing. I do not know Mr. Portman but have heard about him.'

'Do you know Sir Robert Harlow? Did you meet him with Nevile in August last at the King's Head near Butcher Row? Had you not there communication about reviving the Long Parliament? And of preparing a petition for taking off the excise and against a standing army?'

'I am acquainted with Harlow but have not met him for a long time. I had no meeting [i.e. conference] with Sir Robert Harlow at any time. I was not at the King's Head in the Butcher Row at any meeting in August last. I was at no meeting where there was any discourse about making a petition to this Parliament.'

'Had you not a meeting with the same persons at a house near the water-side by Millbank? Was not Mr. Pretty there? Do you know Mr. Pretty? When did you see him? Was there not an oath of secrecy proposed? Did you not agree to choose, and to meet as, a private committee to ripen business? Who were in it? How often did you meet?'

'I do not know one Mr. Pretty, but I know a Mr. Petty who is connected with the Duke of Buckingham. I was never at any meeting at Millbank.'

'Do you know of no invitation sent to disbanded officers and purchasers of Crown lands to repair to this town before the 10th of next month? Of no designs to seize the gates of the City? Do you know of no attempt to be made upon the Lord General [Monk]? When were you at the Spanish Ambassador's house?'

In other words the examining committee got no change out of the Major, who preserved undimmed his reputation for taciturnity and for not betraying his true associates.

Harrington, who was examined by a committee of three—the Earl of Lauderdale who was his kinsman, Sir George Carteret and Sir Edward Walker—was much more loquacious but no more informative. Lauderdale began by inquiring about his relations with Wildman.

LAUDERDALE: 'Do you know Mr. Wildman?'

HARRINGTON: 'My Lord, I have some acquaintance with him.'

LAUDERDALE: 'When did you see him?'

HARRINGTON: 'My Lord, he and I have not been in one house together these two years.'

LAUDERDALE: 'Will you say so?'

HARRINGTON: 'Yes, my lord.'

LAUDERDALE: 'When did you see him last?'

HARRINGTON: 'About a year ago I met him in a street that goes to Drury Lane.'

LAUDERDALE: 'Did you go into no house?'

HARRINGTON: 'No, my lord.'

LAUDERDALE: 'Come, this will do you no good: had not you, in March last, meetings with him in Bow Street in Covent Garden? where there were about twenty or more of you; where you made a speech about half an hour long that they should lay by distinguished names and betake themselves together into one work, which was to dissolve this Parliament, and bring in a new one or the old one again. Was not the meeting adjourned from thence to Millbank? Were you not there also?'

HARRINGTON: 'My lord, you may think, if these things be true, I have no refuge but to the mercy of God and the King.'

LAUDERDALE: 'True.'

HARRINGTON: 'Well then, my lord, solemnly and deliberately with my eyes to Heaven I renounce the mercy of God and the King if any of this be true, or if ever I thought or heard of this till now that you tell me.'

Harrington then went on to swear that he had never met 'Barebones' except at his leather-seller's shop, that he knew Nevile well but had only met him in the most respectable company, and that he had never heard of Portman, the Fifth Monarchy man. He concluded his examination by inquiring why 'being a private man he should so meddle in politics?' True, he had written on them, as had Plato, Aristotle, Livy and Machiavelli. But had not Aristotle been permitted to praise democracy under Alexander the Great? Had not Livy spoken of a Commonwealth under Augustus Caesar and Machiavelli under the Medici? And under which ruler had he himself in fact written of the ideal Commonwealth? Under a usurper, Oliver Cromwell.

Despite all these emphatic denials the Government was convinced that Wildman and Harrington were the leaders in a widespread conspiracy to overthrow the Restoration Government. On 19th December Clarendon delivered a message from King Charles II to the House of Lords, which was duly conveyed to the Commons, stating that 'diverse discontented persons are endeavouring to raise new troubles,' and gave some details of what he had discovered from his informers and the interrogation of the prisoners. The two Houses decided to appoint a Joint Committee, in which the Lords were represented among others by the Bishop of London and the Duke of York, and to it Clarendon submitted his evidence.

According to his first report there was a Committee of Twenty-one which met at Nonsuch House, Millbank, St. Martin's le Grand and elsewhere to organize the plot. The committee, he said, represented seven different parties: three for the Commonwealth, three for the Long Parliament, three for the City, three for the ruined purchasers of Crown lands, three for the disbanded army men, three for the Independents and three for the Fifth Monarchy men. Their first step had been to choose candidates for Parliament in the general election, and he attributed to their machinations the election of the two Independents and two Presbyterians for the City of London. When this statement was made in the House of Commons, the City members referred to indignantly stood up and denied the aspersion. The committee's next move was to have been to frame a petition to Parliament to ask for liberty of conscience and a preaching ministry. There was also a rumour current of an Inner Council of Seven, a republican high priesthood, closely bound together by oaths of secrecy. This, however, did not figure in Clarendon's statement. Clarendon added that 'though he had certain information of the times and places of their meetings, and particularly those of Harrington and Wildman, they were nevertheless so fixed in their design that not one of those they had taken would confess anything, not so much as that they had seen and spoken to one another at these times and places: which obstinacy he thought must need proceed from faithfulness to their oath.'

Although Parliament had been sufficiently impressed by this account to keep the Coldstream Guards in town and to appoint the Joint Committee, it was obvious that more specific accusations than those would need to be forthcoming to induce the Commons to assent to what the King appears to have wanted—a standing army. After all, what were the conspirators alleged to have done? To have formed an election committee in London and to have drawn up a petition for liberty of conscience. Was this treason? Clarendon went away to find something more convincing to tell the Joint Committee. Within three weeks he had obtained what he wanted—or at least all he could get.

The following was his much-improved story. One of the prisoners, Colonel Salmon, he announced, had inadvertently disclosed the truth. In the first place a list of a hundred and sixty officers of the disbanded army had been found on him when he was arrested; in the second place, he and Wildman had contradicted each other. Wildman had said that he had not seen Salmon for twelve months and Salmon said that he had seen Wildman the day before. Salmon had confessed that he had asked for a pass for Wildman, and Wildman said that he knew nothing of it. Clarendon then added his story of the original anonymous informer who, he said, had himself been on the Committee of Twenty-one. According to this man's account, 'some of the late King's murderers were entertained in France, Holland and Germany and were in correspondence with foreign princes and were collecting arms.' This information, Clarendon said, had been confirmed 'by intelligence from abroad that never failed.' There was also an independent story from Huntingdon, the birthplace of Oliver Cromwell, of 'many who met there under the name of Quakers that were not so, that ride in multitudes by night to the terror of His Majesty's good subjects.' The Joint Committee approved the decision of the King to put two troops into Shrewsbury and two into Coventry and asked that Lambert and Vane should be brought to trial. But that they were impressed with the evidence proffered by the King's ministers seems doubtful. For the committee stated that 'they had reached no resolutions or opinions about the matter and thought fit to leave the business to the wisdom of both Houses of Parliament.' The arrested Republicans were kept in prison and the two Houses then turned again with goodwill to complete the Corporation Bill and an Act of Uniformity to crush dissent for ever.

Harrington and Wildman were never given a trial, but were held in the Tower on the warrant of the Secretary of State. This fact alone makes the evidence against them suspect. If it was really good, why did not Clarendon produce it in court? If it was circumstantial, why did the Joint Committee not act more vigorously? Harrington's life-history as a timid and peaceful theoretician who was devoted to Charles I and submitted to Cromwell and who wrote 'whatever is violent is not secure or durable' hardly fits in with the picture of chief architect of a desperate rising in 1661. On the other hand, Mary Ellis's evidence seems conclusive that he and the other old Republicans did in fact frequent Nonsuch House, and it is likely enough that there were many discussions about the chances of regaining religious and political liberty through normal political activity and possibly speculation, based on information acquired from the post office officials, about the prospects of the restored monarchy maintaining itself. Wildman's career of constant plotting makes that much more plausible.

Harrington paid the price for continuing to associate with his old friends of the Rota Club. After he had been in the Tower for some six months his sisters applied for a writ of habeas corpus, requiring that he should be brought to trial, whereupon he was removed from the Tower and shipped out to the rocky island of St. Nicholas near Plymouth to prevent the application of the writ; here close confinement undermined his health and even his mind. Finally he was released, but only the devotion of a wife and the loyal friendship of Henry Nevile made his last years of life tolerable. He died in 1677 but a shell of his true self. He lives on in the record of English history as the greatest republican thinker of his age and the inspirer of many later political thinkers—a philosopher who had the misfortune to live in times of crisis and bitter political revenge. Wildman also had to pay the penalty, but the many hardships that he now had to endure in the Tower and elsewhere could not break the body or the spirit of this taciturn and unremitting worker for a freer form of government.

Mrs. Lucy Wildman, who had already served her apprenticeship in caring for her husband's business affairs during his term of imprisonment by Oliver Cromwell, now exerted herself again on his behalf. At the end of 1661 she petitioned the King for a good doctor to visit her husband since he had fallen very ill after six weeks' close imprisonment in the Tower. A month later she submitted a second petition that she might visit him since he had 'many suits of law pending.' Mr. Secretary Nicholas duly accorded permission to Lucy and the lawyers to visit him from time to time in the presence of a warder and instructed the clerks of the Council that she might have access to her husband's chambers and his closet at Parsons Green, evidently one of their homes. There seems to have been an interval of some months before Wildman, like Harrington, had his friends apply for a writ of habeas corpus. Habeas corpus was a long-established common law right which compelled the gaoler to produce the body of a prisoner with the date and cause of his detention to the judgment of the court issuing the writ. By an Act of 1641 its application was specifically extended even to imprisonments by order of the King or Privy Council. In practice there were several ways of avoiding the writ. In Harrington's case his biographer Toland records, when his sisters applied for a writ, 'it was at first flatly denied, but afterwards when it was granted and duly served his warder came one day to his sisters at

Westminster and acquainted them that between one o'clock and two o'clock that morning their brother was put on board a ship to be transported he knew not whither, without any time given him either to see his friends or make provision of money, linen or other necessaries.' Not until a fortnight later did they discover what had happened to him, and it seems to have been due rather to the courtesy of the deputy governor of St. Nicholas' Island than to any process of law that he was well treated there and finally released.

Presumably some time in 1662 Mrs. Wildman also sought a writ of habeas corpus, whereupon, to circumvent the writ, Wildman was likewise removed, together with John Ireton and Major Creed, to the Scilly Isles. The King's orders for their removal from the Tower to the Duke of York's yacht were received on 5th July. They were taken in the yacht to St. Mary's castle, where Dr. John Bastwick had been imprisoned in the reign of Charles I for his vigorous attack on the authority of the bishops. On 13th August 1662 Sir Francis Godolphin, who was Governor of the Scilly Isles, visited St. Mary's castle and saw the prisoners, who, he told Sir Edward Nicholas, disliked their change from the Tower and 'pretended innocency and expectation of discharge.' In the following year Lucy Wildman vainly petitioned that her husband 'who is in a very infirm condition by being a year a close prisoner in the Tower and half a year in Scilly should be released on bail or allowed to travel beyond the seas.' But it was not until 1666 that Wildman left Scilly and then only for Pendennis castle, Cornwall, whither he was conveyed by a frigate. Here at length he was granted certain concessions in consequence of the unceasing efforts of his wife. His only son John, now a youth in his teens, was permitted to share his father's exile, and the Major was allowed to have a servant. The younger John Wildman's devotion had evidently begun in the Scilly Islands, for it is noted on his tombstone at Shrivenham that 'his filial piety was such as made him prefer confinement for many years with his father a prisoner of State in the Island of Scilly in the reign of Charles II to the full injoyment of his liberty.' A little later the Governor of Pendennis castle was told that he might allow Wildman to go outside the castle and take the air in company with a warder, provided that he did not go too far. In October, 1667, the welcome news of release came after nearly six years in prison. The Governor was then instructed to set

Wildman at liberty 'on good security to repair to London within three weeks and present himself to Mr. Secretary Morrice, give security to keep the peace, and attempt nothing against the Government.'

We may reasonably associate the greater freedom allowed to Wildman in prison and his subsequent release to the fall in 1667 of the Earl of Clarendon from power. Clarendon had always been rightly suspicious of Wildman's attitude to monarchy. Undoubtedly it was he who had Wildman put away out of the reach of habeas corpus. One of the accusations made against him in this very year was that he had sent persons 'to remote islands, garrisons and other places thereby to prevent them from the benefit of the law.' After his downfall more attention was paid to writs of habeas corpus and in general a policy of greater leniency was practised towards political and religious dissenters. Moreover the Duke of Buckingham, who had now suddenly become influential at Court, was Wildman's old friend and associate.

We must now turn back to see how political affairs had changed and how plotting had progressed during Wildman's imprisonment.

CHAPTER XV

PLOTTERS AND TREPANNERS

The good old cause revived a plot requires
Plots, true or false, are necessary things,
To raise up commonwealths, and ruin kings.
DRYDEN *Absalom and Achitophel*

WILDMAN's term of imprisonment in the Tower, the Scilly Isles, and Cornwall coincided with the last years of the political supremacy of the Earl of Clarendon. Clarendon was an austere, honest and patriotic gentleman whose loyalty to the monarchy was beyond question. When, soon after the Restoration, he discovered that his daughter Anne was with child by James, Duke of York, and the question of marriage was raised, he said he 'would rather his daughter should be the Duke's whore than his wife' and talked of sending her to the Tower and even having her executed. However, James and Anne Hyde were married and Clarendon became, in the words of a leading modern historian, 'the last great Minister not a soldier who stood almost above the level of a subject.'

Clarendon's strongest claim on historical fame is that he succeeded in restoring his master to the English throne without foreign money or foreign bayonets. But between 1661 and 1667 he suffered from two misfortunes. In the first place, since he was the First Minister (although by no means Prime Minister in the modern sense) he was blamed for a series of political miscalculations for which he was not much more than nominally responsible. For example, there is good reason to believe that he never thoroughly approved of the series of repressive measures imposed by the Cavalier Parliament upon the dissenters; yet they were named the Clarendon Code. Equally he was no advocate of the coming disastrous war against the Dutch and had little or no control over its finances; but the mismanagement of the war was laid at his door. Clarendon's second misfortune was that he had outlived his time and become an anachronism. He would have made an ideal minister at the Court of Charles I, where his sobriety, virtue and staunch Anglicanism must have commended themselves to that highly respectable monarch. But Charles II's sexual conduct won the Chancellor's open disapproval, and Clarendon soon made an enemy of Lady Castlemaine, the King's mistress, and her rakish men friends. Furthermore, Clarendon looked upon the exuberant Cavalier Parliament with the same jaundiced eye with which he had regarded the rebellious Long Parliament twenty years before. His view was that Parliaments should certainly be seen but not be heard more frequently than was avoidable. As to the other organs of political opinion, like the Press and the coffee-houses, he would have done away with them altogether. In the disbanded soldiery grumbling over their tankards in the East End taverns he was accustomed to detect again the revolutionary rumblings of '42. Hence he employed every resource in his power—denial of habeas corpus, the torture chamber, the licensing system, the over-anxious J.P.'s and the county militia—to eliminate all expressions of radical opinion. He participated in and infected the court with the general state of high-strung tension and heightened the nervous fear that the Restoration was not a final settlement and that the old Cromwellian soldiers would rise again. It has sometimes been suggested that because of this overpowering fear Clarendon deliberately forged or faked the stories of 'plots' which he gave out to the world. There is no solid evidence for this view. But it is obvious that with his mind so shaped he would not trouble to give the same impartial and judicial examination to testimonies against alleged republican plotters as he would have done, say, to Chancery documents on real estate.

In 1662, however, Clarendon—having satisfactorily disposed of Wildman and Harrington—'stood between the furious Churchmen and their victims.' One reason for his attitude seems to have been that he believed the Presbyterians were less likely to plot revolution in concert with the Republicans if their religious freedom was to some extent preserved. He strove in vain to mitigate their sufferings, for Parliament disregarded his views, and the only result of his efforts was to alienate the Presbyterians while displeasing the Churchmen. On 19th May the Act of Uniformity became law, compelling every place of public worship to use the Common Prayer Book as revised in an anti-puritan sense by Convocation, and obliging all incumbents of livings to declare their acceptance of its doctrines. On St. Bartholomew's Day, 24th August 1662, some twelve hundred clergy who had refused to abandon their beliefs were expelled from their livings, and dissent was transformed into nonconformity. At the same time the Licensing Act had been passed with his approval, and freedom of thought and freedom of worship were simultaneously suppressed.

In the same year the Government finally liquidated the republican leaders. In April, 1662, largely through the efforts of Sir George Downing, himself an eminent ex-Cromwellian and now ambassador at The Hague, three more regicides—Okey, Barkstead and Corbet—were seized in Holland and brought over to England to be executed. In 1660 a certain Mr. Thomas had moved in the Commons to have 'somebody die for the kingdom as well as for the King' and named Sir Henry Vane. In spite of an earlier petition of the two Houses to spare his life the Government now in 1662 decided it was dangerous to allow this incorruptible Republican to live on. A case was made out against him and on 14th June he was executed. So boldly did he conduct himself on the scaffold that drums and trumpets were loudly sounded to drown his last words. The more enlightened Royalists felt that the King had lost more than he had gained by his death. General John Lambert escaped with imprisonment for life. A rumour circulated that if Lambert had been condemned to death the old soldiers would have risen and put him at their head. It is likely enough that the death of Lambert would have disturbed the old soldiers more than that of the civilian Vane.

By the end of 1662 the Republicans and old soldiers had thus been deprived of all their leaders, who were dead, in prison, or abroad. At the same time the nonconformist ministers entered a kind of Christian ghetto, in utter exile from all public life. In the official mind these two groups were lumped together as desperate enemies of the régime, and chapel meetings were invariably regarded as hives of conspiracy. The new religious persecution contributed to the violent and nervous state of public opinion which made magistrates and government servants ready to accept any rumours of plots. In December the trials of Thomas Tonge and others were to demonstrate to the satisfaction of Parliament how grave were the dangers of a policy of toleration.

On 31st October 1662 Samuel Pepys noted in his diary: 'Public matters are full of discontent what with the sale of Dunkirk [acquired by Cromwell and sold with the full approval of the King's Council but blamed specifically on Clarendon] and my Lady Castlemaine and her faction at Court; though I know not what more they would have than to debauch the King, whom God preserve from it! And then great plots are talked to be discovered, and all prisons full of ordinary people, taken from their meeting places last Sunday. But for certain some plots there have been, though not brought to a head.'

On the very day that Pepys wrote, the Government was informed that a group of desperate conspirators, representing all the non-conformists from Fifth Monarchy men to Congregationalists except the Presbyterians, had gathered in St. Michael's parish, Cornhill. Their plans were stated to be far-reaching. They aimed, it was said, at deposing and killing the King, seizing Whitehall, the Treasury and the City Chamber, kidnapping the Duke of York and the Duke of Albemarle, securing Windsor castle, overthrowing the Government, and restoring the Commonwealth. The central engine of this ambitious undertaking was alleged to be a Council of Six which met at the Wheatsheaf Tavern in Thames Street. The persons actually put on trial were Ensign Thomas Tonge, a distiller, George Phillips, Francis Stubbs, a cheesemonger, James Hind, a gunsmith, John Seller, a compass-maker, and Nathaniel Gibbs, a feltmaker—a poor lot but the best the police could find. The chief witness against the prisoners was William Hill, a clergyman who had collected his information under pressure from Major-General Richard Browne, a recent Presbyterian Lord Mayor who was now engaged in showing his loyalty by the energy of his activities against the London nonconformists. Hill deposed that money and arms had been collected and that General Ludlow was in Cheapside, waiting to head a rising. Thomas Tonge, confronted with the rack in the Tower, confessed that he had been a member of the Wheatsheaf Council, but subsequently retracted. Others, though tortured, refused to confess. At the trial, which took place on 11th December, evidence was given by Phillips, who admitted that he had heard treasonable words spoken by Hind, who turned King's evidence, by Bradley, a professional spy, who, it is said, distributed half-crowns to out-of-work officers and was rewarded for his help by being made a King's Messenger, and by Captain Baker, an indigenous knife-grinder, who, Ludlow said, was bribed by Bradley. The two Secretaries of State appeared at the trial and said in general terms that they had received intelligence of a plan for a rising. The Solicitor-General was concerned to show that 'this is no trepan but a sober truth.' The four men who refused to confess were hanged, drawn and quartered, and the two others were later reprieved.

Was it indeed a 'trepan'? Bradley and Hill were notorious *agents-provocateur* or 'decoy ducks,' as they were then called. Riggs, who was given £40 a year for his pains, was an obvious liar, and Ludlow, the alleged head of the plotters, was no nearer Cheapside than Switzerland. In their speeches from the scaffold only Tonge admitted his guilt: 'I have sometimes been in some men's company where I have heard them contriving the business for which I am to die: and that which led me to join with them was this: I was and had for some time been in the army; and I have looked upon this cause to be good.' But he denied any intention to murder the King, and the other three condemned men admitted no more than that they had been guilty of listening to treasonable discussions without reporting them to the authorities. There is good ground for supposing that the Presbyterian, Sir Richard Browne, deliberately encouraged Hill to spy among the old soldiers and to smell out plots, and it is perhaps significant that Hill maintained that no Presbyterians were implicated. As in the earlier cases, it is likely enough that there was vaguely treasonable talk and vaguer treasonable plans propounded in the London taverns, but that the grandiose conspiracy outlined by the Solicitor-General was a reality no one who reads the reports of the trial and the testimonies can seriously believe.

The witnesses at Tonge's trial were in agreement that the conspirators were Republicans. Hill said that the revolt was aimed against Popery and monopolies and was for liberty of conscience and a Free Commonwealth. The unreliable Riggs said that Tonge had given him a paper in which the great benefits that they had enjoyed under a Commonwealth were outlined; Bradley said a design to alter the existing Government was intended; and Tyler spoke in detail of the machinery for a new Commonwealth of which he had heard from Tonge.

Bradley the spy and Baker the turncoat tinker, delighted with their success against Tonge, now proceeded, as their great successor Titus Oates did later, to denounce alleged plotters on every side. In accordance with their information a large number of old Cromwellian soldiers and others were arrested and, as was usually the case, one of these offered to turn King's evidence and made yet further denunciations. And so the ball rolled on. The accused men rightly asserted that Baker was an unmitigated liar and, as it proved, the information supplied was too improbable to justify the Government in bringing anyone to trial or in executing any other plotters at this time. But in June of the following year, possibly through information acquired earlier, Alexander Johnston of Waristoun, a prominent and long-proscribed Scottish Covenanter, was seized at Rouen and denounced before the Scottish Parliament in the early summer of 1663. Johnston was the uncle of Dr. Burnet, who declared in his *History* that his uncle was 'so disordered both in body and mind that it was a reproach to a Government to proceed against him: his memory was so gone that he did not know his own children.' Although he was a friend of Lord Lauderdale, Charles II's Secretary of State in Scotland, and although he offered to make every possible submission, he was beheaded.

Four days after the execution of Tonge, King Charles II published his Declaration of Indulgence, announcing that he wished to modify the severity of the Act of Uniformity. The alleged plots furnished Charles with an excuse for a move which he knew would be unpopular with his loyal Anglican subjects and was disapproved in particular by Clarendon. The Declaration, the King stated, was 'designed to quiet the rising disorders.' It denied that the King intended to violate the Act of Uniformity or to establish military rule under the pretence of plots. But although the Declaration chiefly promised liberty of worship to nonconformists and stated that Roman Catholics 'are not to expect an open toleration,' its main purpose was unquestionably to benefit the Catholics, to whom Charles was very sympathetic. The King's long sojourn in Catholic countries, his gratitude to the English Roman Catholics for fighting for his father in the civil wars, and the growing influence of Catholics at his Court contributed to his decision. In October, 1662, Sir Henry Bennet, who was later created Earl of Arlington, had superseded old Sir Edward Nicholas as chief Secretary of State, and although he was not himself a Roman Catholic, he became the leader of a ministerial group which was neither Anglican nor Presbyterian in outlook and encouraged Charles to throw off the tutelage of his hidebound Lord Chancellor. Bennet was not above enlisting the influence of the beautiful Lady Castlemaine, who herself professed to be a Catholic, and his genuine application to his work and his knowledge of foreign affairs made him a dangerous rival to Clarendon.

In this Declaration of Indulgence, which was therefore approved by Bennet, Charles asked that an act of parliament should give effect to his desire for toleration. But when Parliament met on 18th February so threatening was the storm that Charles—always more resilient than his brother James was to be—bowed before it. Consequently the nonconformists were deprived of any hope of freedom to worship and the authorities were everywhere tortured by dread of fresh 'risings.' The year 1663 was filled with stories of plots; and spies, turncoats, and informers did a roaring trade.

Undoubtedly there was plenty of genuine discontent, and the more extreme dissenters were goaded almost beyond endurance. Without liberty to write or preach or worship, or even to earn a living, they had little enough to live for. In Ireland the Cromwellian settlers, who had been deprived of their lands at the Restoration, planned an attack on Dublin castle. They were headed by Colonel Thomas Blood, a Cromwellian soldier of Presbyterian descent, who was afterwards to acquire wider notoriety by stealing the Crown jewels from the Tower of London and being pardoned for his audacity. Blood's scheme was to enter Dublin castle under the pretext of petitioning the Lord Lieutenant, the Duke of Ormonde, to overpower the guard, secure the castle, and rally the discontented elements against the Irish Government. The plotters were betrayed and several arrested, but Blood escaped arrest disguised as a Quaker, and flitted about the obscurer corners of Dublin, terrifying Ormonde.

In England, on the other hand, a great plot alleged to have been discovered at Muggleswick Park, Durham, in the same month of March, 1663, was nothing more than a lying accusation levelled by an unscrupulous informer against a peaceful Baptist meeting. Nevertheless nine persons were arrested and a careful watch was instituted over the nonconformists in Durham, Northumberland, and Yorkshire. Sir Thomas Gower, the High Sheriff of Yorkshire, in particular concentrated his energies on unravelling plots and sent out spies and 'decoy ducks' throughout the North to bring him news of republican schemes. By this means the famous Yorkshire Plot of 1663 was discovered.

The leader of the first part of the Yorkshire plot was Dr. Edward Richardson, who was the so-called Anabaptist Dean of Ripon under the Commonwealth and now had a medical practice in Harrogate. Richardson must either have been an accomplished liar or deceived by others. Many afterwards suspected that he too was an *agent-provocateur*, but he seems to have been merely an irresponsible extremist. He announced that Lambert (who was in prison) and Ludlow (who was still in Switzerland) were ready to head a rising; that he had met a Committee of Secrecy in London, consisting of Major Wildman, Henry Nevile, and others; that Colonel Hutchinson would head a revolt in Nottingham, Colonel Birch in Lancashire, and that they had 'great strength' in the west. A number of local fanatics seem to have been persuaded by this farrago of nonsense and a declaration was drawn up, promising to restore the Long Parliament, overthrow the bishops, obtain a Gospel Ministry and abolish all unpopular taxes. The idea of the conspirators was not apparently to remove the King, and indeed according to the story of one of the conspirators they had intended to declare 'for King and country and their word was to be freedom.' Meetings were held in Harrogate and elsewhere, and a scheme was adumbrated to attack York on 9th August. Full reports of all these alleged plans were conveyed to Gower by his spies, a hundred persons were arrested, trained bands were raised, the Duke of Buckingham, Lord Lieutenant of the West Riding, marched north, and Richardson fled abroad to become a preacher at Amsterdam.

This was not all, as it should have been. Through his arrests Gower now acquired fresh agents to suborn incautious Yorkshire nonconformists into treasonable utterances and hare-brained plots. One of these was a Major Greathead, who had been an officer under Lambert, and who gave it out that he would become a

N

colonel and command a new rising. He was to send his old comrades to the scaffold for £100 down. Others genuinely involved in conspiracy were Captain John Atkinson, known as the Stockinger, Captain Thomas Oates, and Ralph Rymer, middle-class men worth £400 a year in rents. The wildest stories were set in circulation: large forces from Holland, it was said, were to land at Bridlington; a thousand Quakers were ready to fight; there was a bank of money available in London and seven thousand men waiting in Wiltshire. When enough intelligence of this sort had been collected, the authorities acted, and on 10th October Gower told Sir Henry Bennet that 'all the heads of the fanatics were privately seized' and that there was no real danger, as all the recent rumours had originated from one man (presumably Richardson).

Only two days after this, however, Greathead and Ralph Oates, another informer—a man who would have perjured himself against his own father had he been allowed—brought off their biggest coup. Greathead had prevailed upon Oates to summon all his friends at one time and in one place 'in great secret.' Thus on 12th October, a little before midnight, twenty men 'with odd arms,' headed by Oates, met in Farnley Wood; but they gathered only to disperse; and they dispersed only to surrender. In January, 1664, fifteen men were executed for treason, and later Richard Oldroyd, known as the 'Devil of Dewsbury,' also went to the scaffold. Others were sent as prisoners to Tangier, and the Government was satisfied that a far-reaching conspiracy had been stifled. How many or how few were guilty it is almost impossible to say. The general complaint of the prisoners was 'that those who had witnessed against them were the persons that drew them into doing what they did.'

One other consequence of the Government's 'clean-up' of 1663 was to unearth a certain amount of republican or anti-monarchical literature which was then in circulation. Roger L'Estrange, the newly appointed Surveyor of Imprimery, appointed to enforce the Licensing Act, was able to justify his appointment by arresting a group of printers who had been responsible for printing the speeches of the executed regicides, for reprinting some of Milton's tracts, and also for printing two widely read pamphlets, one called *The Phoenix or Solemn League and Covenant* and the other *Mene Tekel or the Downfall of Tyranny.* John Twyn, who had printed *Mene Tekel* (said to have been written by Captain Roger Jones), at the instance of one Giles Calvert in a Smithfield eating-house (note how Smithfield remained a republican centre), admitted that it was 'mettlesome stuff,' and at his trial for treason, which took place in February, 1664, a witness said it was 'too foul to be repeated but in substance.' According to the indictment, the pamphlet stated that the supreme magistrate was accountable to the people, and that the people should enforce their right to govern as against the King and royal family. This pamphlet seems to have derived something from Milton's *Tenure of Kings and Magistrates. The Phoenix* also urged that arms might be used against the King because he had failed to abide by his promise to uphold the Covenant. Twyn was condemned to death and the other printers were fined, pilloried, and imprisoned, but nevertheless *Mene Tekel* and *The Phoenix* continued in circulation. Whether or not these pamphlets were connected with the so-called Farnley Wood plot, as L'Estrange alleged (Twyn was arrested three days before the meeting in the wood), they were plainly dangerous propaganda to get into the hands of cashiered soldiers resentful of injuries.

When Parliament met in March, 1664, the King devoted much of his opening speech to the plots of the previous year; he asked that the Triennial Act of 1641 (which ensured that a Parliament should meet every three years) should be repealed lest the authority of the present Houses should be called into question or future conspirators be able to pretend that they were an unlawful assembly. The Cavaliers were also encouraged by the 'Yorkshire Plot' to resume their congenial task of outlawing the nonconformists and passed the Conventicle Act which declared that any meeting for worship containing more than four persons in addition to members of a family was an illegal meeting punishable heavily by law.

King Charles in his speech also made special reference to the 'desperate men in most counties and a standing council in this town from which they received their directions.' Two Councils of Six were in fact mentioned in connexion with the Yorkshire plot; one was said to have been headed by Thomas Blood and a friend of his named John Lockyer; another (which has already been mentioned) was described in detail by a witness named Richard Walters, who himself had obtained the story from the notorious Dr. Richardson. Walters was a miserably frightened little Yorkshireman, who was so terrified at his arrest that he began accusing everybody he knew indiscriminately, and even caused his own wife to be imprisoned and informed against his closest friend. He twice swore that the Council which directed the plot consisted of Wildman, Nevile, Major Salway, Colonel Hutchinson, Oliver St. John, Lowther (presumably the Westmorland Royalist), and the cautious Bulstrode Whitelocke. On this fragile evidence of a wholly improbable council, Salway, Nevile, and Hutchinson were arrested. The first two were easily able to prove their innocence and had to be released, but Hutchinson, although he had not been in communication with any of the suspects and had lived in blameless retirement felling trees and reading the Epistles to his family, was committed to the Tower and later died in a Kentish prison. Wildman of course was safe in the Scilly Isles, but despite the glaring improbability of the tissue of lies another effort was made to implicate him in this plot through his old servant, William Parker. Parker, in spite of the Nonsuch House episode of 1661, was evidently still at liberty and was now following the trade of barber. One Thomas Tyrell laid information in October, 1663, at the time of the unravelling of the Yorkshire plot, that Parker was in correspondence with his former master as well as with Henry Marten, now in prison at Berwick. However, Thomas Tyrell senior sent a covering letter to Sir Edward Broughton, Keeper of the Gatehouse prison, stating that his son was 'rude and disorderly' and that his information should be treated as of doubtful value. Even Wildman's worst enemies might have found it hard to picture him sitting in his solitude in St. Mary's Island in the Atlantic spinning the webs of the inept Yorkshire plot.

One other event which concerned Wildman took place in 1663. Although Henry Bishop's contract for the post office had been for seven years he suddenly terminated it in April, 1663, and sold the remainder of his lease for £8,000 to Daniel O'Neale, the King's Groom of the Bedchamber. Numerous though the complaints against Bishop's administration had been, he was a good Postmaster-General and was the inventor in England of the postmark on letters. Whether the termination of his contract was due to a suspicion that he was implicated with Wildman in the plotting of 1661 or whether Wildman, being in prison, had to withdraw his financial backing is not clear. But Wildman was unquestionably Bishop's *alter ego*, and just as his assistance had been needed to establish Bishop as the first Restoration Postmaster-General, so Wildman's removal from London to the Scilly Isles spelt the end of Bishop's useful—if checkered—tenure of his office.

CHAPTER XVI

THE 'CREATURE' OF BUCKINGHAM

Wildman . . . a false fellow to everybody.
SIR WILLIAM COVENTRY

Wildman . . . the wisest statesman in England.
THE SECOND DUKE OF BUCKINGHAM

THE year 1663, it has truly been said, marks the end of the first period of Restoration conspiracies. Henceforward domestic unrest and foreign disturbances were frequently linked. In 1664 both Houses of Parliament petitioned the King for redress of their grievances against England's chief commercial and colonial rivals, the Dutch. Captain Robert Holmes was thereupon dispatched with royal authority to seize the Dutch trading station of Goree in West Africa, and an expedition under Captain Nicholls was sent out to capture the American town of New Amsterdam, better known to-day as New York. These deliberate attacks on the Dutch empire—or reprisals, as the English Government called them—led directly to war which was officially declared against the Dutch in February, 1665. The English Government was now concerned lest the Republicans who fled abroad five years before should join with their friends at home, profit by the universal confusion, and attempt to revive their lost cause, And although there was much unnecessary panic, as was natural in war-time, hope certainly stirred in the breasts of the leading exiles. After all, were not the Dutch themselves Republicans?

The chief of these exiles were Algernon Sidney and Edmund Ludlow, both of whom had been opposed to Oliver Cromwell's dictatorship and were abroad at or soon after the restoration of Charles II. Sidney's father was a royalist earl and his brother was reputed to be the real father of Charles II's favourite bastard, the Duke of Monmouth, although he did not dispute the King's claim to paternity. Neither Algernon's upbringing nor even his political principles, as later expounded, necessarily prejudiced him against a moderate form of monarchy. When the Restoration took place he had been in Sweden negotiating a treaty as one of three commissioners sent by the republican Council of State. He then wrote: 'Since the Parliament hath acknowledged a king, I know and acknowledge I owe him the duty and service that belongs unto a subject and will pay it. If things are carried on in a legal and moderate way, I had rather be in employment than without any. If I am trusted, I shall perform my duty with as much fidelity and care as any that I have ever undertaken in my life.' Nevertheless he chose to wait abroad until he saw what course events at home would take. What he heard, he disliked. Although he had not been excepted from the Act of Indemnity, he deliberately expatriated himself because he refused to 'submit, recant, renounce and ask pardon.' He went to live in Rome; but the suspicion aroused by his conduct, sayings, and writings caused him to be pursued vindictively by the triumphant Royalists; he was forced to leave Italy in 1663, and in the autumn he became the guest of Edmund Ludlow, the other important republican exile, at Vevey in Switzerland. Host and guest did not agree, and after Sidney had presented Ludlow with a pair of pistols of beautiful Italian workmanship, he left for nearer home. Sidney, who loathed intolerance, gradually grew more and more hostile to the Restoration Government, and after further wanderings he arrived at The Hague in the early spring of 1665, hoping to arrange to regain his country's freedom with the arms of a foreign Power—thus anticipating by over twenty years the proposals of the patriots of 1688.

Since to Ludlow, even more than to Sidney, republicanism was a religion, the Royalists immediately after the Restoration showed their fear of this solid republican soldier; he was excepted from the Act of Indemnity, £300 was offered for his arrest, and he fled to France. Thenceforward the Government's agents were constantly on the look-out for him. We have seen how his name was regularly mentioned in connexion with the alleged plots of the first three years of Charles II's reign. He was then reported to have been seen alike in London, Canterbury, and in Somerset, but in fact he never left Switzerland where he settled under the protection of the Government of Berne. For although he had no scruples about the methods which might be used to overthrow the monarchy, he was far too cautious to help or to become the mere tool of England's foreign enemies. The reasons which he urged against the plans of

Sidney and the pro-Dutch party were twofold. Firstly, he said that the Dutch were not to be trusted because of the way in which they had surrendered the regicides in 1662 and, secondly, he was afraid to risk arrest or assassination. In March, 1664, attempts were made upon the lives of the exiles by an Irishman named Major Riordane and in August, John Lisle, one of the Swiss regicide colony, was murdered at Lausanne. These incidents further discouraged Ludlow from venturing into active conspiracy.

With Sidney all was different. He was agog for action. He pressed John De Witt, the Grand Pensionary or chief executive of the Dutch Republic, to invade England and Scotland, and he also negotiated with the Amsterdam authorities who, he thought, might be willing forcibly to turn England once again into a Free Commonwealth. But De Witt was afraid of a long war and was said to think England would be a more formidable enemy as a republic than as a monarchy. Besides Sidney, other exiles were optimistically plotting in Holland. William Say, another leading English Republican, for instance, wrote from Amsterdam at this time that things were 'so well prepared to answer the good ends we all desire that nothing seems to be wanting but hands to set the wheels going.' Ludlow, though not unhopeful, was still doubtful, and his doubts were justified by the final breakdown of the Sidney-De Witt conversations.

Meanwhile the English Government naturally got wind of the activities of the exiles and feared the worst. Even before the war officially began the rumour reached it that the exiles were trying to concert action with the discontented parties in the north of England and that Ludlow and Major-General Desborough were among the ringleaders. Desborough was rearrested in February, 1665. Although in July the Secretary of State Arlington was assured 'there is no cause for fear unless some desperate Commonwealthsmen avail themselves of the present distress of the poor to excite tumults,' that month all cashiered soldiers and old officers were again ordered out of London. A little later the Great Plague forced the Court itself to leave the capital. Brave old Albemarle was put in charge of Whitehall while James, Duke of York, hastened north. In August Albemarle announced that he had discovered a gigantic plot in London and the signal having been given, wholesale arrests were made throughout the kingdom.

Besides London, Yorkshire and Scotland were regarded as the chief danger points. Three men, including Major-General Monroe, were arrested in Scotland; strict instructions were sent to the Earl of Derby, the Bishop of Durham and the Deputy-Lieutenant of Northumberland to be on the watch; Captain Roger Jones, the reputed author of *Mene Tekel*, and eight others were arrested and sent to the Tower. But in York all was reported to be quiet; Sir William Coventry assured Arlington that 'there was no great danger of risings since most dangerous men were secured.' However on 1st September Albemarle ordered yet another round-up. He had been informed that a number of desperate officers had intended to seize the Tower by taking boats across the moat, scaling the walls, and surprising the guards. Their supposed object was to kill not only the Governor of the Tower but Sir Richard Browne, Albemarle himself, and the King (although he was not in London). The day chosen for this ambitious enterprise was 3rd September, selected apparently not so much because it was the anniversary of Oliver Cromwell's most famous victories as because it had been declared a lucky day in Lilly's almanac and because the planets foretold the fall of the monarchy. Several persons were arrested, but although Samuel Pepys listened to part of the examinations of the prisoners, he found nothing of importance about them to record in his comprehensive diary. Thus stimulated, the vigilance of the police was doubled. An ex-Cromwellian Governor of Poole in Dorset was arrested; he at first refused to say whether he was sorry for being what he had been, but later recanted and swore he was no plotter; a Captain Gower 'who came into the country in order to work the southern part was providentially secured.' At Lincoln castle alone fifty-five persons were imprisoned and the Governor of Berwick was warned to be ready to receive 'disorderly English Quakers.' Arlington, however, was told that 'nothing can be made out against the persons now in York castle, though all are enemies to the King.'

When Parliament, still evacuated on account of the Plague, met at Oxford in October, the Lord Chancellor, after surveying the English naval successes in the Dutch war, devoted a portion of his speech to the plotters at home. He thanked the 'good General for his vigilance' and asserted that 'by the confessions of many their wicked design is enough manifested and ready for justice.' Nothing very specific was described in the way of 'designs.' Parliament was sufficiently impressed to pass the Five Mile Act, yet another restriction upon the freedom of nonconformists, whose ministers were now driven from their former parishes.

It would be tedious to relate all the rumours of plots and plans that reached Whitehall in the winter of 1666—tales, for instance, of the 'insolent Quakers' and of bodies of men 'expected to land from Holland.' We may notice, however, that Major Greathead, who had earned £100 for provoking the Yorkshire plot of 1663, having tasted blood caused new information to be laid before the Duke of Buckingham against a group of Yorkshiremen, headed by a physician, who were said to be recruiting troops of a hundred horse in Derbyshire and Lancashire for use against the Government. A few men were executed. In April, 1666, Colonel John Rathbone and seven other former Commonwealth officers were condemned to death at Old Bailey for their part in the so-called Tower of London plot. They were hanged, drawn, and quartered on 30th April. They stated on the scaffold that 'they never saw the face of the witnesses in their lives and they were trepanned to speak some words and to hear others speak and not reveal it.'

Meanwhile in Holland, after the Dutch navy had suffered defeat at the Battle of Lowestoft, John De Witt grew more enthusiastic for enlisting the co-operation of the English Republicans. The King of France, who by treaty was obliged to support Holland against England, asked Sidney and Ludlow to go to Paris to discuss possibilities. Ludlow refused on the ground that Louis XIV was scarcely the ruler to restore English liberties; but in March Sidney went and demanded a hundred thousand livres as an earnest of goodwill. Louis offered twenty thousand and nothing came of it.

In 1666, called by the poet Dryden Annus Mirabilis—the Wonderful Year—the English were defeated at sea, losing three admirals and eight thousand men, but this was offset to some extent by the victory known as St. James's Fight on 25th July, eight weeks later. In September further confusion was caused by the Great Fire of London which was attributed by the *London Gazette* to the Republicans. Information of plots again began to pour in from all sides. The only rising which took place was that of the Cameronian Scots, who declared for the King and Covenant and were easily defeated in the Pentland Hills. In the following year, although the 'oppressed sects cried out as loudly as ever' and certain pamphlets, including another version of *Mene Tekel*, were circulated, the country remained calm. Plague, fire, heavy war expenses, small progress at sea, and, it was said, corruption in high places, induced the Government to seek peace. Negotiations were opened at Breda; the navy was reduced in size and ordered to engage only on commerce destroying. With England thus weakened and disarmed panic was widespread and rumours of republican invasions grew afresh. At Dover a fleet was daily expected to sweep across the Channel commanded either by Ludlow or Richard Cromwell. Aphra Benn, that typical Restoration authoress, was sent across to Holland to supplement the Government spies there and she soon persuaded Colonel William Scot, the unworthy son of a regicide father, to sell information about the exiles; but the only thing of interest she learned from him was that Sidney was preparing a tract against monarchy and in defence of a republic. In June, 1667, the people were 'much perplexed to hear that the Dutch vapour so filthily in the Thames.' Taking advantage of the English naval disarmament, a Dutch fleet had entered the Thames and—supreme insult—towed away the half-burnt hulk of the *Royal Charles* from its moorings. Peace was concluded soon afterwards on 31st July and the net result of all the efforts of the republican exiles was for a few of them to have fought in the Dutch fleet and for their plotting to have brought fierce persecution not only upon the old Cromwellian soldiers but upon harmless Quakers, Baptists, and other nonconformist sects at home.

By the Treaty of Breda England by no means gained the objects for which she began the war. She retained New York and New Jersey, but she lost territory in Africa and trade in India. The settlement was so indecisive that another war seemed likely, for it was widely felt that the English monarchy had been worsted by the Dutch republic. A scapegoat was sought and found in the Earl of Clarendon. The enemies whom he had accumulated during his seven years as First Minister fell upon him without mercy. He had lost the favour of the King—whose ingratitude was like that of Charles 1 to Strafford or of Queen Anne to Marlborough—and he had long alienated the Cavalier Parliament, which indeed he would have liked to dissolve. That year, suddenly bereft of his wife and deprived of the protection of his son-in-law, he carried on a lonely struggle against a band of voracious enemies. In August he was relieved of his offices and, after proceedings for impeachment had begun, he left the country which was henceforward to be governed by a group of statesmen known to history as the Cabal.

To the fall of Clarendon John Wildman owed his release from prison. The new ministers, either because they were attached to Roman Catholicism or because they were indifferent to religion altogether, approved a policy of toleration so far as the laws permitted. With the end of the Dutch war the suspects who had been arrested and thrown into prison by hundreds were gradually released; the system, commonly practised in war-time, of committing alleged plotters to prison without trial and ignoring writs of habeas corpus was relaxed or abandoned. But in all probability Wildman was particularly indebted for his release to the Duke of Buckingham, the 'B' of the Cabal.

Buckingham had enjoyed many curious adventures during the period of Clarendon's supremacy. He had never entirely severed his relations with the Republicans and Levellers whose acquaintance he had made in the sixteen-fifties, and he was said to have treated the old officers who were associated with the so-called Farnley Wood plot with as much leniency as he could command in his capacity of Lord Lieutenant. He employed as one of his chief agents a man named Braithwaite, who was known to have been a Cromwellian, and there were not wanting spies and informers to accuse Buckingham, whenever they dared, of plots against the Government. But he rapidly won the favour of the more light-hearted section of the Court and stood impervious to blackmail or threats. He was closely related to the King's mistress, the Countess of Castlemaine, with whom, however, he managed to quarrel, and his versatile talents as composer, song-writer and playwright as well as dabbler in chemistry and alchemy made him a general favourite in the very high society circles to which his immense riches in any case gave him easy access. Unlike his rival, Arlington, his political ambitions were directed by passion rather than by cunning and sustained by brilliance and not hard work. His comical behaviour during the naval war—he took a showy part in the battle of Lowestoft—his love affair with Frances Stuart, who even denied the suit of the King, his subsequent notorious liaison with the unscrupulous Countess of Shrewsbury, and his imprisonment

GEORGE VILLIERS, SECOND DUKE OF BUCKINGHAM
A portrait by Sir Peter Lely

in the Tower for pulling off a fellow peer's wig in the House of Lords, would have blighted the reputation of a poorer or less plausible man. But the impression that he made upon all and sundry as 'the finest gentleman of person and wit I ever saw' (as Sir John Reresby described him) enabled him to emerge unscathed from all his scrapes. Early in 1667, for instance, he was accused of treason for having written a letter to an astrologer, Dr. Heydon, about the King's horoscope. Braithwaite, whom he had always protected, testified against him and Dr. Heydon. Although Heydon, even after torture in a dungeon, swore to the Duke's innocence, a warrant was issued against him in May; but for two months he evaded arrest, sleeping by day and moving from place to place by night. Ultimately the King grew 'as weary of the prosecution as the Duke was of concealing himself to avoid it.' Buckingham surrendered at the end of June. Confronted by Arlington with the evidence, Buckingham said that Dr. Heydon was such a silly fellow that he would not trust him with a tallow candle. Two of the witnesses against him mysteriously died and the damning evidence of the letter to Heydon which King Charles himself had sworn was in Buckingham's own handwriting was now admitted by that fickle ruler to be in fact in the handwriting of Buckingham's sister. The charges fell to the ground; and believing, rightly or wrongly, that the whole affair had been organized by Clarendon, whose policy he had always opposed, Buckingham devoted himself with zest and success to bringing about Clarendon's downfall.

In the years which elapsed between the fall of Clarendon and the emergence of the Whig and Tory parties a decade later, Buckingham was at first the chief royal counsellor although he did not hold any office until he purchased the Mastership of the Horse after the death of Albemarle. He was by no means Prime Minister in the modern sense; indeed, in so far as his natural indolence permitted him, Charles II was his own Prime Minister and liked to play off his advisers against each other. Buckingham's personal programme was as much a mystery to his contemporaries as it has proved to be to later historians. One thing only is certain, and that is that he was a genuine advocate of toleration for nonconformists. Was this because his marriage with the daughter of the Presbyterian General Fairfax brought him into touch with dissenter circles?

Was it to gratify the King? This at least seems unlikely because he was no lover of Roman Catholics and was the declared enemy of James, Duke of York, whose conversion was at this time imminent. Was he, then, a true hater of intolerance or a convinced believer in philosophic indifference, an early devotee, as his laboratories at York House might make one suspect, of the 'research attitude' to religion? His friendship with John Wildman, whom he publicly received into his company soon after his release from prison, may not a little have affected his outlook. Apart from religion, his main policy seems to have been to maintain his supremacy at home with the help of his talents as a courtier and his renewed friendship with the Countess of Castlemaine, while in foreign affairs he determined to revenge his country's humiliation upon the Dutch by promoting an alliance with King Louis XIV of France.

In resenting the defeat by the Dutch, Buckingham for the time being saw eye to eye with the House of Commons which, although still the same Cavalier assembly that had been elected in 1661, was beginning in its wrath to breathe that air of independence that had been enjoyed by the Roundhead Parliament of 1642. The members did not rest content with impeaching Clarendon; they demanded and exacted the right to investigate thoroughly what they conceived to be the mismanagement both of the navy and of the national finances. Confronted by the angry members, Charles II, who earlier in the same year had resisted the Commons' claim to inspect the national accounts, suddenly gave way and permitted the appointment of a commission to examine them, taking evidence on oath. John Wildman, two months out of prison, was nominated one of the Commissioners. Let Samuel Pepys tell the story. Here are some entries in his diary:

'*December 7, 1667*:

'Somebody told me this, that they hear that Thomson with the wooden leg, and Wildman, the Fifth-Monarchy man [*sic*], a great creature of the Duke of Buckingham's, are in nomination to be Commissioners, among others, on the Bill of Accounts.

'*December 8, 1667*:

'Sir William Coventry tells me that he hears some of the Thomsons are like to be of the Commission for the Accounts, and Wildman, which he much wonders at, as having been a false fellow to everybody, and in prison most of the time since the King's coming in.

'*December 12, 1667*:

'Walked to my booksellers, and there he did give me a list of the twenty who were nominated for the Commission in Parliament for the Accounts; and it is strange that of twenty the Parliament could not think fit to choose their nine, but were fain to add three that were not in the list of the twenty, they being many of them factious people and ringleaders in the late troubles; so that Sir John Talbott did fly out and was very hot in the business of Wildman's being named, and took notice how he was entertained in the bosom of the Duke of Buckingham, a Privy Counsellor; and that it was fit to be observed by the House, and punished.'

And not even Buckingham's reported observation that Wildman was 'the wisest statesman in England' could induce the House of Commons to approve his appointment.

In May this obstreperous session came to its close and the Commission of Accounts bent itself with energy to exposing financial mistakes, while another committee investigated the administration of the Navy so effectively that three eminent officials were compelled to resign and the Secretary for the Navy was later expelled the House of Commons. At the same time the Commons still set their faces unflinchingly against any lessening of the prerogatives of the Church of England. But the Duke of Buckingham stuck to his guns. His own 'cabal' was said to consist of Major Wildman, Dr. John Owen, Cromwell's chaplain, and other former Republicans 'so that some say we are carried in Oliver's bucket.' According to Lord Conway, 'the Duke heading the fanatics and guided by their counsels, thinks to arrive to be another Oliver.' Consorting with these old-fashioned elements of political society was not, however, Buckingham's sole occupation. He was far too much of a dilettante to become a successful dictator. One January morning the Earl of Shrewsbury, at last provoked beyond endurance by Buckingham's intrigue with his wife, fought a duel in which he was wounded and from the indirect effects of which he afterwards died. Only the friendship of the King saved Buckingham from the consequences of this scandalous episode. Later that year Sir William Coventry, the ablest of Clarendon's

opponents, who was ousted from the fickle royal favour by Buckingham, challenged his successful rival to a duel, but this was stopped
through fear of another tragedy. After the first duel Buckingham
retired for a day of humiliation at Wallingford House 'in the
manner and as zealously as ever General Fleetwood performed his
exercise there.'

Throughout the rest of the year Buckingham carried on a
double policy of trying to separate the King from the Catholicizing
Duke of York and of keeping in touch with the Republicans and
nonconformists. 'It is said,' quoted the well-informed Pepys, 'that
Buckingham do knownly meet daily with Wildman and other
Commonwealth men; and that when he is with them, he makes the
King believe that he is with his wenches.'

Whatever the truth may have been about Buckingham's own
political views, we may detect in his party—the party of 1668–1669
—the historical link between the Interregnum Republicans, on the
one hand, and the Exclusionists who tried to bar the Duke of York
from the throne, the Rye House plotters, who tried to accomplish
the same end by force, and, finally, the parties which achieved the
revolution of 1688. In Wildman the Leveller, Wildman, who
conspired against Oliver Cromwell, Wildman, the client of the
Duke of Buckingham, Wildman, the Rye House plotter, Wildman,
who was to come over with William of Orange, is to be found the
typical figure—it may be, if we knew enough, the most influential
figure—of all those who bound together the two great seventeenth-
century revolutions. Behind Buckingham at that time stood better-
known figures, including Ashley, himself an ex-Cromwellian, who
as Earl of Shaftesbury founded the Whig party, and Danby, a
future Prime Minister, father of the Tories, but none was more
symbolic of this period of our history than Wildman.

Buckingham's instability and unreliability were to be his undoing. In the political race he was outmanoeuvred by the subtler
tactics of the Earl of Arlington. By 1670 Charles II had abandoned
the policy of toleration in return for a cash payment from the
House of Commons, had resisted the temptation to rid himself of
his barren Queen, and had concealed from Buckingham the
negotiation of the Secret Treaty of Dover in which he promised
Louis XIV of France that he would declare himself a Roman
Catholic. Finally a Second Conventicle Act against Nonconformists

—a kind of postscript to the Clarendon Code—was enacted. Although Buckingham survived for another four years as a leading statesman and courtier his programme (such as it was) was doomed. England was now no place for those who believed in liberty of thought or who opposed despotic monarchy. In July, 1670, John Wildman obtained permission for himself, his wife, and son to travel abroad. He was to return to an England torn by faction and ripe for conspiracy.

CHAPTER XVII

THE POPISH PLOT

Be wise, ye Sons of Men, tempt God no more
To give you kings in's wrath to vex you sore:
If a King's Brother can such mischief bring,
Then how much greater Mischief is a King.
Attributed to ANDREW MARVELL, 1677

WHATEVER their differences over Roman Catholicism may have been, all Charles II's advisers were agreed in 1672 on renewing the war against the Dutch. Only Clifford and Arlington, the Catholic or crypto-Catholic members of the Cabal, had actually signed the Secret Treaty of Dover whereby Charles had promised the French King in return for substantial financial assistance first to declare himself a Roman Catholic and then to make war on the Dutch. Later Buckingham was duped into signing a sham treaty for the deception of the public in which no mention was made of religion and the subsidies allotted in the Secret Treaty towards the cost of converting England to Roman Catholicism were assigned to paying for the coming war. In the event both Charles II and Louis XIV concurred in the postponement of the religious clauses of the treaty, and in March, 1672, the two allies fell upon the Dutch republic. As a prelude to the war the English Court demanded the arrest of Lieutenant-Colonel Joyce, an exiled Republican, who as Cornet Joyce had seized Charles I on Oliver Cromwell's behalf in 1647. The Dutch compromised by ordering his arrest and allowing him to escape.

At the same time Charles II published, on his own initiative, a second Declaration of Indulgence as a partial concession to the Roman Catholics as well as the nonconformists. His still Anglican though less Royalist Parliament resented this, forced him to withdraw, and substituted a Test Act which required all office-holders to take the sacrament according to the rites of the Church of England. This meant that the Catholic Duke of York had to leave his command as Lord High Admiral and that Clifford resigned his office as Lord Treasurer. The non-Catholic ministers shared in the general unpopularity of the Government that derived from a war which was unwelcome as well as unsuccessful.

Buckingham threw himself with all his usual spasmodic ardour into the naval actions against the Dutch. Indeed the entire Cabinet volunteered for active service. Denied a command, Buckingham in 1672 hired a little craft of his own which made him independent of a posting upon a warship and thus contributed his mite to the campaign in the teeth of official remonstrances. Later, however, he tired of this form of patriotism and went over to persuade William of Orange, who at the time of the Dutch republic's peril had been chosen its leader, to make peace on the French terms. He assured William's mother, the Princess Royal, that 'they did not love Holland as a mistress but as a wife,' to which the good lady not unnaturally replied, 'Truly, I think you love us just as you love yours.' The hit was pertinent, for Buckingham's mistress, the Countess of Shrewsbury, had just borne him a child whom Buckingham had publicly acknowledged, and, assuming royal prerogatives, had christened 'Lord Coventry,' and was later to bury in Westminster Abbey.

The Dutch by heroically flooding their dykes and holding their own at sea prevented the complete destruction of their country by Louis and Charles. The House of Commons, which disliked France and feared the Catholicizing tendencies of the Court, began to seek scapegoats for the King's policy. Just as the first Dutch war of Charles's reign resulted in the dismissal of Clarendon, the second ended in the fall of the 'Cabal.' Ashley, now become Lord Shaftesbury, was dismissed in November, 1673, and in January, 1674, Buckingham and Arlington were invited to explain their handling of the nation's affairs under threat of impeachment by the House of Commons. Buckingham's defence did not satisfy his critics and the Commons petitioned the King to dispense with his services. The House of Lords then turned to concern itself with the fallen favourite's private morals. Provoked by the ceremonial burial of 'Lord Coventry,' the House ordered the judicial separation of Buckingham and his mistress (who had in any case tired of each other) and the forfeiture of £10,000 to the King.

By this time Buckingham's fantastic extravagances had reduced his fortune to a low level. His lawyers were hard pressed to find a fund to meet this new claim. Six years earlier Samuel Pepys had noted that although the Duke's rent roll averaged £19,600 a year he had a margin of only £4,600 left free for his personal expenditure. The loss of all his offices and perquisites on his dismissal, even after he had disposed of them for a lump sum, was a severe shock to his financial system. He was compelled to retire to his country house of Cliveden to recuperate mentally and financially before returning to politics.

It is in connexion with Buckingham's finances that we learn of Wildman's return to England from his trip abroad. In June, 1675, Brian Fairfax, a relation of Buckingham by marriage (who was later to become his biographer) invited Wildman to collect on his behalf his arrears of salary as Buckingham's employee. These arrears amounted to over £500 and Fairfax appointed Wildman his 'lawful attorney to ask and receive all and every sum and sums of money whatever due unto me from his Grace.' This was a perfectly friendly arrangement, for Fairfax was Buckingham's intimate friend and Wildman was now also Buckingham's own solicitor and trustee. To safeguard what remained of his property Buckingham had appointed several trustees including, besides Wildman, Thomas Sprat, his chaplain and future Bishop of Rochester, and Sir Robert Clayton, an eminent London alderman and magistrate, to supervise the administration of his estates and pay him a trust income of £5,000 a year. But Wildman's resumed relations with Buckingham were far closer than those of a solicitor; they also embraced politics, as they had done before Wildman went abroad.

The King's Government was now directed by the Earl of Danby, a Yorkshireman, who, largely through Buckingham's influence, had been appointed Lord Treasurer in succession to Clifford in 1673. Danby soon abandoned his patron and indeed took over one of his offices, the Lord Lieutenancy of the West Riding, after his disgrace. Danby had a mind and a programme of his own. He wanted to rally the old Cavaliers with the cry of 'Church and King' and secure the Commons' support for the Government both by bribery and by an oath of non-resistance to the King. The Duke of Buckingham opposed this fresh Test Act and clamoured for the dissolution of Parliament, which had now sat for fifteen years. In the autumn of 1676 Major Wildman was observed at Edmonton with the Duke drinking a cup of tea to a new parliament and 'to all those honest gentlemen of it that would give the King no money.' Even the existing Parliament was so distrustful of the King and Danby that it was not summoned for a period of fifteen months between November, 1675, and February, 1677, and when it met Buckingham at once appealed to an Act of Edward III's reign to show that since Parliament had not been called for over twelve months it was automatically dissolved. 'Statutes of the realm,' he observed, 'are not like women, for they are not a jot the worse for being old.' It is a reasonable assumption that this legalistic and antiquarian argument was suggested to Buckingham by Wildman, whose familiarity with early Edwardian statutes has already been noticed. Although Buckingham was supported by Shaftesbury and two other peers, the House of Lords deemed the line of reasoning an insult to Parliament and threw them all into the Tower. Buckingham emerged safely a few months later, this time through the good offices of Nell Gwyn.

Buckingham now entered with undimmed enthusiasm into opposition to Danby and the Court. The immediate subject of political controversy was foreign policy. England had withdrawn from the war against the Dutch in 1674, but Louis XIV had continued to exert all his military resources to compel William of Orange to submit to a humiliating peace. In 1677 by one of his sudden but temporary changes of outlook Charles II had consented to the marriage of his niece Mary, daughter of James, Duke of York, to William, and the House of Commons, which had been roused by the all-embracing ambitions of Louis XIV, was demanding war against France in aid of the Dutch. Under these circumstances Louis XIV tried to keep England neutral by encouraging the Opposition to deny Charles II monetary support on the ground that additional taxation would be used to pay for a standing army which would be a danger to Parliament's own independence. At the same time Louis maintained close contact with the English King and negotiations were opened for Charles to become a mediator between the French and the Dutch. Two French ambassadors were supplied with ample sums of money to stir up intrigues and embroil the two English political parties with each other. It came as a painful shock to later English historians to discover that the fathers of the Whig party (the name by which the Opposition to Charles II became known in 1680) were on the pay-roll of the tyrannical Louis XIV and the facts have enabled other historians to contend that Charles II was no more (or less) unpatriotic than his political opponents. In the end Charles tried both policies—of intimidating Louis XIV and of selling his services to him—without much success; and the Dutch States-General and Louis ultimately made peace for the excellent reason that both were tired of fighting.

Among those who accepted money from Louis XIV was the republican exile, Algernon Sidney, who had been allowed to return to England in the autumn of 1677 to see his father before he died; his political influence was indirect since, obtaining permission to stay, he unsuccessfully contested a number of constituencies during the years 1678 and 1679. Buckingham did not, it seems, accept money for his own use, but told the French ambassador that he could employ it usefully to summon the old Cromwellians, Republicans, discontented seamen and other subterranean elements to resist Charles II's scheme for a standing army. Since Wildman was now in close touch with Buckingham, it is likely that he was the intermediary between Buckingham and the remnants of the republican party of twenty years earlier.

What had happened to the republican movement in the decade which had passed between Wildman's release from his Cornish prison and these years when it was being linked as a radical wing to the rising Whig party? The relaxation of severity which followed the dismissal of Clarendon had persuaded all but fanatics to cease plotting, and the ending of the second Dutch war had made the authorities less credulous of informers. Nonconformists could now hold their meetings undisturbed and the only faintly heard criticism of the King was that he was favouring 'Papists.' On 22nd August 1667 the Government was informed that 'the fanatics in the North, disappointed of assistance from abroad by the King's peace, set store by the belief that the King is a Papist and propose to rebel in defence of religion.' At the beginning of the next year a pamphlet called *Vox et Lacrimae Anglorum* was published in which the predominance of Popery, the persecution of the sects, and the decay of trade were grouped together as popular grievances. But the nonconformists resented the imputation to them of republicanism. In a letter written by a nonconformist named John Lerie to the King in April, 1670, he outlined their point of view. The nonconformist gatherings, he said, are open and not like the meetings held by Venner, the Fifth Monarchy man, behind closed doors ; the nonconformists disowned Venner and abhorred his principles; all they wanted was freedom from the bishops to exercise their faith in peace. The King, as usual, was lackadaisically sympathetic. While the police search for Edmund Ludlow and Richard Cromwell was optimistically continued throughout England, Charles published his second Declaration of Indulgence, and even after its forced withdrawal in 1673, the puritans were never persecuted as they had been before the disgrace of Clarendon. Only in Scotland, where a scheme for toleration had broken down, were there substantial rumours of a republican rebellion during the second Dutch war, but the aims of the West Scottish Presbyterians, who first fought on the Pentland hills and were later dispersed by 'bloody' Claverhouse, were essentially ecclesiastical and little concerned with purely political changes.

The secular republican leaders had been only gradually released from prison. Wildman, with Buckingham's influence behind him, was privileged; Salmon and Butler were not released until 1670, Overton in 1671, Miles Corbet in 1676, and Major Creed not till 1679. These men drifted slowly but surely into the political camp directed by Shaftesbury and Buckingham. Shaftesbury was of course an old Republican himself. This graceful, ambitious, capable man, with his narrow, intelligent face and aquiline nose, had had his life soured less by disappointments in his career than by a virulent cyst in the liver which caused a continuous dull pain. He had fought against Charles I and had been a member of the republican Council of State before Cromwell became military dictator. He does not appear to have been opposed to monarchy in principle and, according to one account, his quarrel with Cromwell was due to a rebuff when he asked to marry one of the Protector's daughters. He held the offices of Chancellor of the Exchequer and Lord Chancellor under Charles II but never really agreed with the King's foreign and domestic policy. In 1675, after his dismissal from the post of Lord Chancellor, Lord Digby had said to him: 'You are against the King and for seditions and factions and for a Commonwealth, and I will prove it. . . .' This Digby signally failed to do and Shaftesbury was awarded £1,000 damages for slander. It is nevertheless true that Shaftesbury was a Republican in the current sense of those days, since he believed in a tightly controlled constitutional monarchy; and in the newly formed political clubs of the City—Shaftesbury's famous 'Green Ribbon' Club, which met at the 'King's Head,' the gatherings at the 'Green Dragon' in Fleet Street and the 'Sun' at the Royal Exchange—the old Republicans now began to creep out of the shadows. In the coffee-houses, which the Government had more than once tried to suppress as centres of political disaffection, murmurings were heard against the growth of 'Popery' and the royal friendship with France.

A belief that there was more behind the French alliance of 1671 than had been made public had filtered down by this time from high places. In 1677 Andrew Marvell, one-time assistant to Milton and friend of James Harrington, published anonymously his *Account of the Growth of Popery and Arbitrary Government in England*, which was printed in Amsterdam and was a deliberate attack on the Court party as 'forwarding a design to change the lawful Government of England into an absolute tyranny and to convert the established Protestant religion into downright Popery.' The 'invisible League' struck up with France in 1670 was broadly described and readers were urged to deliver England from 'privy conspiracy.' In satires published about the same time (which may or may not also have been written by Marvell) the acknowledged Roman Catholicism of James, Duke of York, who had in 1673 married a 'Popish' second wife in Mary of Modena, was used more directly as an argument against monarchy:

'Be wise, ye Sons of Men, tempt God no more
To give you kings in's wrath to vex you sore:
If a King's Brother can such mischief bring,
Then how much greater Mischief is a King?'

In 1675 in reaffirmation of the virtue of the Restoration a statue of Charles I on horseback was put up at Charing Cross. Marvell wrote an imaginary dialogue between this horse and a horse in the Stocks Market, Woolchurch, which bore Charles II on its back:

Charing Cross: 'But canst thou divine when things shall
be mended?'
Woolchurch: 'When the reign of the line of the Stuarts
is ended.'

216

Charing Cross: 'Then England, rejoice, thy redemption
draws nigh;
Thy oppression, together with kingship,
shall die.'
Woolchurch: 'A commonwealth, a commonwealth we
proclaim to the nation;
The Gods have repented the King's
Restoration.'

In the same year that Algernon Sidney returned to England,
1677, the King told a courtier that half of the members of the
parliamentary opposition aimed at subverting the Government and
bringing in a Commonwealth again. In the west of Scotland the
quartering of the Highland Host on the Lowland Presbyterians
roused the old Covenanters to a pitch of disloyalty. 'Speak, O
people' was the cry of the preacher there, 'what good the king has
done since his homecoming, yea, hath he not done all the mischief
a tyrant could do, both by his life and laws?' But the divisions of
the Covenanters into monarchists and Republicans proved their
undoing, and when they rose in rebellion they were defeated by the
Duke of Monmouth at Bothwell Bridge in June, 1679. Thus in the
writings of Marvell and his imitators and in the political stirrings
of Algernon Sidney, Wildman and their followers in the London
taverns republican ideas lived on, while the speeches of the new
Opposition under Shaftesbury with their virtual claims to parliamentary sovereignty, so reminiscent of the speeches of the Long
Parliament, once more brought to the Court fears of a reviving
republican movement.

In the late summer of 1678 Buckingham set out for Paris, accompanied among others by his bosom friend, Sir Ellis Leighton, whom
Pepys described as one of the best table companions in the world.
The Duke gave it out that the object of their journey was romantic,
and he spread the rumour that when he reached the French
capital he was 'shut off with some kind of females.' But his presence
in Paris during the hot months of August and September, when
fashionable society deserted the town and the Court was at
Fontainebleau, raised the suspicions of the English Government;
and the presence in his suite not only of his solicitor, John Wildman,
but also of the Republican, Henry Nevile, suggested that he had
political aims in view. Wildman, by general testimony, had

become a close friend of Algernon Sidney since his return from exile, and Sidney, as we have seen, was working to obtain money from France to promote republican projects. Louis had, however, no reason for supporting an English republican movement now that the Dutch war was over, and Buckingham's party returned empty-handed. Soon after this curious episode the Duke virtually disappeared from the political scene. The reasons why this hitherto daring and untrammelled grandee abandoned politics at the moment when the opposition movement against Charles II was reaching its pitch of ferocity are obscure even to his biographers. The most likely explanations are that a real shortage of money—even though his affairs were now under Wildman's ever careful management—prevented him from playing an extravagant part such as suited his temperament, and that dislike and jealousy of Shaftesbury, now unquestionably the leading figure of the Opposition, determined him to retire from a sphere in which he loathed to take a secondary place. Wildman therefore had perforce to transfer his allegiance to Shaftesbury, but there was no quarrel with Buckingham, whose trustee he remained, and as late as 1683 he was contesting a claim for arrears from the workmen who built Buckingham's Cliveden mansion.

Politics apart, Wildman and Shaftesbury had a common approach to religion. In the reign of Charles II, when dissent was driven underground and there were not a few Vicars of Bray among the Anglican parsons, agnosticism or belief in natural religion was spreading among the upper classes. Indeed this period was in some respects not unlike our own, in which many leaders of society either frankly (in private) confessed themselves agnostics or found refuge in the firm and comprehensive faith of the Roman Church. There is a story of a conversation about religion between Shaftesbury and Wildman which must belong to this period:

'The Earl of Shaftesbury was one day conversing with Major Wildman about the large number of religious sects in the world and they finally reached this conclusion: that notwithstanding the infinite divisions caused by the interest of priests and the ignorance of the people all wise men are of the same religion. A lady who happened to be sitting in the same room sewing caught this last remark and pricking up her ears demanded in some concern what that religion was? "Madame," retorted the Earl, "wise men never tell."'

Shaftesbury now climbed to the pinnacle of power as a result of the Popish plot which was discovered by Titus Oates in the autumn of 1678. Oates was an Anglican clergyman who had been thrown out of a naval chaplaincy for immorality. But a long and impressive chin which distracted attention from his shifty eyes and short neck, a real familiarity with the teachings of the Spanish Jesuits, acquired during a somewhat checkered early career, and an entirely imaginary doctorate of divinity in the University of Salamanca, combined to make the Privy Council attend to his disclosures. The story that he unfolded was that the Jesuits were plotting to murder the King and overthrow the Government and to convert the country forcibly to Roman Catholicism under the monarchy of James, Duke of York. He asserted that the plan was finally agreed to at a Jesuit 'consult' held in the White Horse tavern in the Strand on 24th April 1678. This tissue of lies was, as things proved, to result in the judicial murders of Jesuits and other Catholics, to enforce the exile of the Duke of York, to destroy the Cavalier Parliament, to raise Shaftesbury to power, to create the party system in England, and to imperil the very throne itself. But if the words of a perjured informer were to have these sensational results, the Government of Charles II had only itself to blame. From the very beginning of the reign the trade of informer, stool-pigeon, and spy had received official support and remuneration. To their accusations had been owing the judicial murders of poor London tradesmen like Thomas Tonge. Indeed the very name of the chief informer was no novelty in the history of the reign, for another Oates had been one of the witnesses who had furnished the tainted evidence of the alleged Farnley Wood rising of 1663. Some English historians have tried to draw a distinction between the early 'Republican' plots and the Popish plots, assuming the genuineness of the former and the fraudulence of the latter. It cannot be too strongly stressed that there is no basis for such a distinction. In all the plots disclosed in Charles II's reign there was some element of truth and much of falsehood. And there is no question that a Popish plot actually existed; but it was not the plot described by Titus Oates and it dated not from 1678 but from 1670. The policy of the Secret Treaty of Dover by which Charles II agreed to accept foreign money and employ troops to convert the English nation to Roman Catholicism was a Popish plot of such awe-inspiring magnitude and so entirely contrary to the wishes of Parliament or even of Charles II's leading ministers that it had to be kept a deadly secret. It may be, as some historians have urged, that Charles never intended to keep his word to Louis XIV, but there the agreement was in black and white. News of it had leaked out and Marvell's *Growth of Popery and Arbitrary Government*, published the year before Titus Oates's appearance, had already warned the politically conscious of the dangers of an English Court subordinated alike to Paris and Rome.

Oates, together with his fellow informer, Dr. Tonge, not only laid his accusations before the Council but also before a London magistrate named Sir Edmund Berry Godfrey. One of the many mysteries of a still mysterious affair is why Oates thought it necessary to go to Godfrey with his depositions at all. Was it out of distrust for the Privy Council and simply as a precaution or had it another and more sinister purpose? Godfrey was known to be the friend of Roman Catholics and, among others, of Edward Coleman, the Roman Catholic secretary of the new Duchess of York. Godfrey is said to have been so perturbed by the character of Oates's depositions that he warned Coleman, who promptly destroyed all his more recent correspondence. One suggestion that has been made about the motive for Oates's dealings with Godfrey is that he intended to blackmail the magistrate—possibly into revealing and betraying the secrets of his Catholic friends. A fortnight after Godfrey had taken the depositions he disappeared from his house and on 17th October his body was found face downwards and transfixed by a sword at the foot of Primrose Hill. A coroner's jury found that it was wilful murder, and a reward of £500 having been offered, two new informers came forward to declare without much plausibility that the murder had been planned in Somerset House, the London residence of the Duke of York. The clarion cry went forth throughout London that Godfrey had been murdered by Jesuits to keep secret the facts of the Popish plot. The country was convulsed with fear and hate and acclaimed Oates a national hero. Some letters which Coleman had failed to destroy and which talked vaguely of projects for Catholicizing England seemed completely to confirm the details of the plot; and the curious fact (which we now know) that a Jesuit 'consult' was actually held and attended by James, Duke of York (although not at the White Horse tavern but at St. James's Palace), on the date named by Oates gave the Catholics at Court a dangerous secret which they were compelled to conceal. Parliament had now met and it was decided to send five Roman Catholic peers to the Tower; a Bill was passed to prevent Catholics from sitting in either House; Coleman was executed and three Jesuits sentenced to death; and accusations against Charles II's unfortunate Portuguese Queen were freely made.

At this time another and more reputable informer in the shape of a former ambassador at Paris appeared to charge Charles II's chief minister, Danby, with conspiring with the French King. Danby may be considered to have been a little unlucky in this, first, because he had never thoroughly approved of Charles's secret negotiations with Louis XIV but had rather been forced into them, and secondly because not a few of his accusers in the Commons were tainted since they themselves had taken money from the French ambassador to aid their political ends. However, impeachment and execution faced the minister. To save Danby and the Duke of York and perhaps his Queen, Charles prorogued and later dissolved the Cavalier Parliament, which had sat for eighteen years —longer than any in our history.

That the Parliament in which Charles II had once rejoiced should now be dissolved by him out of fear is a measure of the changes of eighteen years. The Parliament had begun its career as an exuberantly Royalist, Anglican, and nationalist assembly. But although by-elections had materially altered its composition and some of its members had grown wiser as well as older, it had not really changed radically in its political convictions. It was Charles who had changed. His negotiations with Louis XIV, now widely suspect, his friendship for Catholics and to a less extent for nonconformists, had estranged the members from him. The mad spell of cruelty, engendered by fear aroused by the Popish plot, was merely a logical culmination of the discontent caused by earlier policies. There is something to be said, and it has been well said recently, for Charles II's point of view. The Commons made inadequate financial provisions for the increasing expenses of government, especially in war-time (although it should be noticed that Louis XIV's grants were never very large nor covered the Treasury's deficiency), and there is no reason to suppose that Charles ever intended to become the placid instrument of the French King's diplomatic ambitions. Granted, however, the existence of a fervently anti-Catholic and anti-French Parliament controlling the purse, harmony between the executive and the legislature was impossible. And so now at last the ghost of Charles I's Long Parliament, which the courtiers had dreaded for many years, again stalked Westminster—a ghost which the ruling powers had vainly tried to exorcise by hanging the Cromwellian soldiers who had talked treason in the taverns.

Henceforward Charles II and his advisers took the line of 'anything but a repetition of 1641'; Shaftesbury, who had exploited the Popish plot, said in effect 'Remember '41!' According to Lord Halifax, Wildman acted as secretary of a committee of the Lords, under the direction of Shaftesbury, which met at Wallingford House in the Whig interest to see what political profit might be made of the opportunity 'to carry on some long-hatched design of their own.' And Wildman, together with Henry Nevile, Richard Salway and Algernon Sidney, 'men well known for their Commonwealth principles,' now prepared to stand as parliamentary candidates in the second general election in the reign of Charles II.

In spite of the enormous difficulties of electioneering in those days when there was only one polling station in each constituency and immense powers for sharp practice or even fraud rested in the hands of the sheriffs, the Country party, as the opposition to the Court boldly called itself, or the Whig party, as it was soon to be known, organized and won a decisive victory. The courtiers, or pensionaries, were ousted as friends of France, 'Popery' and national enslavement. The King, always resilient, hastened to acquiesce in the electoral facts. He sent James, Duke of York, abroad into exile, accepted the resignation of Danby, dispersed most of his old advisers, and announced that henceforward his policy would be guided by a remodelled Council of which the Whig leaders constituted the majority and the Earl of Shaftesbury was the president. Here therefore appeared the seed of Cabinet Government; the King accepted the result of the general election by choosing ministers from the party majority. But Charles acted thus only the better to repulse the Whigs later. Moreover a division at once showed itself in the Council when the question of the succession to the throne was raised. The problem was how to persuade Parliament to acquiesce in a Roman Catholic successor to the throne in his brother, James, Duke of York, as Charles had no legitimate children and—because he steadily refused to divorce his wife—seemed unlikely to have any. Shaftesbury wanted James to be excluded from the throne and the Crown to pass on to his Protestant children as if he were dead. Lord Halifax, a witty political trimmer whose family mansion had been destroyed by the Roundheads during the civil war, put forward the alternative solution of imposing limitations on James's rights as monarch which more or less reduced him to a cipher in the hands of Parliament while allowing him to retain the empty pomp of the title. The scheme of limitations was nearer republicanism, both theoretically and practically, than exclusion. According to Burnet, Halifax argued for the benefit of his republican friends that exclusion 'kept the monarchy still, only passing over one person, whereas the other brought us really into a commonwealth, as soon as we had a popish king over us.'

Wildman was not elected a member of this new Parliament, but when he became a member of Parliament later he voted against the Exclusion Bill, no doubt because he was convinced that the system of limitations was more akin to a republic. At the same time exclusion seemed to most people a more violent break with tradition, for it was a condemnation of the hereditary principle. For this reason it was opposed alike by the King and the majority of the House of Lords—themselves hereditary rulers. But the Commons were rabid for exclusion. They looked at the problem in a simple, straightforward way. They detested 'Popery' and distrusted the fanaticism of James. After pushing on with the impeachment of Danby, reaffirming their belief in the Popish plot, and showing further material gratitude to Titus Oates and to the betrayer of Godfrey's alleged murderers, they passed an Exclusion Bill by 207 votes to 128. At this point the King struck. He realized that the policy of compromise and moderation had failed. Parliament was prorogued after a sitting of four months and later dissolved. Three months later Shaftesbury, who had been furious at the prorogation, was dismissed from the Council, and both Charles and James wrote begging letters to Louis XIV to ask him for money to preserve the succession to the English throne in a Roman Catholic King.

Charles saw correctly enough from his own point of view that his object should be to gain time so that the effects of the Popish plot might wear off. Already in July Oates had suffered a rebuff when Sir George Wakeman, the Catholic physician to the Queen, was acquitted of the charge of plotting to poison the King. A new election was held, and since it again went against the Court, Charles boldly prorogued the new Parliament for an entire year. During that time the London mob worked off its excitement in an orgy of 'Pope burning.' Shaftesbury overreached himself by vainly trying to indict James and the King's French mistress for treason—and Oates's salary was reduced by ten pounds a week.

The year 1679 was notable for some slight revival of the production of anti-Government political literature, such as had been printed in the first years of Charles II's reign. The Licensing Act of 1662, renewed in 1664, had expired in June, 1679. Roger L'Estrange's commission as Surveyor of the Presses ran out; and although licensing provisions were renewed by royal proclamation in October, the temporary lapse encouraged the reappearance of unlicensed printers. Elizabeth Calvert, the printer of *Mene Tekel*, issued various pamphlets to prove that the Great Fire had been started by 'Papists.' An effective seditious pamphlet published at this time, called *An Appeal from the Country to the City*, advocating the claim to the throne of Charles II's illegitimate Protestant son, the Duke of Monmouth, caused a sensation, and this was later supplemented by an even more famous pamphlet on the 'Black Box' which was supposed to contain the proofs of Monmouth's legitimacy. But the real Republicans, like Wildman and Sidney, never thought much of Monmouth except as a convenient counter to the Duke of York, and surprisingly little republican literature appeared. While there were many Whig newspapers or newsletters about the Popish plot, the only work which may be called republican was Henry Nevile's *Plato Redivivus*, published in 1680.

Nevile's book was written in the form of a Socratic discussion between an Englishman, a doctor and a noble Venetian. The argument begins by pointing out that neither the prince nor the people is to be blamed for the decay of government; for this is caused by no account having been taken in the constitution of recent changes in the distribution of property. All governments are liable to become corrupt if the State fails to make political power accord with the actual division of property within the community.

Hence a civil war can provide no remedy for the evils from which England is suffering nor can the succession of the Duke of Monmouth nor even the establishment of a democratic republic. In England, the argument continued, sovereign power resides in the three estates—King, Lords, and Commons; but the King's powers are excessive; for example, his assumption of the right to make peace and war is a usurpation, more especially since the King's holdings of property have been reduced steadily. 'That which is undoubtedly the King's prerogative is to call and dissolve parliaments; to preside in them, and to put in execution as supreme or sovereign magistrate . . . all laws made by them as also the common law.' Nevile maintained that the King had been invading the rights of the Commons who, since the decline of feudalism, owned an increasingly large share of the national land. As the laws cannot be executed owing to the usurped powers of the King, these powers —of making war and peace, of controlling the militia, of nominating officers and of controlling the revenue—must be taken from him and put into the hands of councils, one-third of whose members must be changed yearly. Parliaments ought to meet, regardless of a royal summons, every year; peers should be chosen by Parliament; members of the councils should not belong to the Privy Council; and the two Houses should approve of ministers appointed by the Privy Council. Thus Nevile, although asserting that he was against a revolution and in favour of a limited monarchy, wanted to leave the King with virtually no powers, rights or duties.

Unlike *Plato Redivivus*, Algernon Sidney's book on politics was only published posthumously after the revolution of 1688. But his *Discourses concerning Government* were undoubtedly completed about the same time as Nevile's book. They were written in refutation of Filmer's *Patriarcha*, published in 1680, which outlined the extreme royalist doctrines of divine right and non-resistance. After dealing with Filmer, Sidney states that the best form of government varies with the conditions of the country. Real democracy is suited only to the convenience of a small town 'accompanied with such circumstances as are seldom found.' But in every nation there is a natural aristocracy, for 'God has raised them above all whom He has made to excel all.' Speaking of the late English republic, he says that it had 'produced more examples of pure, complete, incorruptible

and invincible virtue than Rome or Greece could ever boast.'
Those kings only are natural heads of the people who are good,
wise, and seek to advance no interest but that of the public. 'I hope
to prove,' he wrote, 'that of all things under the sun there is none
more mutable and unstable than absolute monarchy; which is all
that I dispute against, professing veneration for that which is mixed,
regulated by law and directed to the public good.' Like Nevile's
monarch, Sidney's constitutional ruler is carefully controlled. He
is bound by law, the people are the fountain of law, and he must be
deposed for corruption or the abuse of the law; he is bound also by
the law of nature. What Sidney really wanted in England was a
monarch with extremely limited powers, advised by a council of
the natural aristocracy, and administering laws promulgated by
the people. Hence, as Professor Gooch has said, 'the Sidney of the
Restoration is, strictly, not a republican at all.' But his political
views, like those of Nevile, form a link between the English
Commonwealth and the coming revolution, and in practice it can
scarcely be doubted that if the opportunity had presented itself, both
authors would have tried to re-establish a republic. Somewhere
about the same time Wildman too was commissioned to draw up a
new English constitution, which unfortunately has not survived.
He was the friend of both Sidney and Nevile. But as the keen
Harringtonian of 1659 and enemy of the extreme aristocratic
republican view, he undoubtedly preferred Nevile's approach to
a very limited monarchy to that of Sidney.

When Parliament, elected a year before, at last met in October,
1680, it at once turned again to the schemes of exclusion. Super-
ficially the political atmosphere in the autumn of 1680 resembled
that of 1648. Never since 1659 had the republican movement been
stronger. Henry Sidney, brother of Algernon and English
ambassador at The Hague, Sir Leoline Jenkins, one of the
Secretaries of State, and James, Duke of York, all thought that the
establishment of a republic was almost inevitable. The French
ambassador in England reported home that men like Buckingham
and Algernon Sidney were preparing for civil war—and he had
reason to do so since Sidney had personally urged upon him the
need to convert England into a republic. Henry Nevile's book had
revived the doctrines of James Harrington. In Parliament a variety
of proposals for reducing the monarchy to a shadow by exceedingly

drastic limitations on the prerogative were favourably discussed. In the Lords it was seriously suggested that if the Duke of York came to the throne, he should have no right of veto on Bills and the legal capacity only of a minor, and that in the meantime he should be banished the kingdom under penalty of death if he returned. This programme was thoroughly approved by Sidney and the Republicans, but met with opposition from Shaftesbury and the Prince of Orange, who, as the husband of James's daughter, Mary, the next heir to the throne, would undoubtedly have preferred exclusion to any tampering with the royal prerogatives.

But most of these revolutionary constitutional proposals were put forward somewhat mildly after exclusion had been temporarily defeated. For the Earl of Halifax by brilliant oratory secured the decisive defeat of the Exclusion Bill in the House of Lords. The Commons took their revenge by impeaching Lord Stafford, one of the five Catholic peers sent to the Tower for complicity in the Popish plot. The judicial murder of this aged nobleman was the last success of Titus Oates and marked the end of the Popish plot, one of the most disgraceful episodes in the history of the House of Commons and of the English Bench. On 29th December Stafford was executed; on 10th January 1681, when the Commons were happily engaged in passing a resolution that the Fire of London of a dozen years earlier was the work of the 'Papists,' Black Rod knocked at the door and the second Exclusionist Parliament was dissolved.

The wisdom of Charles ii's policy (from his own point of view) of resisting exclusion by prorogation and dissolution was proved by the Whig party's loss of some seats in the general election of 1681. On the other hand, John Wildman at last became a member of Parliament. He had first faced the hazards of seventeenth-century electioneering no less than twenty-seven years earlier as a young man eager to overthrow the military dictatorship of Cromwell and replace it by a democratic republic. Now, ally of Shaftesbury and Sidney, he was chosen member for Great Bedwin in Wiltshire. He still had the same object in view and as a first measure sought to destroy the discredited royal line of the Stuarts.

The third Exclusionist Parliament was summoned by the King to meet at Oxford instead of at Westminster so that it might be freed from the intimidation of the London mob who had been politically organized by Shaftesbury. The French ambassador had noted earlier the danger to monarchy of an alliance between the City and the Commons, and the great historian Ranke has called the City 'a republic at the King's side.' Charles made a final attempt to reach terms with the Oxford Parliament by coming out openly for the policy of limitations, a policy which, as we have seen, was preferred by Wildman and the Republicans to that of exclusion. The Whigs, however, who had flocked to the city in armed bands, so fearful were they of the loyal regiments, stuck to the full rigour of exclusion. Charles, cheerful as ever (he had housed a selection of his mistresses in the Oxford colleges during his visit) ignored all threats. On 22nd March he concluded a verbal treaty with the French King for a fairly generous subsidy (Louis XIV thought it well worth his while to back the Roman Catholic James's succession) and six days later Charles flung down the gauntlet by dissolving, not proroguing, his last Parliament. In the next eighteen months the country drifted towards civil war.

THE RYE HOUSE PLOT

... One of Cromwell's majors [*sic*] Wildman, a bold and desperate fellow.
ROGER L'ESTRANGE, 1684

WITH the abrupt dismissal of the Oxford Parliament began the clever and successful, if unscrupulous, Tory counter-offensive against the Whigs. A resurgent royalist rank-and-file, embittered children of the Cavaliers, determined that concerted parliamentary opposition to the King's Government, hitherto unknown in English history save as a prelude to revolt or revolution, should no longer be tolerated. Previously, in his days of political weakness, Charles II had stomached every possible insult to his prerogatives, but now, when his opportunity was ripe, he laboured to crush his domestic enemies. 'I will stick by you and my old friends,' he told a leading Tory squire, 'for if I do not, I shall have nobody to stick by me.' He moved forward as the Popish plot grew more and more discredited. The Court party decided to make the law courts the instrument of their revenge upon the Whig grandees. The Lord Chief Justice Scroggs, who had presided over the Popish plot trials, was summarily ejected from his post and replaced by a complacent royal nominee, Sir Francis Pemberton. But one main obstacle yet remained in the path of royal vengeance—the juries of the City of London—whose independence (or partisanship, if you will) nobody could intimidate, for they were appointed by the Whig sheriffs. They showed their mettle when the first victim chosen to satisfy the Tory wrath—Stephen College, a Protestant joiner—came up for indictment.

College, who was said to have been closely associated with Sir Thomas Player, the City Treasurer, and Sir Robert Clayton, Wildman's fellow trustee, both eminent Whigs, was accused of treason for uttering seditious words in Oxford during the meeting of Parliament and, among other things, for singing a ribald ballad to the tune of 'I am a senseless thing.' A Middlesex Grand Jury, unimpressed by the evidence of shuffling informers, threw out the bill. Thereupon a mean device was adopted; the place of the trial was changed to Oxford, that traditionally Tory stronghold, on the ground that the alleged acts of treason had been committed there. Titus Oates tried to defend College, but his evidence was considered to be of no worth when proffered in favour of a man whom he believed to be innocent. College was found guilty and executed— a first Whig martyr. Just before the execution of College one Fitzharris, an Irishman, who had been mixed up in the Popish plot and was suspected by the Whig politicians of having been suborned by the King's friends to spy on them, was hurried to the scaffold with his lips still sealed. Then in July, 1681, the royal advisers struck their most daring blow. Shaftesbury, the Whig chief, was arrested and put in the Tower on a charge of high treason. The ground on which he was arrested was the discovery in his cabinet of a paper undated and unsigned and not in his own handwriting, containing a pledge to resist the accession of a Popish king to the throne. In November of the same year John Dryden exerted the full force of his poetic and satirical genius on the side of the Tories, lashing the Whigs in his *Absalom* (Monmouth) *and Achitophel* (Shaftesbury); and in the following month Argyll, the Whig 'uncrowned King of the Highlands,' was put on trial in Edinburgh and sentenced to death merely because he had ventured openly to qualify his oath of allegiance to the Crown.

Yet the Court was not able to achieve the full measure of its revenge. For, in spite of the biassed summing up of Chief Justice Pemberton, the Grand Jury marked the bill of indictment against Shaftesbury 'ignoramus' ('we take no notice of it') and Argyll was smuggled out of prison by his stepdaughter and fled by way of London to Holland. Shaken by these rebuffs the royal advisers made up their minds to carry the City of London over to their side by hook or by crook. They demanded the surrender of the City Charter to the Crown so that a new one, modelled in the Tory interest, might be substituted for it. But they found a quicker way of reaching their ends. If only the annually elected sheriffs were Tories instead of Whigs, there need be no more 'ignoramus' juries selected. It happened that in 1682, owing to the splitting of Whig votes, the Lord Mayor of London was a Tory and his assistance in an ingenious scheme was invoked by the Court. He was prevailed upon to resuscitate an obsolete custom which enabled the Lord

Mayor to nominate one of the sheriffs simply by drinking to him at an annual feast. He raised his glass to a wealthy Tory freeman and thereby claimed to exercise his ancient mayoral prerogative. Aghast at the audacity the Whigs were thrown into confusion, and with the aid of the Privy Council and the judges, after four months of litigation and recriminations, two Tory sheriffs, North and Rich by name, were established in office and stayed there. Thus for the following year the three principal City officers were Tories. The fate of the 'ignoramus' juries was settled and the Whig leaders in fright for their lives turned from open opposition to secret confabulations on insurrection.

The origins of the Whig consultations about the prospects of rebellion which now began can be dated roughly from the time when North and Rich were nominated sheriffs. It is true that Wildman had been accused of 'carrying on long-hatched designs' when he was secretary of the Wallingford House committee; and it is likely enough that on the two occasions when the King had been taken seriously ill in 1679 and 1680 there had been hurried Whig meetings to consider whether a Roman Catholic king should be allowed to mount the throne. But the confessions of the less unreliable informers, as well as of two men who were put to death for treason, concur in dating continuous discussions from this moment. Now was the time when all established Whig and republican plotters rallied to the aid of the party, and Major Wildman was foremost among them.

The first thing that Wildman did after the nominations of North and Rich was to republish a thirty-two-year-old pamphlet on *London's Liberties* in the hope of reminding the freemen of the City that all of them had an historical right to take part in electing the Lord Mayor and sheriffs of London. This, however, was but a pill to stop an earthquake. In October, 1683, another Tory Lord Mayor was elected and the surrender of the City of London Charter again demanded. In February, 1683, the case to test the validity of this demand came before the King's Bench. In the same month Wildman received a visit from Nathaniel Wade, a Bristol lawyer of Whig persuasions, at his new London home in Little Queen Street. Wade gave it as his opinion that the judges would give a verdict in favour of the surrender of the charter. Wildman said he thought not, but 'if they do, we know what to do next.' If

Wade's report of this conversation is genuine—and it bears the stamp of probability—Wildman by that date was familiar with plans to resist the Government by force. But who besides Wildman knew of them?

It is an ancient subject of historical controversy how far the Whigs of Charles II's reign committed themselves to an insurrection in the winter of 1682–3. Later Whigs, when their party had been hallowed by years of constitutional respectability, were reluctant to admit that the founders of their party, which had in any case derived its pristine strength from the unsavoury business of the Popish plot, should so soon have turned to revolutionary action. Both Charles James Fox and Lord John Russell wrote books in which they attempted to prove that their predecessors were entirely innocent of conspiracy, although they allowed that they might have engaged in conspiratorial talk. Indeed one of them, William Russell, ancestor of Lord John Russell, in a letter written to be shown to King Charles after his death, did not deny that 'he had heard many things and some things contrary to my duty.' But, as later historians argued, the evidence for the deliberate planning of insurrection by the Whig leaders was derived from professional spies whose words were tainted and who often contradicted each other; and, they added, even those supposed conspirators who fled the country—or in one case committed suicide—when information was laid against them did so not because they were conscious of guilt but because they could not trust the impartiality of the remodelled law courts and the Tory juries bent on their destruction. A great deal of evidence has been published, some of it only recently, since Fox and Lord John Russell wrote, but the problem is still open to debate. The most damning argument in favour of the reality of the insurrectionary movement was that when James II succeeded to the throne exactly the kind of plans which were said to have been concerted by the accused Whigs in 1682 and 1683 were actually put into effect. Monmouth's rising of 1685 and the Glorious Revolution of 1688 were in fact carried out largely in the same places and by the same men who were named in the treason trials of 1683. It is also to be observed that the Duke of Monmouth, who, because of King Charles's devotion to him, went in little danger of his life and had no impulse to lie, confessed that a conspiracy had been on foot, while various pieces of evidence independently collected after Monmouth's invasion in the reign of James II and produced after some of the earlier condemned conspirators were dead, tended to confirm in a general way that plans for a rising had been worked out in the previous reign. The fact that a seasoned plotter like Wildman was at the centre of the various groups engaged in this treasonable talk or activity shows that the cabals went beyond tap-room aspirations.

In the autumn of 1682 the opposition was divided into four main groups. In the first place there was Shaftesbury and the exclusionists. Shaftesbury at this time deliberately intended to embark upon a civil war to prevent James, Duke of York, from becoming King, and egged on the Duke of Monmouth to discover how far his popularity as the Protestant 'son' of Charles II might be used to enlist military support in the provinces. Earl Russell was likewise an exclusionist but seems to have distrusted Shaftesbury. Arthur Capel, Earl of Essex, was also a vehement exclusionist but not an enthusiastic supporter of Monmouth. In the second group came Monmouth himself, a weak man, very susceptible to flattery, the pathetic hero of a generation of novelists; his entourage included Sir Thomas Armstrong, Robert Ferguson, an unstable Scottish preacher and plotter, Francis Charlton, a lawyer, and Nathaniel Wade. The third group consisted of Republicans who had always preferred strict limitations on the King's rights to the policy of excluding James from the throne: they were led by Algernon Sidney, whose courage and intellectual daring exercised a fascination upon John Hampden, a grandson of the hero of the first civil war, and upon the Earl of Essex. The fourth group contained men like Lord Grey of Wark and Lord Howard of Escrick (whom we met as Wildman's enemy during the Interregnum) whose interest in conspiracy was qualified by a profound regard for the safety of their own skins. There were also a number of underlings who had little or no connexion with the Whig aristocrats, some of whom, like Captain Rumbold and Captain Walcot, were old Cromwellian officers of genuine republican sympathies but several of whom, like Robert West, a Middle Temple lawyer and his friend, Colonel Romsey, faced both ways, and while provoking others to treason were ready to sell their information to the Government at the earliest opportunity.

John Wildman, although himself a Republican and therefore most closely linked with the section of the opposition led by Algernon Sidney, was almost the only politician who had intimate relations with all four groups. Ferguson said that he had several important conversations with him, although he distrusted him because he was at that date an antagonist of Monmouth. He was, as we have seen, a friend of Shaftesbury; and West alleged that he had at least one meeting with him, although he admitted that among the lower order of conspirators Wildman trusted only Rumbold. In the statements made by West and his fellow informers at the trials of the Whig leaders it was frequently asserted that an insurrection had been planned by a Council of Six consisting of Russell, Essex, Sidney, Monmouth, Hampden, and the traitor Howard. But in the depositions taken before the trials Wildman was also said to have belonged to the directing Council. It is improbable, in view of the relations between Howard and Wildman during the Interregnum, that they would have been members of the same secret committee, but in any case there is small reason to believe that the Council of Six ever existed. The idea of a secret Council of Six manufacturing but not participating in plots was part of the stock-in-trade of all informers throughout the reign of Charles II. We have seen, for instance, how two Councils of Six were mentioned as being concerned in the Farnley Wood plot of 1663 (to one of which Wildman was said to have belonged, although he was at the time a prisoner of State in the Scilly Isles). Russell emphatically denied that he was a member of such a council, and it seems unlikely in the extreme that the genuine Republicans would have worked in harmony with the self-interested Monmouth, the exclusionists, and the serpentine Howard, of whom every one was said to be 'shy.' All that happened for certain was that on two occasions some of the leaders of the different groups drifted into a wine shop to receive a message from Lord Shaftesbury when he was in hiding in London at the end of 1682.

Shaftesbury's scheme to exploit the popularity of Monmouth, 'the Protestant Duke,' against the unpopularity of James, 'the Popish Duke,' broke down because Monmouth could never be persuaded to fight his supposed father and because he had not the requisite strength of character and purpose for a pretender to the English throne. When Monmouth went on a tour, known as a 'progress,' in the north of England in the autumn of 1682, Shaftesbury hoped that he would seize the opportunity to find out whether or not the country was ripe for rebellion. Monmouth duly visited Staffordshire, Cheshire, and Lancashire in all pomp and obtained an enthusiastic reception from the crowds by winning races both on horse and on foot; he presented the plate which he won at the Wallasey races to his little godchild Henrietta, the mayor's daughter; and in general he courted popularity rather than danger, preferring the habits of princely graciousness to those of conspiratorial research. Such tactics were too obvious to escape the notice of the authorities. His activities were closely followed by the Serjeant-at-Arms and he was ultimately arrested at Stafford as a disturber of the peace. When he was brought back to London he protested that the warrant was illegal and after much remonstrance he obtained his release on bail. Shaftesbury urged him to return at once to Cheshire and start a popular rising against the Government. Monmouth, to Shaftesbury's unconcealed disgust, refused. 'The Duke of Monmouth,' declared the Earl, 'is an unfortunate man, for God has thrice put it into his power to save England and thrice he has failed her.'

Monmouth's unwillingness to grasp his chances—if such they were—strengthened the hopes of the republican party which, under the direction of Sidney and Wildman, was once again becoming a reality. Shaftesbury himself, weighed down by his disappointment, seems momentarily to have contemplated organizing a rising with his invisible army of ten thousand 'brisk boys' from the City of London and declaring for a republic. According to Lord Howard (whose words are roughly confirmed by Grey and Ferguson who wrote their stories independently) Shaftesbury said, 'We are for a Commonwealth and he [Monmouth] hath no design but his own personal interest and that will not go down with my people now.' But another warrant was issued for Shaftesbury's arrest and he was forced into hiding, whence he twice communicated with his friends through an agent who delivered his messages to them in Thomas Shepherd's wine shop in Abchurch lane. He pressed upon them the desirability of an immediate rising on an agreed day, but those who were present did not consider that the state of political feeling either in the north-west or the west of England made any such attempt in the least hopeful.

Moreover on 24th October a final blow fell upon the Whig interest when Sir John Moore was succeeded by yet another pliable Tory as Lord Mayor and by the end of November, despairing of any immediate move, Shaftesbury fled to Holland. His new centre of conspiracy was destined to be his last. On 21st January 1683 Shaftesbury's life of tireless intrigue and tergiversation came to a sudden, if not unexpected, close, in an Amsterdam merchant's house. He died disappointed but smiling.

The flight and death of the Whig leader put an end to all real hopes of a rising against King Charles II by the united forces of the opposition. Henceforward the plans for a rising broke down because of an irreconcilable division between the followers of the discredited pretender Monmouth and the supporters of the revivified republican movement. One of the minor informers estimated that two-thirds of the opposition were for Monmouth and one-third for a Commonwealth. There is no serious evidence that any concerted preparations were made for an armed outbreak, although there was much subversive talk. Algernon Sidney, who had not taken part in the discussions before Shaftesbury's death, now recommended the dispatch of a reliable messenger to Scotland to discover whether an agreement could be reached between the English opposition, the Covenanters, and the supporters of Argyll. He suggested that some representatives of the Scots should come up to London nominally in order to talk over the affairs of the recently established colony known as Carolina but really to investigate the prospects of rebellion in England. Meanwhile Argyll himself, who was still in Holland, talked largely of invading England if someone would pay him £20,000 to buy munitions and hire ships; he later reduced his demands to £8,000, but nobody was willing to offer him even that. The Scots were in any case concerned only about the preservation of their own religion and independence and were otherwise indifferent as to which Government ruled in London. The English conspirators were thus thrown back on their own devices.

Wildman took a leading part in the negotiations with the Scots and afterwards. Being on not unfriendly terms with all sections of the Whig opposition he was looked upon as their 'chief oracle' and 'entrusted to prepare and draw up a remonstrance of the grievances and oppressions of the kingdom and how far the King had invaded and subverted the laws even to the changing of the constitution.' That is Robert Ferguson's story. According to other accounts Wildman was invited to draw up a specifically republican manifesto. In any case remonstrances were his *forte*. Had not his pen been employed against Cromwell thirty years earlier and against Charles I another five years before that? He set to work with a good will. This particular manifesto has not survived. Rumbold told West that Wildman had shown him a draft which he intended to have printed and distributed as soon as an insurrection took place and that Wildman had said the manifesto was 'bold but safe, set forth our grievances plainly, but kept within the law.' This latter statement attunes with his character as we know it, for he was always a cautious conspirator. By his fellow Republicans he was valued not only for his ready pen and constitutional lore but also for his reputed wealth. It was hoped and believed that if ever a rising should occur, he would be the paymaster. The informer West had a story, which he repeated on several occasions, that Ferguson had told him (all these stories were third-hand) that if he wanted £100 to buy arms all he had to do was to send a note to Major Wildman. But Wildman insisted that the only one of the lower order of conspirators with whom he would deal was Captain Rumbold. Rumbold (so West's tale ran) was duly sent at five o'clock in the morning to the Major's house, only to find that the Major had gone out of town an hour before without leaving any orders about the money and West had to collect it direct from Ferguson. Certainly Wildman was generally regarded as a suitable agent to buy arms, for there is pretty reliable evidence that two years later he had that reputation among Monmouth's entourage at a time when rebellion awoke in the realm of action.

Another of West's stories about Wildman was that in March, 1683, he had met Wildman on the Exchange and—evidently in an effort to penetrate the Major's notorious taciturnity—observed that he had a plantation in America 'where the churchmen never had had a footing' and that he intended to go there if he were driven from England. The Major retorted, 'Keep here, and don't talk of being driven out—drive them out.' 'I do not see how that can be done,' returned the ingenious West. 'It may be done, and must be done, and shall be done,' said the Major fiercely—and left it at that.

The episode on the Exchange obviously referred to Wildman, but that West's stories about him cannot be readily trusted is shown by another entirely inaccurate recollection of West's. He asserted that Major Wildman had maintained a regular correspondence with the Earl of Argyll and 'did me the honour to order that the Earl's letters to him should be directed to me and left at the South-wark Coffee House in Bartholomew Lane.' West was not un-naturally puzzled at this inexplicable sign of trust on the part of the cautious Wildman—'the making use of my name who was almost as obnoxious a man as himself was so weak a piece of policy as a man of less grimace than Major Wildman would scarce have been guilty of.' Grimacer or not, Wildman's reputation as a plotter will not be affected by this story. For we know that Argyll's letters were in fact addressed not to Major Wildman but to an old Cromwellian officer named Major Holmes who used the alias of 'Master West.' Some of these letters were intercepted by agents of the Crown, and West, having heard an inaccurate version of the events, embodied it in his testimony to impress the King with the fullness of his knowledge. It merely proves to posterity, as it should have proved to the Court of Charles II, what an unscrupulous liar West was.

So much for Wildman's part in the so-called insurrection plot. He was in the autumn of 1682 the only link (apart perhaps from Robert Ferguson) between the various consultative groups; after Shaftesbury's flight he threw in his lot with the Republicans and was the closest associate of the single-minded Sidney; and he was regarded as pamphleteer in chief, a potential paymaster and buyer of arms.

We now come to the 'Rye House murder plot,' the disclosure of which threw light on the discussions about insurrection. On 13th June 1683 Josiah Keeling, a bankrupt Anabaptist oilman—*alter ego* of Dr. Tonge—came forward with his lurid revelations, later to be confirmed and elaborated by Robert West, most astute of the informers, and by Colonel Romsey, an old Cromwellian officer and a tax collector at Bristol. West himself was a barrister of the Middle Temple, a confessed student of Machiavelli, and was described by a contemporary as 'a witty and active man full of talk, believed to be a determined atheist.' Here is the tale they told. The Rye House was a strong moated building named after a near-by meadow and situated in Hertfordshire some eighteen miles from London. Under it ran a road from Bishop's Stortford to Hoddesdon which was occasionally, but by no means invariably, used by King Charles when he went to or from the Newmarket races, as he was accustomed to do twice a year, in the spring and autumn. The house had recently come into the possession of a maltster named Richard Rumbold through his wife. The alleged plot, to which Rumbold was a party, was to shoot the King from the house as he returned from Newmarket in March, 1683. Three or four men, it was asserted, were to hide behind a wall with blunderbusses in their hands and murder in their hearts to shoot at the postilion and horses as soon as the King's coach came into sight; if the horses did not drop, two men disguised as labourers were to pull an empty cart across the lane to block the coach. Then one party was to engage the guards and another to kill the King and the Duke of York. The scheme, it was explained, failed because of a miraculous fire that broke out at Newmarket and obliged the King to return to town a week earlier than had been expected. The plotters were caught on the hop and so there was no murder. According to West, no attempt could be made at such short notice because horses could not be bought on a Sunday without exciting suspicion. It was not suggested that any figure of political importance was concerned in the plot. The would-be murderers were stated to number six or seven; besides the informers were Captain Walcot, who was alleged to have agreed to command a group of men who were to confine their activities to an attack upon the King's armed guards since he 'would not attack naked men'; Rumbold, owner of the Rye House; and Richard Goodenough, who had been an under-sheriff in the City of London and was said by his servant to have been in favour of a good honest Commonwealth as in Oliver's days. An astrologer refused to take part because he could not ride, but averred that the portents were excellent. Romsey, himself an informer, blandly confessed that he had been allotted the role of actual murderer. But was there in fact any such murder plot at all? There is not the slightest reliable evidence that a plan for the assassination of the King and Duke ever existed outside the imaginations of a few men. It is one of the great historical myths. A close study of the evidence leads to the conclusion that the plot originated as a figment of Wildman's imagination, and when the idea was abandoned by him was picked up and embroidered by West and Romsey and was indirectly responsible for sending a number of innocent men to the scaffold.

The first suggestion of a plan to murder the King on the road to Newmarket dates from as early as July, 1678, when an informer reported a coffee-house conversation in Bartholomew Lane about 'a good ambush' when the King and Duke went to Newmarket and 'two hundred men brisk and fit for business' who 'could do the work.' A year after this the idea was again mentioned during one of the Popish plot trials, that of Sir George Wakeman, the Queen's physician. Fifteen months later a certain Charles Rea came forward and stated that Wildman had been talking in general terms of the need to kill the King. According to his information, supplied to the Government in April, 1681 (just after the dissolution of the Oxford Parliament), Wildman said to him several times, 'We have had enough of a king and especially such a one as this is—there never was so bad a one in the world.' It would be, so Wildman told him, 'no sin to cut him off.' Thus, if Rea is to be trusted, the idea of murdering the King was revolving in Wildman's mind two years before the discovery of the alleged murder plot. Nearly a year later another informer, John Fitzgerald, who had been mixed up in the Popish plot, bore witness that he had heard Major Wildman and Colonel Sidney 'speak several treasonable expressions.' He also stated that Dr. Tonge, the first inventor with Oates of the Popish plot, had observed that 'some noblemen had told him that the King was to go to Newmarket in March, 1680, and that there was a general intention and design to cut off the King before he could return.' Thus we have it that the plan of murdering the King on his way to or from Newmarket in March was commonly discussed in the political underworld in 1680 and 1681, that it derived from the fertile imaginations of the Popish plot informers, and that Wildman knew of it.

We must now turn to the evidence provided in the 'confession' of Robert Ferguson. Ferguson is one of the most peculiar figures among the many political oddities of the late seventeenth century. Beginning life as a minister of the Church of England, he became a successful Presbyterian preacher and vehement anti-Royalist plotter. After spending the reigns of Charles II and James II as a pamphleteer, political busybody, and plotter against the Stuarts, he ended his career as a virulent Jacobite schemer devoted to the exiled Court. His 'confession' is one of the chief pieces of evidence about the circumstances of the Rye House plot. It was written, after several of the principal characters were dead, towards the end of the reign of James II. Ferguson's biographer believed that this document found its way into the British State papers in the reign of William III. A careful search in the Record Office has not yielded the original document, and certainly there is no trace of its ever having been among the papers of James II's reign. Nevertheless, judging merely by internal evidence, the 'confession' bears the stamp of authenticity, and it is not materially contradicted by any other reliable information. Ferguson claimed in it that he was always a consistent enthusiast for an insurrection on behalf of the Duke of Monmouth. He was therefore opposed alike to the plans of Shaftesbury and of Sidney and worked to thwart any scheme to murder the King, a design to which his hero Monmouth was also unflinchingly opposed.

Ferguson states, without mentioning Wildman by name but obviously referring to him, that it was from Wildman that he first heard of a murder plot:

'The first man of note and consideration from which I received the light into it . . . was a gentleman that is at present [1688?] at Amsterdam and who is esteemed a great statesman and excellently versed in the laws of England, tho' never accounted very friendly to kingship. For having long been acquainted with him and meeting him occasionally at a friend's house, we entered into a discourse of the posture of affairs and of the councils which the King seemed to be eagerly pursuing; whereupon he largely represented to me the danger that the nation and all who had asserted the liberties of the people were brought into, with the necessity of doing something speedily for preventing our being arbitrarily destroyed and for hindering the subversion of the ancient legal Government; and having declared the hazard, folly and impracticableness of thinking to engage people in a general insurrection . . . he added that the only thing which remained to be rationally attempted . . . in the pursuing and executing whereof there would be less danger in that it needed only to be imparted to a few, was to employ the zeal and courage of some brisk lads to destroy the King and Duke, whom he expressed by the name of the Stag that would not be impaled but leapt over all the fences, which the care and wisdom of the author of the Constitution had made to restrain them from committing spoils.'

This talk took place in the autumn of 1682, and Ferguson says that he at once took steps to frustrate Wildman's plan. Later, however, he says that Wildman himself abandoned it because he had by then entered into consultations with Sidney and Essex and saw genuine hope of achieving his political ends not by murder but by insurrection. There was thus, in Ferguson's view, not the slightest danger of King Charles II being assassinated in March, 1683; the Newmarket fire did not save him: 'I dare positively affirm that if he had remained there a month longer he would have come back with as much security as at the time he did.'

But the seed sown by Wildman had germinated in the brain of Robert West. From the time of the dissolution of the Oxford Parliament this shady barrister had been mixed up in the lower realms of Whig endeavour. College had asked that West should be one of his attorneys. It is evident that West had got to hear of Wildman's ideas and of his change of mind. In one of his numerous statements West informed the King that Rumbold had told him that 'the Major grew a very unintelligible man; for he had first encouraged him to undertake the assassination of the King and Duke and afterwards seemed to dissuade him.' Whether Rumbold really said this or not does not matter; what matters is that West's statement shows that he was familiar with Wildman's views. Around them he wove his story of the Rye House plot. Together with his friend Romsey he started talking grandiloquently to Walcot and Rumbold and Goodenough, all of whom were reluctant to make any move, of the necessity for murdering the King—which West called the 'lopping point' as distinct from the 'general point,' meaning the insurrection. Rumbold's ownership of the Rye House lent colour to West's detailed revelations about the plot. He also got hold of a half-witted joiner named William Hone. Of the other informers who came forward or confessed later no fewer than five of them—Romsey, Whitlock, Waller, Bourne and Holloway—said that they had heard of the murder plan originally through West and two others said that they had it from Keeling. Yet West and Keeling were the very men who 'betrayed' the plot to the Government. The most likely explanation is that they first invented the story of the Rye House plot and then they exposed it. Nor are their reasons for this manoeuvre hard to seek. Let us examine what they were.

Keeling appeared with his story first. But before he went to the authorities on 23rd June 1683, he opened his mouth widely in a City tavern. In July, Captain John Phelps and seven other persons testified that they were in the Fleet tavern in Cornhill before the discovery of the plot and Keeling told them that 'he was very much solicited by a great person whom he was to meet that afternoon to do some business for which he was to have a place of £160 a year; he was also stated to have said that he was disobliged by his friends and would be revenged on them.' West himself admitted that Keeling had betrayed the conspirators for money. Rumbold in a letter to West written after his escape abroad referred to 'that villain Romsey, the Duke of York's spy and trepan.' As for West himself no one had a good word to say for him. What evidently happened then is that Keeling decided to lay his information first and to take his would-be fellow stool-pigeons, Romsey and West, by surprise. But they acted quickly and hastened to confirm the tale of the Rye House plot that they themselves had concocted out of Wildman's ideas, which he had derived in turn from the plot factory of Oates and Tonge. West had the sense to get Rumbold out of the country lest his testimony about the ownership of Rye House should ruin his story. He also had the grace to try to save the life of the imbecile Hone who would keep on saying that the intention was to kill the King and save the Duke of York— a meaningless plan for republican or anti-Popish conspirators. Probably Hone had some fuddled notions left over from the days of the Popish plot. But Walcot, although he denied both at his trial and in his speech from the scaffold that he had contemplated the murder of the King, confessed that he had listened to treasonable talk and was sent to his death by the lying testimonies of West, Keeling and Romsey. Together with Hone and later Holloway he was convicted for his part in the imaginary plot. Rumbold was killed on the battlefield two years later, so that his evidence is denied to posterity. Such were the small fry involved in the Rye House plot. But three of the informers—later to vanish back into the murky darkness from which they had stepped on to the pages of history—created such a prejudice in the minds of the hand-picked Tory juries as to assist the judicial murders of Russell and Sidney, of whom they knew nothing whatever, for they never met any prominent Whig but Wildman.

On 1st June 1683 the Mayor of Newcastle notified Secretary of State Jenkins in London that he had arrested a man named Pringle who had been attempting to embark for abroad and was carrying seditious papers and letters written in cipher. On examination Pringle proved to be a Scotsman named Alexander Gordon of Waristoun and the deciphered letters were found to relate to a possible rising and to be destined in all probability for the Earl of Argyll in Holland. This information predisposed the Court to accept Keeling's story when he appeared on 13th June, after he had first secured a pardon for all treasons, murders and the like which he might have committed. After hearing Keeling's account of the Rye House plot, the Earl of Sunderland, the other Secretary of State, observed that the King, who 'is least inclined to think that he is in danger, cannot doubt the truth of the depositions.' The confessions of West and Romsey a few days later clinched the matter so far as the Government was concerned and orders were given for the arrest (in addition to that of the minor characters directly concerned in the 'murder plot') of Sidney, Russell, Wildman, Monmouth, Ferguson, Grey, Armstrong and others. Although five hundred pounds was offered for their capture, Ferguson, Grey and Armstrong escaped. Extensive search was made for arms in Bristol, Coventry and other towns, and a hue and cry was raised. On 28th June Wildman was committed to the Tower of London. Three days before, the Earl of Abingdon, Lord Lieutenant of Berkshire, had informed Secretary Jenkins that he had heard in Oxford that a certain person called Colonel had been hiding for several days at Becket, Wildman's country seat. (This may have been Rumbold or some other Republican.) Jenkins gave orders that the house should be searched as Wildman was now lodged in the Tower. Before his arrest Wildman sent his tailor out of town on horseback to fetch his wife and no doubt to warn her to destroy compromising papers. He rode by way of Reading and reached Mrs. Wildman on the Tuesday (26th June). Reduced perhaps to a state of imperturbability by her husband's numerous escapades, she told the messenger that she would not start for London until the Thursday.

Meanwhile Wildman was interrogated by an official committee. No records of his examination have survived. Evidently nothing incriminating was unearthed at Becket, but in his London house two cannon were discovered in the cellar. These, Dr. Burnet relates, were 'two small field pieces' formerly belonging to Wildman's old friend and employer, the Duke of Buckingham, now living in retirement, which Wildman had taken from York House when it was pulled down. These pieces were 'finely wrought, but of little use . . . they were laid on ordinary wooden carriages and no way fitted for use.' But they were duly taken to Whitehall and put on view as undeniable proof of the rebellion which had been prevented by the vigilance of the authorities. They were in fact the only arms ever found in connexion with the supposed rising. West declared that the arms, which had been ordered and paid for, remained in the factories. But there was no proof of their existence. The Government also laid hands on a certain Benjamin Summer who reported a conversation that he had held about the plot with a man named Doller. Doller had declared that Major Wildman was a cunning fellow and would outwit them, for he had been too cunning for Oliver. And so it proved.

The testimonies of West, Romsey and Keeling and the crowd of minor informers, although valuable against the ruck of old Cromwellian officers and others whom they had trepanned, were of no worth in a court of law against the leading Whigs. But on 9th July, Lord Howard of Escrick, who also had been arrested, offered a confession which contained direct and not hearsay evidence against Russell and Sidney. He also asserted in a general way that 'Wildman was very forward in the work.' He added that he himself had told Wildman that what was needed for the insurrection was guns, and alleged that in reply Wildman had said that they would be furnished with two Drakes by a friend, and Howard thought that those Drakes might be the small pieces found in Wildman's house. The Court party now felt strong enough to proceed with the trials and first tried out their informers against Walcot, who was duly convicted of high treason. On 13th July the trial of Earl Russell followed. The trial was interrupted and Russell's case prejudiced by the news that the Earl of Essex had committed suicide in prison. Romsey and Shepherd swore that

Russell was present at a meeting at Shepherd's house where plans for a rising were discussed—although they contradicted each other about whether there was one meeting or two—and Lord Howard gave evidence of Russell's complicity in the Scottish negotiations. Dr. Burnet swore that Howard had told him earlier that Russell had no knowledge of the plot. Nevertheless Russell was found guilty. Every effort was made, by bringing money and influence to bear on the highest circles of Court society, to secure a reprieve for this Whig aristocrat. But the most the King would concede was that Russell should be beheaded instead of hanged. The Earl maintained his innocence to the last, kissed his wife saying, 'Now the bitterness of death is past,' and on the morning of 21st July went bravely to his execution. John Rouse, a sea captain, who admitted he listened to treasonable talk, and the unfortunate half-wit Hone were also done to death. After that, although there was a rumour at the end of the month that Sidney, Hampden and Wildman were to be brought to trial at Old Bailey, no further move was made by the Government until November.

The truth was that the evidence available against these influential figures was extremely weak. It was only because of Russell's apparently accidental visit to Shepherd's wine shop that the two necessary witnesses were found to testify against him. After much thought the King's legal advisers, always notable for their ingenuity rather than their scruples, discovered a way to attack Sidney. In his house the manuscript of his *Discourses* had been unearthed. It was suggested that passages from these republican writings might be employed in place of one witness, while Howard was to be the other. On 21st November, therefore, he was brought to trial. Like the strong legalist he was, Sidney fought the judges and the Attorney-General step by step, denied that the authorship of his republican writings was proved or indeed provable, and swore that he was guilty of no treasonable act. The jury, however, was convinced that if he were the author of republican literature, he must have been guilty of the most wicked forms of treason. He died, as even James, Duke of York, admitted, 'stoutly and like a true Republican.'

The publication of Algernon Sidney's speech from the scaffold and the report of the trial, in which West and Romsey were shown to have contradicted each other, made a considerable impression in the City. Howard, too, at this time began to feel some remorse at swearing away the lives of his friends. And it was decided not to stretch the evidence or test the credibility of the witnesses to obtain further victims. Against Wildman there was no direct evidence. Howard could only swear that he had heard of Wildman's complicity through Shaftesbury; Romsey said that West had told him about Wildman's activities; West repeated his stories obtained from the exiled Rumbold and Ferguson or made up lies; even James Holloway, who was later persuaded to confess what he knew on being seized in the West Indies, could only say that he had heard about Wildman from his Bristol friend, Nathaniel Wade, who had the wisdom to remain in Holland. Thus there was no shred of evidence against Wildman except the two rusty cannon found in his cellar. In August, 1683, Romsey wrote to his patron, the Duke of York, suggesting that Charlton, one of Monmouth's friends, who had just been arrested, should be interrogated about Wildman's part in the conspiracy, who was 'privy to all.' But Charlton kept his mouth closed. In October the Privy Council ordered that a full inquiry should be made into where Wildman's gun carriages were manufactured and where they were found, but nothing fresh was forthcoming. Throughout his period of imprisonment Wildman was therefore able to carry on with equanimity the various business transactions in which he was always engaged. His wife was allowed to visit him in the Tower from time to time. She had begged for permission to visit him 'as often as it shall be needful to preserve her life and recover her health.' 'His advice to her,' she explained, 'she having been afflicted with many great sicknesses, has been many times the only means to preserve her life.' She had, she complained, 'been denied access to him and his advice and help . . . and for want of his assistance she was most likely to lose her life.'

During his stay in the Tower of London, which had now been his occasional residence for many years, he was concerned in negotiations with the Duke of Beaufort on a manor he had at Leominster which he had acquired from Buckingham; and he was questioned on his trusteeship for an estate belonging to a certain Thomas and William Hussey. On 28th November, a week before Sidney's execution, he was brought before the King's Bench on a writ of habeas corpus and bailed out on a recognisance of £1,000.

Roger L'Estrange, the one-time royal censor and semi-official journalist, set himself to spy on the prisoners released on bail, who included Charlton and Hampden, and reported that on the night of their release they 'made very merry together' at Wildman's house, while Henry Nevile, another veteran Republican, also welcomed the escape of his friends. Ten weeks later, on 12th February 1684, Wildman was finally discharged, 'there being no evidence against him.' He was luckier than Hampden, who was accused not of treason but of misdemeanour, and fined the impossible sum of £40,000. That same year Holloway was arrested in the West Indies and Sir Thomas Armstrong in Holland; the former was induced to confess what he knew (which was little enough) and the latter was put to death as an outlaw. With Armstrong's death the judicial holocaust of Charles II's reign came to an end.

How far were the men who gathered in Shepherd's wine shop and elsewhere to make political plans in 1682–3 and who paid for their outspokenness with death or imprisonment genuinely anxious to establish a republic? Even those victims of the imaginary Rye House murder plot who confessed on the scaffold that they had been entangled in treasonable talk made no explicit statement of their aims. All wanted to enforce the exclusion of the Roman Catholic Duke of York from the throne, but it is beyond question that they were not in agreement over what form of government or which governor they wanted in his place. But there can be no doubt that there was a movement in favour of the restoration of a republican system. A group of the old Roundheads and some Independents definitely wanted to see a Commonwealth ruled by the 'natural aristocracy of the nation.' An estimate that one-third of the opposition to the Court party consisted of Republicans has already been given. Rouse declared before his death that some of the 'conspirators' were for the Duke of Monmouth, some were for a Commonwealth, and a very few for the Duke of Buckingham. Besides Sidney and Wildman, Walcot, Rumbold, Goodenough and perhaps Hampden wanted to set up a republic. After the death of Sidney, Essex and Walcot, it was Wildman, Nevile and a certain Dr. Cox who kept the light of their 'Good Old Cause' glowing. But in Sidney the party had lost a man of inspired and inspiring faith. To him absolute monarchy was the supreme evil and fear of it still haunted him upon the scaffold. To the end he hoped that God

ALGERNON SIDNEY

After a portrait by Justus van Egmont, 1663

would speedily visit His people to free them from their tyranny: 'I die in the faith that He will do it,' he wrote in his *Apologia*, 'for His cause and His people is more concerned now than it was in former times. The lust of one man and his favourites was then only to be set up in the exercise of arbitrary power over persons; but now, the tyranny over conscience is principally affected, and the civil powers are stretched unto exorbitant heights for the establishment of popery.'

The ever-watchful Roger L'Estrange reported some stirrings in republican quarters in the spring of 1684. 'A great many new faces,' he told Secretary Jenkins, 'come lately to town, full and frequent meetings, and some persons taken notice of that cannot be understood to have any business here [in London] but mischief . . . as one of Cromwell's majors, Wildman, a bold and desperate fellow.' Again, he reported in March, 'there is something a-brewing more than ordinary. Sir Samuel Bernardiston [a Whig alderman], Dr. Cox, Henry Nevile and Major Wildman are exceedingly busy, back and forward, up and down, within these three days.' In particular he noted that Wildman visited a woman 'disguised as a man' in Vere Street; he 'commonly stays two or three hours, sometimes longer.' This intelligence need not have been a conclusive proof of treason. It is known, however, that about this time, in the spring of 1684, old Edmund Ludlow in Switzerland received the last of a long series of appeals from his republican friends in England to come over and head a rising. Nathaniel Wade went to Vevey and suggested that Ludlow should direct an invasion of the West of England. But without substantial preparations the scheme was obviously hopeless. Wildman and his associates had therefore to await the accession of James II in order to achieve their revenge upon the Stuarts. The event came sooner than was expected. On 1st February 1685 King Charles II had a seizure, the ultimate payment for a merry life. Before he died he received extreme unction from a priest who had saved his life after the battle of Worcester. He rallied once, but on 6th February, while bonfires to celebrate his recovery were burning in York, the King followed Algernon Sidney into the unknown. Wildman lived on to plot another day.

CHAPTER XIX

TOWARDS REVOLUTION

... the people have a right supreme
To make their kings; for kings are made for them.
All empire is no more than power in trust,
Which when assumed, can be no longer just.
Succession, for the general good design'd,
In its own wrong a nation cannot bind;
If altering that the people can relieve,
Better one suffer than a nation grieve.

DRYDEN *Absalom and Achitophel*

WHEN at the age of fifty-three that obstinate bigot, James II, succeeded to the English throne, he found that his brother had left him a most satisfactory heritage. The Whigs, who had done their utmost to deprive him of his monarchical power, were broken and dispersed and their leaders were dead. The Government's successful tampering with the municipal charters contributed to the election of another enthusiastically royalist parliament in the fourth month of his reign. An ample revenue was promised. There was only one cloud in the blue sky. James II was a Roman Catholic king—the first such ruler since Bloody Mary—and Parliament was as faithful as ever to the Church of England. When the House of Commons met it immediately asked for the enforcement of the penal laws against James's fellow-worshippers. But King James was firm in his desire for the toleration, if not the predominance, of Roman Catholicism in his kingdom. True, he had thrown a sop to the Church of England when he told his Privy Council on his accession that he would always take care 'to defend and support the Church as established by law' and that he knew 'the laws of England are sufficient to make the King as great a monarch as I can wish.' But he provocatively celebrated mass with the doors of his chapel open and rebuked those Anglican preachers who impertinently denounced 'popery.' All this was no doubt natural and even commendable in a faithful adherent of the Roman Catholic Church, but it was a foretaste of the difficulties which were likely to arise with a Roman Catholic King ruling over a country in which the religion of the Church of England remained the only recognized form of worship.

James's enemies foresaw that sooner or later the country would be torn asunder by this religious conflict, and the men who had striven in every way, both constitutional and revolutionary, to prevent his coming to the throne began to make ready to fight him once more. There were soon gatherings in 'little cabals' where the possibilities of rebellion were discussed. But again, as in the insurrectionary councils of 1682, opinions were divided. In London the Republicans, led by Major Wildman and his cousin, Major Disney, and working in liaison with Whigs or semi-Republicans like Delamere, Trenchard, and Charlton and others who had survived the Rye House prosecutions, though ready to use their chance when it came, could not but see that Charles II had left the throne too securely entrenched for an immediate rising in England to be practicable. Wildman had better hopes of instigating an effective campaign against James in Scotland, where the Covenanters were being persecuted more severely than ever, to such an extent that the new reign was being spoken of as the 'killing time,' and where the exiled Earl of Argyll, who was meditating revenge on James from his Frisian estates, was believed to possess tremendous influence.

Argyll had indeed for some months been making general preparations for an invasion of Scotland and was sanguine enough to hope to achieve success unaided. He had some financial resources placed at his disposal by a widowed lady who had long been one of his admirers. But it was urged upon him that an alliance with his fellow exile, James's supposed nephew, the Duke of Monmouth, might contribute usefully to this enterprise. There were consequently comings and goings to this end. Monmouth was at first reluctant to disturb himself. Had not the poet Dryden written of him that though none were 'so beautiful, so brave' as he,

> 'In peace the thoughts of war he could remove
> And seem as he were only made for love'?

He was now dallying pleasantly with his mistress, Lady Henrietta Wentworth, and scribbling jejune but pacific verses:

'We'll to our bowers
And there spend our hours.
Happy there we'll be,
We no strifes can see.'

And it was with some difficulty that Argyll and the Reverend Robert Ferguson induced him to contemplate quitting his bowers for the field of battle.

Wildman had never admired or trusted Monmouth, who, after all, had behaved badly over the Rye House plot, but he had thought fit to keep in touch with him after the failure of the rebel schemes of three years before. Lord Grey of Wark, when he was in the position to offer Monmouth an appointment as general in the Brandenburg army towards the end of Charles II's reign, considered it advisable to acquaint Major Wildman with the offer, 'whom I thought most likely to convey it to the Duke of Monmouth.' Wildman, however, clearly knew Monmouth for what he was, a weak, extravagant and credulous man, whose head was easily turned by flattery and who, were he victorious over James, would be likely to become at least as despotic as Charles II. Wildman could see, on the other hand, that the bitter lessons of Charles's and James's reigns were gradually alienating the Scots altogether from monarchy, a form of government to which they had been so faithful in former years. Sir Richard Lodge wrote that 'the Scottish conspirators [of 1685] had no intention of supporting Monmouth's pretensions to the throne, and most of them were in favour of a republic.' Sir Patrick Hume, who was one of Argyll's chief advisers, bluntly asked Monmouth whether he intended to lay claim to the Crown in the event of the success of an invasion and Monmouth ambiguously replied that he would accept any place in the Commonwealth which the people might bestow upon him. Hume then observed that they found that many of his best friends in England were 'jealous of his aspiring to the royal dignity,' since monarchy had been so much abused that they were entirely disgusted with it as a political institution. It was upon the unwritten understanding that a republican form of government should be introduced in the event of success that a formal alliance was concluded between Argyll and Monmouth and that preparations were pressed forward for invasion. Argyll, who had indeed already expended £10,000 on the purchase of ships and arms, was in a hurry to set off, but Monmouth had only what he could beg, borrow, or raise by pawning his mistress's jewels, and was anxious, before making a move, to discover what assistance his friends or potential allies could afford before hazarding all upon so perilous an expedition with but a handful of men and weapons.

There is every reason to suppose that—unlike in 1688—the impulse for an invasion and rising in the first months of James II's reign came almost entirely from the exiles, whose precarious position in Holland, natural impatience, and ignorance of the situation in England and Scotland alone made their decisions comprehensible. James's opponents in London, who maintained contact with the exiles since they knew how things stood at Whitehall and Westminster, did their utmost to dissuade Monmouth from his rash venture. As soon as they learned of Argyll's plans at the beginning of the reign they dispatched one Robert Cragg, alias Smith, to discover the exact state of affairs. Lord Grey of Wark in his thoroughly unreliable confession to James II after the Monmouth invasion asserts that Cragg was sent by Wildman with an encouraging message that 'if Monmouth only landed with a switch in his hand, he could march unmolested to Whitehall. This of course is sheer nonsense. Cragg himself stated that he never even spoke with Wildman unless he was a mysterious gentleman whom he once met in the dark in Lincoln's Inn Fields and to whom he gave an account of 'all things.' Cragg was sent by Major Disney simply on a mission of discovery, and such information as Cragg possessed about Wildman was obtained second-hand from Disney. Cragg returned to London after his first visit to Holland and reported to Disney that everything had been settled and that Monmouth demanded money and help. Disney was discouraging. He said the money could not be raised and that the people in England were 'cold.' Cragg went back with the message and saw Monmouth himself. Monmouth was very angry 'and seemed to lay great fault upon Major Wildman who would govern everybody and did believe that he was the cause of backwardness in others— he was always the governor of Mr. Hampden and the rest—but he should not govern him in this affair.' Monmouth added that Wildman liked nothing of anybody's doing but his own and told Cragg in extreme anger that 'he thinks by keeping his own purse-strings fast to hinder me in this thing, but he and they shall be mistaken.' A bystander remarked that Wildman probably expected to be a Chief Minister of State—Lord Chancellor perhaps—and suggested cynically that Monmouth might send him a Dutch butter-print for a seal. Cragg was sent back with urgent instructions that Monmouth's friends in London must raise £5,000 or £6,000 for the expedition. It was suggested to him that he should apply to Sir Samuel Bernardiston, who, as we have seen, belonged to Wildman's republican group. Monmouth also ordered Wildman, Colonel Danvers, and the rest to hold regular meetings to discuss what might be done to assist him and to press on Lord Delamere and Lord Macclesfield to prepare for a rising in Cheshire. Wildman and Delamere were also asked to send over an agent. Cragg reported these instructions to Disney, who saw Wildman and said that they were perturbed that the Duke should remain unshaken in his determination to move at so unpropitious a time. The main source of their concern lay apparently not so much in the hopelessness of invasion—to which it seemed that Monmouth and Argyll were committed beyond possibility of withdrawal—as in the old difficulty about what form of government was to be established after the invasion had taken place. Not unreasonably Wildman and his friends were against risking their lives and property merely to substitute James Monmouth for James Stuart. They were shocked that Monmouth and the exiles should conclude a scheme for the government of the nation without the knowledge or approval of any of the people in England; this, Wildman averred, was calculated to offend 'the gentry,' for 'to this day they knew not what he intended to set up or declare.' Until Monmouth let them know what were his political ideas, he should not have a penny. Disney said that he was himself of Wildman's opinion that 'it was madness to pull down an old house before they knew how to build a new one.' So Cragg once again returned to Amsterdam with this unappetizing information and Monmouth disgustedly laid the whole blame on Wildman, 'who obstructed everything.'

Robert Cragg was not the only intermediary between Wildman and Monmouth. Henry Ireton, son of Cromwell's friend with whom Wildman had contended in the famous Putney debates nearly forty years earlier, was also engaged in this capacity. He happened, he related afterwards, to meet Monmouth accidentally in Rotterdam and Monmouth asked him to go to England with a confidential message for Wildman. Wildman was to be asked to raise a mortgage of £4,000 on an estate belonging to Monmouth called Moor Park. Ireton, however, was arrested before he could deliver this last message.

At the end of April, 1685, soon after James II had been crowned in Westminster Abbey, the Earl of Argyll set sail on his desperate invasion of Scotland with a band of followers inspired to save their native land from idolatry and slavery. Argyll was accompanied by two Englishmen, Ayloffe and the one-eyed Richard Rumbold, owner of Rye House, while two Scotsmen, Ferguson and Andrew Fletcher, were left as a counterpart to go with Monmouth. The authorities at Amsterdam, who were themselves not unsympathetic to the republican cause and anxious to spite William of Orange, a monarchist, had kept a blind eye on the preparations for the expedition. Under the name of Mr. Carr, Argyll had purchased three ships and hired crews of Dutchmen who had been told that their job was to carry merchandise to Italy. After the tiny and camouflaged armada had set off, the wind changed in its favour and the ships went forward with such rapidity that some thought that 'the witches had sold Argyll a wind.' The Dutch sailors were then notified that their destination was the west coast of Scotland and that their merchandise was military stores, news which they were said to have learned without surprise. Meanwhile Monmouth, who had promised to follow in a fortnight, still scratched around for resources and sent further messengers to England.

After Argyll had sailed, Monmouth dispatched three envoys to England. The peripatetic Cragg was again ordered to go to London and instruct Disney, Wildman, Danvers and the rest to hold daily meetings and to prepare for a rising in London as soon as Monmouth landed. Wildman was also asked to send down five or six horses for Monmouth's personal use to the west country, where the landing was to take place, and to get into touch with Lord Delamere, a Whig who was influential in Cheshire, to induce him to concert a rising there. A second messenger named Captain Matthews was sent to Cheshire to give the signal for the rising, but he was told to stop and see Wildman on the way. Matthews was given a piece of paper that had been indented, which matched another piece in the Major's possession, as proof that he did in fact come from Monmouth on urgent business. After Matthews had seen Wildman, he wrote to Monmouth that Wildman spoke to him 'only in hieroglyphics and was something shy of the matter, but told him that he believed he would find the Cheshire gentlemen in another humour.' A third messenger, named Christopher Badscomb or Battiscomb, was ordered to go to Somerset and make the necessary arrangements there.

There is a good deal of controversy and contradiction over Wildman's feelings about the latest series of messages. Since the evidence is all derived from confessions extorted from the men who were arrested or captured after the failure of the expedition, it is almost impossible to extricate the truth. Wildman seems to have wanted Monmouth to wait until the whole attention of the English Government was distracted by Argyll's invasion of the west of Scotland, before he landed at the other end of the island. Another version is that he wanted Monmouth to come to London to head a rising there, if Argyll were unsuccessful. In practice Wildman could do very little to help. Ever since the Rye House affair the London Republicans who had been acquitted of treason were under the close surveillance of the Government. If they attempted to organize a rising before Monmouth arrived, they would have been instantly suppressed, and if they waited until the landing was known, they were certain to be arrested as a precautionary measure. In fact they could do nothing unless Monmouth and Argyll achieved a striking military success. There was no immediate source of discontent against James II that they could exploit to win a big following. But the evidence of Dr. Burnet, later Bishop of Salisbury, is decisive on the question whether Wildman carried out Monmouth's request for consultations and proves that soundings were made. 'Wildman, Charlton and some others,' Burnet records, 'went about trying if men were in a disposition to encourage an invitation [to Monmouth]. They talked of this in so remote a way of speculation that though one could not but see what lay at the bottom, yet they did not run into treasonable discourse. I was in general sounded by them.' Moreover, according to Grey, one of the conspirators, Wildman did dispatch some horses to the west and the Duke received a message from Mrs. Wildman that '"Mr. Indenture"' (the pseudonym employed by Wildman on account of his piece of indented paper) 'did assure his Grace that my lord Delamere had gone into Cheshire and that our friends in London were all ready to rise also—as for himself, he was ready to be disposed of by him how and where he pleased.'

There is one piece of independent evidence that Wildman had in fact established contact with Delamere. On 27th May, a fortnight before Monmouth landed with a hundred and fifty men at Lyme Regis, Delamere sent the following letter to Wildman, care of the London Post Office:

'Worthy friend (he wrote),

'I have received yours and am of your opinion that we are near our vertical point, and I fear the decree is gone out against us . . . yet I will omit nothing that on my part ought to be done. I have fixed the militia of this county [Cheshire] and am taking horse for Chester to settle the militia of that city where I expect a good reception. If it be worth the trouble of a letter you shall have it; I hope we have in these parts twenty thousand [who] will stand by us to the last, which is some comfort.

'My service to Mrs. Wildman.

'I am,

'Your most obliged and faithful friend and servant,

'Delamere'

The decree had indeed 'gone out against them.' As early as 19th May a warrant was issued for the arrest of Wildman; Disney was seized on 13th June; and Delamere was arrested later. Argyll's invasion proved a complete fiasco, largely through divided counsels. By that time Monmouth, in express contradiction to his promise to the Scots and Republicans, had assumed the title of King of England at Taunton on 20th June, most of the conspirators had been secured, and Cragg had taken to his heels for the Continent. There was much rejoicing in Taunton on the occasion of Monmouth's self-coronation. A number of young girls belonging to the seminaries kept by a Miss Blake and a Mrs. Musgrave presented to the Duke at his lodgings twenty-seven banners worked with a 'J.R.' (Jacobus Rex—for Monmouth's name, like that of the reigning monarch, was also inconveniently James). He was also given a sword and a Bible. But John Churchill, the future Duke of Marlborough, who was in effective command of the royal army, was already approaching and Monmouth was forced out of

JOHN WILDMAN

Taunton and soon went to his decisive, although not dishonourable, defeat at the night battle of Sedgemoor (5th July 1685).

The severe revenge taken by King James II and his agent Judge Jeffreys, of 'Bloody Assizes' notoriety, upon not only Monmouth's immediate followers but the deluded Somersetshiremen and even the maids of Taunton is a familiar story. Wildman once again escaped—this time by flight. Every effort was nevertheless exerted to collect evidence against him. Cragg, Nathaniel Wade, who was caught in Devonshire after the battle, Henry Ireton, and Lord Delamere were also exhaustively cross-examined about him, but none of them could or would produce really damning evidence. Cragg had to admit that he had never actually spoken to Wildman but only to Disney. Wade, whose life was the price of his information, had a long rigmarole about Wildman which was summarized in the sentence: 'Major Wildman of Berkshire was a man much concerned as an abettor and assistant to advise, but gave him no money for which he had heard Monmouth curse him.' Henry Ireton related how he once heard Wildman complain that there were some people on the other side of the water

'who were so uneasy under their ruined condition that nothing would satisfy them but that everybody must be a rogue with them and a rascal, unless to help them people in London would run themselves into ruin also; and he desired me that if I should at any time see anybody that conversed with these people I would endeavour that they might be told from him that it was nonsense to think of trading [rising] for there is no fair, no mart; no people to buy; and then he added, you understand me, don't you? To which I replied I understood as much as I cared for understanding, which was, that he desired people should be patient under what they had brought upon themselves, and he answered yes.'

Although Ireton added that this conversation was long before the rebellion, it was calculated rather to obtain Wildman's acquittal than to convict him of complicity in the Monmouth invasion. Finally, Delamere, who knew most, kept his mouth shut and would admit no more than that he knew Wildman and had last seen him at his house in Queen Street on the day of the meeting of the new Parliament (19th May). Afterwards, to Jeffrey's disgust, Delamere was acquitted in a trial by his peers, at which Lord Churchill as junior baron gave his verdict first. As late as 23rd August the authorities were still trying to collect evidence against Wildman and found a certain John Jones, a cabinet-maker, who, however, could claim only that he had heard from Disney that Wildman was opposed to Monmouth's coming and had said that if he did come, it was against the advice of his friends.

On this occasion Wildman wisely decided not to try his luck too hard. Although the evidence against him was confused and contradictory, he fled abroad. On 4th June a proclamation was issued against him and four others who 'having lately absented themselves there is public notice given for the apprehending of them.' Seven weeks later, on 26th July, a proclamation signed by James II was published against Wildman 'as a person suspected of several traitorous practices and conspiracies against us.' In March, 1686, when the rebellion had been finally liquidated and Monmouth and others had paid the supreme penalty, a general pardon was published by James II, but Wildman was specifically exempted from it. He became an outlaw. For although other pardons followed later, Wildman was always excluded and for three years he remained an exile with a price on his head.

Historians, who often elect themselves moral censors in the most obscure cases and deliver judgment on very meagre evidence, have disapproved of the part played by Wildman in Monmouth's invasion. He ought apparently to have placed all his worldly goods at Monmouth's disposal and headed a London rising, however fruitless. This might have been consistent and dramatically effective, but it would clearly have been as foolish as it would have been useless. For these same historians agree that Monmouth's invasion was hopeless from the first—he came too soon or too late. He might perhaps have inspired a big following earlier when Charles II died, although it is doubtful if the Whig party in England had then recovered from the disaster of the 'Rye House plot.' If he had waited until later, he would have been able to profit from the unrest aroused by James's attacks on the supremacy of the English Church and by his undisguised despotism. But to attempt to rebel just after James had given assurances that he would not break the law or attack the Established Church was to invite failure. Wildman saw this plainly, just as he saw that any

Stuart monarch—and Monmouth, after all, claimed to be a Stuart —was unlikely to uphold those principles of political and religious freedom for which he had worked and plotted all his life. If Argyll's boasts had been well founded and the English Government had been distracted by a successful invasion of Scotland, then evidently there would have been a hopeful occasion for a republican rising. In that sense Monmouth's invasion was the final attempt of the seventeenth-century Republicans to introduce the form of government they desired by revolution. When Monmouth, against Wildman's advice, insisted on coming when he did, Wildman did what he could to help. He risked his life, for there is no doubt that had he not escaped abroad a case would have been made out against him and he would have perished on the scaffold. He had been too deeply involved in the earlier plots against James II, when he was Duke of York, to avoid this fate a second time. Soon he was to join the band of outlaws in Holland who were to help to accomplish James's downfall, and he was to preach the doctrines of republicanism in the somewhat unreceptive atmosphere of Prince William's Court.

Monmouth's rebellion has been called 'the last popular rising in the old England.' Afterwards James II hardened his heart. The 'Bloody Assizes,' at which Monmouth's poor and ill-educated followers were punished, were brutal even for those days of fear and uncertainty. Henceforward King James was obstinately determined to be the unquestioned ruler of his land and to revive the pristine glories of the divine right of kings. Looking enviously across the Channel, he saw Louis XIV, the 'Sun King,' at the full height of his power and employing all his resources to fashion his people into a homogeneous, if independent, unit of the Roman Catholic Church. James approved this programme. When the English ambassador at Paris tried to intervene on behalf of certain English Protestants who were now being persecuted in France, his efforts were coldly received and he was swiftly recalled. James's understanding was slow and narrow, but when he reached a conviction he stuck to it, and he assured an intimate that he would never 'do so damnable a thing as deny my religion.' He went much further than that. Not merely did he openly practise his religion but he aimed at employing the Church of England as his agent in securing liberty of conscience and equality of treatment, if not predominance of opportunity, for all Roman Catholics. After Monmouth's rebellion James set forth this policy in a series of uncompromising speeches. But his Tory and Anglican Parliament objected equally to promoting Roman Catholics to high office and to James's proposal to establish a standing army to achieve his ends. James, however, was 'set on his fateful path.' Parliament was dissolved; troops were raised apparently to overawe the capital; a Papal Nuncio was welcomed in London; and the Privy Council was filled with Roman Catholics.

Throughout 1686, King James, in fanatical enthusiasm for his faith and with a magnificent indifference to worldly advice, promoted Roman Catholics to key positions everywhere. Roman Catholics officered the army, a Roman Catholic was put in command of the fleet; a leading Roman Catholic became Lord Lieutenant of Ireland and another Master of the Ordnance. An illegal ecclesiastical commission was set up to silence Anglican critics and even to assist the Catholicizing policy. But by the New Year of 1687 it had become obvious to James that his methods had alienated the Church of England and that he must reach his objectives by other means. Leading Anglican Tories were thereupon thrust from their offices and an appeal was made to nonconformists by the publication of a Declaration of Indulgence which by virtue of the royal prerogative power to 'dispense' with the statute law granted liberty of conscience to all. A coalition of dissenters, renegade Tories and Roman Catholics, was envisaged as a combat team with which to attack the citadel of Anglican exclusiveness.

In our later days of religious toleration King James's plans for liberty of conscience may not unreasonably be admired, whatever may be thought of his despotic methods. But then he created opposition, first, because he plainly weighted the scales in favour of the Roman Catholics who were, after all, only a small minority, making it known that conversion was a sure road to high office; secondly, his methods were too blunt. He preferred to crush discontent instead of removing its causes, and made such unscrupulous use of his prerogative powers as to alienate the normally ruling aristocracy and even to anger the voteless mob. The English aristocracy, almost to a man, refused to acquiesce in a policy which involved the repeal of the existing discriminatory Acts against

Roman Catholics, and the older Roman Catholic families and even the Pope himself warned James that he was pressing too hard.

While James II was thus doing what his brother Charles had failed to do, namely undermine the loyalty of the Tories and the Church of England, a group of Republicans and other exiles in Holland and elsewhere were quietly biding their time. John Wildman first went to Germany before joining his friends in Holland; it was neither to his interest nor to that of his friends to become unduly conspicuous after the Monmouth fiasco. Many had been only too delighted to have escaped with their lives and courted obscurity lest James should persuade the Dutch Government to grant extradition. The adventures of John Erskine of Carnock, a young Scottish Presbyterian student, as they are recorded in his diary, must have been typical. After landing with Argyll and sharing in his defeat, he was sheltered by various friends and relations in Scotland and then hidden among the coal cargo of a three-hundred-ton ship while awaiting transport to the United Provinces. On reaching there he was advised to take a course at Utrecht University rather than to live in Rotterdam or Amsterdam. Hence when passing through Amsterdam he thought 'it fit not to be too public, seeing I was not designed to stay in this place.' Soon Utrecht was filled with apparently 'sober and diligent' English and Scottish gentlemen pursuing their studies and closely following the news from England.

Such modest behaviour was unquestionably wise. After Monmouth's rising, Sir Bevil Skelton, the English ambassador at The Hague, received instructions to secure the surrender at any rate of the rebel ringleaders. He was active in the pursuit of this duty. In March, 1686, he even made a sudden appearance at an English church in Utrecht. 'He went aside and read a prayer,' wrote Erskine, 'as if he had been presently designing to seek after the Scots and English fugitives or other disaffected persons, Colonel Danvers, Sir Patrick Ward, etc., with several who were concerned being in church. We could understand nothing that he designed but to make a *bravade*, which was an unsuitable practice for a person in such a place.' However, the appearance was more than enough to frighten the exiles. In the following month Skelton told London that he had heard a report of a fresh plot against James and that he had spoken to William and Mary of Orange about it; but they explained that no permission to extradite English refugees could be granted without the assent of all the States of the Dutch Union. And it was notorious, so Skelton reported, that, just as the Amsterdam Republicans had connived at Monmouth's invasion, so they were now using their influence to protect those of his followers who had escaped. Nevertheless Skelton added that several of the 'lesser criminals' (including young Bernardiston, son of Wildman's friend, and one Joshua Lock) were asking him to secure their pardon. The English ambassador went on to advise Whitehall that pardons should be granted them, provided that they agree to 'making discovery of such things as they knew,' because he had heard that they were contemplating the establishment of a woollen textile factory overseas and he was afraid that, if left in ignominious exile, they would become dangerous competitors with the English manufacturers.

Since most of them kept quietly to themselves not a great deal is known of the Republicans and other exiles in Holland in 1686 and 1687, and the Dutch Government became chiefly concerned with the more numerous French Protestant refugees who hurried across the frontier after Louis XIV intensified his persecution in the autumn of 1685. Erskine, a Scot, noted that he 'did see and was with many English' when he was in Amsterdam. In addition to Danvers, Ward, Bernardiston and Lock, Slingsby Bethel, the former Whig sheriff of London, Major John Manley, Captain Thomson, Dr. Oliver, Captain Hickes, the son of one of the men who were executed in Somerset, Mr. Starkey, and Captain Alsop were among the lesser known English refugees in Amsterdam at this time. Better known names are Robert Ferguson, the Scottish plotter, Sir Robert Peyton, the London Republican, and Dr. Gilbert Burnet, the Whiggish Protestant divine.

According to the confessions of one of the prisoners, Ferguson after the battle of Sedgemoor consulted with a few others 'which way to set up a free State, since Monmouth was no more in being.' This optimistic project, if considered, was soon dropped and Ferguson, after many adventures, found his way in an open boat to Amsterdam. He returned to that town in the early autumn of 1685. Here he and Sir Patient Ward and other Presbyterians were said to pray for Monmouth the martyr's wife and children and in general the Monmouth party was believed to be 'very great and many in Amsterdam.' But there seems to have been some exaggeration in these reports and, on the whole, Ferguson was very discreet after his escape from England. Sir Bevil Skelton was on the look-out for him so as to claim his extradition, and when Edmund Calamy, the well-known nonconformist writer and preacher, visited Amsterdam in 1686, although he tried to meet Ferguson he never found him. However, that summer this unquenchable pamphleteer appears to have pulled himself together, for in July a pamphlet printed in Holland was circulating in London about the villanies of Charles II, so 'foul mouthed' that it was held to be a sure proof that Ferguson was still alive. Henceforward Ferguson busied himself on various pamphlets attacking the Catholicizing policy of James II and aimed at preventing the English nonconformists from lending their support to the King in return for his promise of liberty of worship. Although every possible care was taken by the English Government to suppress seditious newspapers, pamphlets and newsletters of the type commonly read in the London coffee-houses, many pamphlets were being secretly handed about town from the early summer of 1686 onwards, and most of them were written and printed in Holland. By such activities Ferguson managed to convey the impression in Holland that he was a far greater power with the English and Scottish dissenters than he really was.

Although Calamy failed to meet Ferguson at Amsterdam, he met another prominent 'Monmouthian' in Sir Robert Peyton, an extreme Republican who had been associated with Wildman before the rising. In October, when Sir Bevil Skelton was leaving Holland to take up the post of English ambassador in France, Sir Robert Peyton was arrested but avoided extradition since he was a naturalized Dutchman. The following story is told in a contemporary letter:

'A scuffle that happened at Rotterdam in seizing Sir Robert Peyton, who braved the loyal English there, as Mr. Skelton [sic] embarked for England, maketh much noise; the rabble stirred in favour of him, when seized (though he was not in the King's Proclamation) he was forthwith released, and the Amsterdammers appear more fierce than any in his vindication, as being, they say, their burgher; and so it is thought Ferguson and his fellows are, which is the reason they escaped this long.'

Dr. Gilbert Burnet, who was the particular object of James II's animosity among the refugees in Holland, also was made a Dutch citizen after he married a Dutch wife. Burnet, a prominent and able Whig, was not a Republican. He had been sounded on the eve of Monmouth's invasion by Wildman and his friends in London, but, according to his own account, he did not think that a few indefinite fears and dangers and some illegal administrative acts could justify an insurrection at that time or that it was likely to be successful. Nevertheless Burnet thought it wise to leave England before the invasion took place, and after travelling in Italy and Germany he came to Holland, where his reputation as a tolerant theologian and historian brought him into close contact with William and Mary. When in January, 1687, the Marquess d'Albeville, an Irish Roman Catholic, who had been ennobled by the House of Austria for his work in spying on the Spaniards, came as James II's ambassador to replace Skelton, he was instructed to acquaint William with James's displeasure over the protection and shelter given to Dr. Burnet. William replied coldly that since Dr. Burnet had been in Holland, he had not found him doing anything against the King of England. D'Albeville alleged that he had discovered proofs of intrigues between Burnet and the Earl of Halifax, the famous political 'trimmer,' who had been dismissed by James from his post as President of the Council because he refused to consent to the repeal of the laws against Roman Catholics. A clause in a recently confirmed Anglo-Dutch treaty on the subject of rebels and fugitives was involved, but Burnet was protected by his naturalization. William was nevertheless compelled for a while to forbid him the Court. But as political discontent grew deeper in England and James's behaviour alienated him from his son-in-law, Burnet became the chief link between William and the Whigs, on the one hand, and between the Whigs and the extremists like Wildman and Ferguson on the other.

In the early summer of 1688 the political situation in England had become tense and critical. At the end of April James had reissued his Declaration of Indulgence and had given the electrifying instructions that it was to be read in all the churches. This was to try the Anglican doctrine of never resisting the King too high. Seven bishops, headed by the Archbishop of Canterbury himself, petitioned the King to withdraw his order and expressed their opinion that the royal dispensing power on which the two Declarations of Indulgence had been based was illegal. Their petition was printed and circulated and the bulk of the parish clergy thereupon refused to read the King's declaration as they were ordered. The infuriated monarch demanded the prosecution of the bishops for seditious libel. Before their trial, which began on 29th June, the bishops were lodged in the Tower of London, where their plight invoked popular sympathy which communicated itself even to James's army and to the Middlesex Court. Under the impulse of this feeling the jury returned a verdict of not guilty and public rejoicing was widespread. Before the glad news of this acquittal came the Anglicans and Constitutionalists had received another severe shock. On 10th June the Queen was unexpectedly delivered of a healthy son. It was certain that the child would be brought up in the Roman Catholic faith and taught James's rigid conception of kingship. An unending Roman Catholic dynasty could be envisaged. Hitherto the hope had prevailed that James would soon die and be succeeded in effect, if not in name, by his nephew and son-in-law, William of Orange, as husband to the heir presumptive of the throne. The disconcerting event of the royal birth converted many leading Tories to the idea, long fermenting in Whig circles, of sending an invitation to William to rescue England and her Church from King James and his infant.

William of Orange was a realist whose calm judgment of affairs was never to be hurried or distracted. He was a slow, unimaginative man. In person almost a dwarf, he suffered badly from asthma and was constantly in poor health. He had had a defective education, read little, was secretive in manner and narrow in outlook. Despising popularity and eschewing generosity, he was a stern disciplinarian and a hard master. Burnet, who knew him intimately, wrote that he 'had a true notion of government and liberty,' but it is certain that he never understood the English people or their parliamentary system. The paramount consideration in his life was that it was his bounden duty to resist the overweening power of the French monarchy. Hence he entertained the idea of becoming King of England chiefly because he was convinced that by this means alone he could mobilize the full resources of the island State in the struggle for European independence against France.

The first suggestion made to William that he should invade England appears to have come from Henry, Lord Mordaunt, a vain, unstable, adventurous Whig who went over to visit him in 1686. William, who regarded all extreme Whigs as Republicans and distrusted them accordingly, merely said that he would keep his eye on English affairs. After the first Declaration of Indulgence, however, when William had been sounded by James on his attitude to the repeal of the Tests and had refused to give his approval, the Dutch Prince thought it time to send over a trusted envoy to spy out the proffered land. This envoy, the Lord of Dykveld, found James immovable in his intentions and so, by mixing with the opposition, he was able to carry back to his master a number of letters from leading Whigs and Tories expressing their discontent but, on the whole, signifying their lack of power. Nevertheless Dykveld's mission was the beginning of a revolutionary conspiracy which embraced Whigs as well as Tories. In April, before the trial of the bishops or the birth of the prince, Admiral Russell, cousin of the peer who had been executed for his alleged part in the Rye House plot, came over to see William and was told by him that if he received a formal invitation from some of the 'most valued' members of the English public, he would be ready to act by September. The rebellion was thus envisaged before the decisive events of June. But these events were to smooth the path of the highly placed English conspirators. While the London bonfires were burning to celebrate the bishops' acquittal the invitation to William was signed by four rich and influential Whigs and three Tories and carried across to The Hague by another Tory, Admiral Herbert, disguised as a common sailor. Other independent letters and visitors from London brought William assurances of support in his forthcoming errand of mercy. As soon as the invitation was in his hands in July, 1688, he hastened to recruit an army and an armada and make every other preparation for his daring enterprise —the last successful invasion of England.

CHAPTER XX

'A KING FOR THE PEOPLE'

For in some soils republics will not grow:
Our temperate isle will no extremes sustain
Of popular sway or arbitrary reign.
DRYDEN *The Medal*

WILLIAM OF ORANGE's decision to invade England was not, as we have seen, altered or determined by the birth of the Prince of Wales; for he had already given his promise to move against James II in September, if he were to receive satisfactory guarantees from the discontented Protestant grandees. At first he lent no support to the popular view that the Prince was supposititious. On the contrary, prayers were said for the baby in the Princess of Orange's chapel, and an envoy, the Lord of Zulestein, was sent to St. James's to congratulate the proud, if belated, parents. Zulestein, however, reported privately that there was a widespread opinion in London that the birth was not genuine and that the child had been smuggled in by the Jesuits; and Princess Anne, the child's other step-sister, wrote to her sister Mary, throwing all manner of doubt on the circumstances of the royal birth. Thus, although the author of the first pamphlet written in Holland to prove that the birth was an imposture was punished, the story was later adopted by William and his adherents as useful propaganda to precede the invasion of England.

One factor which had induced William to make his critical decision before the birth of the Prince had been his fear of being anticipated by a revived English republican movement. For his reports from England were showing plainly that exasperation was growing in the country against James's autocracy and that a new civil war, on the lines of that of 1642, might again substitute a Commonwealth for the monarchy. If this occurred, William's wife would have lost her right to succeed to the throne. At the end of 1687 Dr. Burnet noted: 'The Prince may find himself eventually compelled to interfere in the affairs of England; since a rebellion of which he should not retain the command would certainly entail a Commonwealth.' Consequently no very warm welcome awaited the English Republicans and 'Monmouthians' who flocked together in Amsterdam and other Dutch towns when they heard of the military and naval preparations on foot for the invasion.

Among other preparations a declaration was drawn up to be published by William on, or immediately before, his arrival in England. The first draft of the declaration was written in Dutch by the Pensionary Fagel on the basis of a wide variety of suggestions sent by the Whig and Tory conspirators in England. Burnet, an able publicist, shortened the draft when he translated it into English. In its new form the declaration stressed England's constitutional and ecclesiastical grievances against King James; it deplored his use of the dispensing and suspending power to override parliamentary laws; it rehearsed the trial of the bishops; it condemned the King's failure to call a parliament and his ignoring of popular petitions; and finally it set out the reasons for suspecting the Queen's 'pretended delivery' of an infant Roman Catholic heir. William signed the declaration on 10th October, but it was not yet shaped into the final form in which it was sent to England.

It was about this time that the saturnine Wildman arrived at The Hague, ever eager to be at the centre of the plot's webs. He soon threw himself eagerly into the task of manufacturing propaganda in the general cause, for he fully realized that the only hope of overthrowing James was to give his support to William. William had the men and the guns; Wildman had but a battered faith and a vitriolic pen. When James had been thrust from his throne, it would be time enough to see what was the form of constitution most nearly suited to the republican ideal which he could hope to establish. Like Ferguson, Wildman could best make his weight felt in the conspirators' camp by boasting his influence with the dissenters. The task of persuading the English nonconformists that it was better for them to throw in their lot with William than with James was not simple. For James in his recent Declaration of Indulgence had promised the dissenters not only liberty of worship but equality of civic rights. The only thing for the Republicans and Orangists to do was to undermine James's credit. A whole battery of pamphlets had already been loosed against the non-conformists to induce them not to support James's catholicizing programme. The Pensionary Fagel had propounded a State paper setting forth William's view officially on the question of religious disabilities, and this had been supplemented by a number of free-lance efforts from Ferguson, culminating in *An Answer to Mr. Penn's Advice to the Church of England*—William Penn, the Quaker founder of Pennsylvania, had acted as intermediary between James and the nonconformists. Many other pamphlets were designed 'to keep the dissenters straight.' Most famous of these publications was Lord Halifax's *Letter to a Dissenter*, published anonymously after the second Declaration of Indulgence had been issued. In this Halifax argued that 'the alliance between liberty and infallibility' was contrary to the nature of things and that 'wine is not more expressly forbidden to the Mahometans than giving heretics liberty is to the Papists.' Wildman developed this thesis in a popular broadsheet called *Ten Seasonable Queries proposed by an English Gentleman in Amsterdam to his Friends in England*. How, ran the second 'query,' can a real and zealous Papist truly be in favour of liberty of conscience? What, he asked, about the persecutions of the Protestants in Savoy and the prosecutions of the bishops in London? Are these not, asked Wildman, unanswerable proofs of the inevitable bigotry of a Popish King?

Having thus established his claim to be heard in Dutch conspiratorial circles Wildman began to express his own views about William's proposed Declaration, very much to the annoyance of Dr. Burnet, the established English propaganda chief. Burnet, who was now meeting Wildman for the first time, wrote of this episode:

'Among the English who came to The Hague was one Wildman, who, from being an agitator in Cromwell's army, had been a constant meddler on all occasions in everything that looked like sedition, and seemed inclined to oppose everything that was upper-most. He brought his usual ill humour along with him, having a peculiar talent in possessing others by a sort of contagion with jealousy and discontent. To these the prince ordered his declaration to be shewed. Wildman took great exceptions to it, with which he possessed many to such a degree that they began to say they would not engage upon those grounds.'

Wildman himself had framed a scheme for the government of England and had also set out his own conception of what the

English Constitution had been in the past and how it had been violated, not only in King James's reign but also in the reign of King Charles II, and he illustrated his argument copiously with 'many authorities from the law books.' On the other hand, he equally employed his legal lore to demonstrate that it was a mistake for William to insist overmuch on the abuse of the dispensing power which, in his view, certainly did form part of the royal prerogative and had been frequently used in the past, especially in a number of patents in which there had been a *non obstante* to one or more acts of parliament. Wildman admitted that this dispensing power had been stretched too far by James, but thought that in itself it could scarcely be made a just ground for levying war on him. He also thought that it was a mistake to lay too much stress on the trial of the bishops, for, as he not unreasonably urged, the bishops had had a fair trial, had been acquitted and discharged—and there was nothing illegal in that. But since in other pamphlets which he was to write after William became King, Wildman took a precisely opposite view on these questions, Burnet was probably right in thinking that Wildman was using his legal and constitutional knowledge in aid of some specially serpentine purpose. It certainly appeared mysterious that a well-known Republican should justify —if only on legal, as distinct from political, grounds—the bloated use of the royal prerogative. Wildman saw, says Burnet, that 'as the Declaration was drawn, the Church Party [that is, the Tories] would come in, and be well received by the Prince: so he designed to separate the Prince and them at the greatest distance from one another, studied to make the Prince declare against those griev-ances, in which many of them were concerned and which some among them had promoted.' Wildman was supported in his extremist aims by Charles Gerard, Earl of Macclesfield, by Lord Mordaunt and many others, but was opposed by the influential right-wing Whigs like the Earl of Shrewsbury, Admiral Russell, and Prince William's favourite Englishman, Henry Sidney, brother of the dead Republican Algernon. They objected that the Prince ought not to refer in his declaration to King Charles II's reign since that would mean the alienation of many of the leading nobility, clergy and gentry. They argued that to secure a bloodless victory they must appeal to as many Englishmen as possible, regardless of party. As to the dispensing power, they maintained it must be regarded as the chief cause of the rebellion, and urged that anyone could distinguish between the legitimate use of this power to dispense with a limited number of acts of parliament in individual cases and a general dispensation of the executive from laws calculated to ensure the safety of the nation and the Protestant religion. Wildman and his friends also objected to the clauses in the Prince's declaration in which he promised to try to promote a reconciliation of all Protestants. That did not mean of course that Wildman was intolerant; on the contrary, he was in favour of wide toleration, but he was not an advocate, as Burnet was, of a latitudinarian Church, which, by reducing the number of fundamental Christian beliefs, would be capable of embracing all Protestant faiths. Wildman, as we have seen, was a sceptic, and it may well have been, as Burnet argued, that he was influenced by the political consideration that a policy of comprehension would so strengthen the Church of England that the State would be henceforward ruled perpetually by his lifelong enemies, the Royalist Anglicans.

In face of these conflicting arguments Prince William adhered to his view that he could not enter into an elaborate and academic discussion of the laws and government of England, as Wildman in his draft declaration had done. William, always a realist, saw that to set out the general and recent grievances against James and to promise to call a free Parliament to remedy them was the tactic best calculated to obtain the maximum amount of support for his invasion. In other words, he was prepared to offer a divided and weary nation just what General Monk had promised a generation before. Nevertheless in deference to Wildman's far-reaching criticisms a few expressions were omitted from the draft signed by William on 10th October and some details, presumably relating to the trial of the bishops and the dispensing power, were omitted, and the declaration was reprinted as amended. Wildman recognized that he had been beaten for the time being and henceforward set his hopes on persuading the Free Parliament, which was to be summoned if the invasion was a success, to take the opportunity to frame a constitution restricting the power of the King in accordance with the circumstances of the day. In the meantime he entered into an alliance with Burnet, Ferguson and the other English political writers at The Hague to prepare for the triumph of William's enterprise.

Wildman now wrote one of the most influential of the pamphlets which were produced in support of the revolution of 1688. It was written with the author's tongue well stuck in his cheek. Although concocted by a freethinker in Holland, it purported to be addressed by the oppressed Protestants of England to William Bentinck, Prince William's friend and confidant at The Hague. At an early point it reminded its readers that 'the truly Noble Monarchy was founded on equal Freedom' which had now been perverted. There was, it said, no hope of a freely and fairly chosen legal parliament being called to put matters right under the autocratic 'Papist' ruler under whom they now groaned, and it concluded by begging William of Orange to protect the Protestant religion and fundamental rights of Englishmen. Hitherto the English Protestants had suffered their wrongs in the name of Christian charity, but unquestionably a King of England ceases to be King when he breaks his mutual agreement with his subjects; here is the full Whig doctrine clearly stated. Moreover, Wildman argued, the Crown ceased to be free when an English King surrendered his powers and rights to the Pope as King John had done and King James was now doing.

In spite of his adverse criticisms of the references made in William's declaration to the trial of the bishops and the use of the dispensing power, Wildman made full, if not undue, play with these convenient arguments in his *Memorial of English Protestants*. On the other hand, he insisted on recalling the shortcomings of King Charles II, which William had excluded from his Declaration. Had not Charles II, he asked, been proved to be Louis XIV's pensioner? ''Tis now notorious to the world that an agreement was made between the French King and his late Majesty of England to subdue and divide the United Provinces.' Louis had been encouraged by James's conversion to Roman Catholicism and had then prosecuted his work of extirpating Protestantism from France; he had further plotted with Charles II to subvert free parliaments as a first step towards the overthrow of Protestantism in England.

But Wildman's two chief points in this pamphlet, which he thrust home with vigour, were that James's reign had been the culmination of a vast anti-Protestant conspiracy, and that the imposture of the birth of the royal heir was part and parcel of that

s

conspiracy. An army of Papists and mercenaries had been maintained, judges had been turned out of office, municipal charters had been attacked, the 'closeting of electors' had been undertaken, the penal laws had been suspended, all in one grand design, engineered by the Jesuits, to root out Protestantism. When James had failed to persuade William to approve the toleration of Roman Catholicism in England, preparations had been begun at the English Court for the fictitious birth. The proofs of a genuine birth, Wildman asserted, would not survive a serious examination. The circumstances of the lying-in were suspicious; none had heard the crying of the child; the circumstances revealed no 'sincere plainness.' And so it was with 'bleeding hearts that in this manifest extreme oppression and danger we beg your Highness's aid to defend the Right of the Crown and the Realm,' and they begged him to come over to enforce the penal laws, to restore the privileges of the City of London, to replace the cashiered officers in their commands, to abolish the Ecclesiastical Commission, to free the electorate from intimidation, and to call a legal Parliament.

The *Memorial of English Protestants* is dated November, 1688, and was therefore presumably written some weeks earlier. According to D'Albeville, James's ambassador in Holland, Dr. Burnet had a hand in its compilation, but no indication of this has been found among Burnet's papers and, in view of the antagonism between Burnet and Wildman at that time and their differing views about the subjects suitable for inclusion in William's Declaration, it seems probable that D'Albeville was mistaken. D'Albeville also noted that there were being printed both in Holland and in England at about this time forty or fifty articles against James II, which were left behind after William's fleet had sailed to be distributed in case of success. Their authors, whom he named, were John Wildman, Gilbert Burnet, and Robert Ferguson, and it was clear that these three diverse conspirators—freethinker, Churchman, and Presbyterian—although they failed to agree among themselves, were the recognized and active chiefs of William's propaganda office.

It is likely enough that Wildman's *Memorial* was out-of-date by the time that it was circulating in England. Already on 22nd October James II had produced and published proofs which to the impartial student are decisive on the question whether his newborn son was genuine or smuggled into the Queen's bedchamber by Jesuits. And by the date of publication William had already landed in England. But news circulated slowly, and unquestionably Wildman's pamphlet had a real influence in converting England to the idea of a Dutchman coming over to rescue her from a Roman Catholic ruler. On 19th October William had made his first attempt to sail with his Protestant armada from Helvoetsluys. Wildman was there but not on the Prince's frigate. A storm arose and dispersed the ships, driving them back into port. No ship was lost in the storm, although a few were damaged and supplies and horses perished. Perforce William had to await a more favourable wind. According to Burnet, Wildman at this point lost his nerve and created new disturbances (following the disturbance he had created earlier over the Prince's Declaration). 'He plainly,' wrote Burnet, 'had a shew of courage but was, at least then, a coward. He possessed some of the English with an opinion that the design was now irrecoverably lost.' They were afraid of facing the English fleet and even suggested that Admiral Herbert should be sent over in advance either to fight it or to carry it over to the Prince's side. William and his advisers withstood this suggestion, and on 1st November all left Helvoetsluys safely upon the perilous crossing. This time the luck was with them and the same winds that blew their ships across the North Sea kept James's fleet helpless in the mouth of the Thames. On 5th November the landing was effected at Tor Bay in Devonshire, and a little later Robert Ferguson, the other professional plotter of the party, convinced that the good old days had returned, forced his way into a Presbyterian chapel in Exeter, marched up sword in hand to the pulpit and preached to a reluctant and astonished congregation from the text 'Who will rise up for me against evildoers?'

For more than a week William remained quietly at Exeter to allow his Declaration, Wildman's *Memorial* and the other popular literature published on his behalf to take their effect. At first his immediate prospects looked thin. The bishop and dean ran away; and men gathered in the cathedral city's streets 'to stare at the well-mounted gentlemen with their negro servants, the Swedish horsemen and the Swiss foot, the train of artillery, and the English, Scottish, French and Dutch soldiery, who made up the motley but formidable array.' Gradually the skilful promises of a Free Parliament and of Protestant supremacy yielded results. When

James II marched at the head of his army to Salisbury to confront the invaders, he began to find that the two ancient pillars of loyalty to the throne, the country gentlemen and the army, were being undermined. From the North came the news of towns being surrendered almost without a shot to the supporters of William of Orange, and from Whitehall he heard that his own daughter, the Princess Anne, had hurried towards the enemy's camp. Henceforward James's vacillations were the undoing of his own side and paved the way for the triumph of William. Remembering his father's death upon the scaffold, James quickly convinced himself that all was lost. First, consumed by sickness and absorbed in prayer, he retreated to London; then, having sent out a commission to treat with William as a smoke screen to cover his withdrawal, he fled to Faversham and unsuccessfully tried to escape to France. He crept back to London to be surprisingly welcomed with bells and bonfires, only to leave his capital again and for the last time a week before Christmas. On 18th December William of Orange entered London, and the day after Christmas he was invited by a representative gathering of Whigs and Tories to take the administration into his hands and to call a Parliament, which since it could not be summoned by royal writ was known as the Convention.

In the Convention John Wildman was elected M.P. for Great Bedwin in Wiltshire, and his son was elected for Wootton Bassett in the same county. The principal question before the Convention was what form the new Government should take. There were some who still contemplated the restoration of James II (now in France) on terms, and at the other extreme there were a few who favoured a Commonwealth with Prince William at the head of the Council of State. But neither of these extremes carried much weight, while between them lay a wide selection of solutions. A large part of the Tory party at first advocated the idea of a regency with William as permanent regent acting for the exiled father-in-law; other Tories wished it to be assumed that James had abdicated the throne and that the title therefore actually passed—since his son was 'supposititious'—to his eldest daughter, Mary, William's wife; William would then be Prince Consort. The advantage of both these schemes, to Tory minds, was that they preserved in theory at least the doctrine of hereditary right. Curiously enough, Wildman and his followers seem to have flirted with the idea of regency on the ground that it would give Parliament some measure of control over the King.

'They thought' (wrote Burnet) 'it would be a good security for the nation to have a dormant title to the crown lie as it were neglected, to oblige our princes to govern well, while they would apprehend the danger of a revolt to a pretender still in their eye. Wildman thought it was a deep piece of policy to let this lie in the dark and undecided.'

Here we have an instance, not uncommon in politics, of two extreme parties temporarily agreeing on a common objective but for different reasons. However the regency plan was soon abandoned, although it obtained a big minority vote in the House of Lords. At this point High Tories and left-wing Whigs parted company. If we cannot have parliamentary supremacy through the myth of a regency, the Republicans urged, then let us have an elective monarchy. The throne had not been abdicated, they argued, for James II had simply fled; the throne was therefore vacant, for James had been deposed because he had misgoverned, and they might now elect whom they chose in his place. Thus, they said, a valuable precedent would be established—or rather confirmed, for had not Charles I been deposed?—that rulers are elected by the people and hold office only during good behaviour. In more than one pamphlet written at this period the view was expressed that William should reign alone, since that would establish for all time the elective character of the monarchy.

Before the Convention met Wildman published a brilliant little pamphlet in support of the republican point of view, entitled *A Letter to a Friend Advising in this Extraordinary Juncture How to Free the Nation from Slavery Forever.* In this pamphlet he argued that since their deposed prince was alive and the existing Government had been dissolved all political power devolved on the people who 'may set up what Government they please.' All constitutional powers, he suggested, should henceforward be jointly conferred on King William, Lords and Commons, including even the right to make war and peace and 'the power of the sword.' This plan (which reduced the monarch to a mere figurehead) meant of course that the new King would have to surrender his right of veto on parliamentary bills: if the King were obstinate about giving up his right of veto then, said Wildman ingenuously, it would be better to place supreme power in the Lords and Commons only—without a 'Controller.' 'The people, after all,' he added, 'is not made for a King, but a King for the people.' If the King does not care for being stripped of his prerogatives 'and is pleased to withdraw himself we must be grateful for his piety, goodness and condescension. . . . Otherwise we must regard it as a divine deliverance.' Practical experience in the House of Commons soon killed all this theorizing.

William of Orange himself emphatically stated that he would neither be a regent nor a prince consort, and since the Whigs had a majority in the House of Commons, the solution was eventually reached that James II had abdicated, that the throne was vacant, and that William and Mary should be invited jointly to occupy it. At the same time a Bill of Rights was presented to the Commons with a clause forbidding Roman Catholics or such as should marry Roman Catholics to succeed to the throne. An additional clause was proposed by which the Electress of Hanover, granddaughter of James I, should succeed Princess Anne in the succession. This clause was strongly and successfully opposed by Wildman and the Republicans.

The revolution settlement was a typically British compromise, unsound in logic but convenient in fact. Wildman's view, as expressed in yet two more anonymous pamphlets, was that the Convention had asserted its supreme and over-riding authority by declaring that the descent of the Crown should henceforward be limited to a Protestant. But it should, he thought, also stress in a public declaration that hereditary monarchy had been re-instituted by the free choice of the representatives of the nation. He further urged the Convention to make a pronouncement on the sovereign rights of the people in a Free State according to the terms of an inviolable social contract. The Bill of Rights, which besides limiting the succession to Protestants abolished the sovereign's right to 'dispense' with acts of parliament, did not go far enough to please Wildman; he would have liked a firmer and bolder statement of constitutional theory. Nevertheless he felt that in the revolutionary settlement his republican views had at least triumphed in part, and the fact that he expounded his most far-reaching constitutional theories in anonymous pamphlets and not in speeches in the House of Commons suggests that he himself realized that he was far in advance of his times. In public he played a more sober part. He represented the House of Commons in a conference which took place between the two Houses on 6th February 1689 to discuss whether James had really abdicated and if his throne were vacant. On the following day, on a motion to declare the throne vacant, Major Wildman said that to prevent anarchy nothing could be better than to nominate the Prince and Princess of Orange as King and Queen of England. This was an accepted Whig decision and in no way remarkable. But that Wildman still maintained his customary opposition to the House of Lords and to the Church of England is shown by the part he took in two other debates. On 8th February he objected that there was no point in wasting time in sending the Bill of Rights for approval to the House of Lords. And on 25th March he seconded a motion for limiting the words of the Coronation Oath to upholding 'the doctrine established by God and Jesus Christ' and not to upholding 'the doctrine established by law' since, he said, it was unreasonable to require the new monarchs to swear to maintain established doctrine when toleration was intended. This motion was defeated, however, and on 12th April William and Mary were crowned.

Wildman was to have his reward for his contribution to the revolution conspiracy. It was at first reported that he had been offered the valuable post of Lieutenant of the Ordnance under Henry Sidney, King William's favourite, who was Master-General. But this office was not to his taste. He preferred to return to the position which he had occupied in deed if not in name in the early days of Charles II's reign, that of Postmaster-General. Philip Frowde, James II's Postmaster, was therefore ousted, and on the day of the coronation Wildman took possession of the General Post Office in Lombard Street.

It has often been said by historians that the Republicans, heirs of the Levellers of 1647 and of the Harringtonian group of 1659, played no part in the Glorious Revolution of 1688. The Republicans, they say, had their last fling in Monmouth's unsuccessful invasion and were then virtually eliminated, a few pathetic and unwanted figures staying as exiles in Holland to cling willy-nilly to the coat-tails of William of Orange. But political history, looked at from the widest point of view, is not concerned so much with the fortunes of members of parties as with the fate of their ideas. And in a large measure it was the Republicans' ideas which triumphed in 1688. In the heated struggles of Charles II's reign the Whigs had stood for exclusion of a particular ruler, the Republicans for limitations on the King's power. Admittedly James was excluded from the throne—that was an essential of political progress—but the reign of William III was also to establish a far more important principle—clearly defined limitations on the King's power, embodied in the Bill of Rights and the Act of Settlement, which was to come after Wildman's death. Moreover, whatever the forms which disguised the realities of the revolution, the thrusting of a King and his son from the throne for a breach of trust and the choice in his place of a ruler who was not even the next heir, made plain that Parliament was the ultimate sovereign. When William uttered his celebrated paradox, 'I am a King in Holland and a Stadtholder in England,' he was admitting that a more genuine republican form of Government existed in England than in Holland, which was nominally a republic. The other principles for which the Republicans had plotted and struggled so long were also being gradually achieved. The nonconformists were granted toleration and the Church of England party ceased to dominate our political life. The House of Lords began to take a secondary place. When the Tories reluctantly lent their support to William of Orange they were in effect acquiescing in political doctrines against which they had fought for forty years.

Wildman, for his part, had, after his experience of the Cromwellian dictatorship followed by the anarchy of the Interregnum, realized that the country was not ripe for that full form of democratic government which had been envisaged by the Levellers. He had recognized (with Harrington) that this could not come about until economic power was more widely distributed among the masses of the people. Consequently he had concentrated his efforts on trying to attain a wider and more balanced distribution of political power which in itself should guarantee the liberty of the average citizen and above all his liberty of conscience, even though he himself was not permitted a direct say in affairs of government. In the end Wildman came to acquiesce (like his friends, Nevile and Sidney) in the idea that a king might have to form a part of the machinery of government, but a king whose rights were pared to the bare bone and who could be deposed for any abuse of the established or even the unwritten laws. Thus the republican movement came to be absorbed into the movement towards constitutional monarchy.

Not to many men is it given, as it was to Wildman, the Leveller of 1647—the anti-Cromwellian conspirator of 1655—the tavern philosopher of 1659—the political prisoner of 1661—the Rye House plotter of 1683—the exile of 1685—to see so many of their political hopes realized.

CHAPTER XXI

POSTMASTER-GENERAL

Now we may call ourselves the freeborn subjects of England ... fully
secured forever from the heavy and insupportable yoke of arbitrary
power.

WILDMAN, 1689

ONE important change had taken place in the English postal
service since Wildman had been first concerned with it in 1660.
In 1680 William Docwra, a London merchant and a sub-searcher
in the Customs House, had introduced a penny post which operated
within the City of London. Hitherto there had been no postal
service between different parts of London. Moreover there had
been only one place in London where letters for the country could
be posted and that was at the General Post Office in Lombard Street.
Consequently those who wanted to send letters and parcels across
London or to post them to the country or abroad but were not
within easy reach of Lombard Street had been obliged to employ
special messengers at considerable expense. Docwra met the need
by setting up some five hundred 'receiving offices' in various parts
of the City and by introducing a service whereby for the sum of
one penny a letter or parcel weighing up to one pound in weight
or being of up to ten pounds in value would be promptly delivered
in any quarter of London; and this penny charge covered not only
the cost of delivery but the insurance of the article delivered.
At first Docwra and his backers lost money by their enterprise,
but soon it began to pay. When it did so, James, Duke of York,
to whom the profits of the post office had been assigned by
Charles II, at once protested that this was an infringement of his
monopoly and brought twenty-two actions against the innovator.
Docwra's undertaking, in which he had invested four thousand
pounds, was filched from him and he himself fined and his family
of nine impoverished. But the country was to benefit from an
improved and enlarged postal service. And the capital's debt to
Docwra was ultimately recognized under William and Mary when
he was granted a pension.

It is not, however, true to say, as one historian of the post office states, that Docwra was also the inventor of the postmark. This was in fact first employed by Henry Bishop, Wildman's crony, the postmaster of 1660, and the Bishop postmark is well known and much sought after by modern stamp collectors.

Even before the amalgamation of Docwra's penny post with the general system, the service had been steadily expanding. Whereas Bishop had paid £21,500 a year for his farm or patent, the Postmaster of 1667 had paid £43,000. In 1694 the revenue of the post office was stated to be nearly £60,000 a year. Assuming that Wildman paid £50,000 or thereabouts for the farm, it may be presumed that he made a handsome profit.

The growing postal service continued to have political significance and the Postmaster-General was responsible to the Secretaries of State, first, for ensuring that the posts were not used as vehicles of conspiracy or treason, and, secondly, for seeing that the letters were tapped for intelligence both about home and foreign affairs. These were necessary measures in those days of constant continental wars and internal upheavals. For instance, in March, 1689, one regiment disobeyed King William's orders, seized the artillery at Ipswich and declared for King James. Wildman had to tell the House of Commons that he had letters every day about 'the ill condition of the soldiers in their quarters,' especially in Berkshire, and of hundreds of leaflets being circulated to 'fright the people with the change of Government.' Later the Jacobite rising in Scotland under 'Bonnie Dundee,' which culminated in the battle of Killiecrankie (July, 1689), James II's campaigns in Ireland, and the war which was declared against France all necessitated the imposition of a strict postal censorship, not only in order to prevent information from reaching the enemies of the Government but also to ensure a good means of obtaining the latest intelligence of the enemy's moves. Wildman as Postmaster-General therefore was responsible for the interception of letters from danger zones and for conveying them to the Secretary of State's office for examination and analysis.

Unlike in modern times, however, during the seventeenth-century wars against France private letters were allowed to pass freely across the frontiers. Although a month after war had been declared a bill was introduced into the House of Commons forbidding all trade with the enemy and although a treaty was concluded in this sense with our allies, the Dutch, there were no restrictions on the ordinary postal arrangements through France except, of course, that treasonable correspondence was prohibited. The packet boats plied between Dover and Calais much as in peace time.

It was Wildman's duty as Postmaster-General to plug this breach in the security system, and since treasonable practices had been his speciality for the past forty years, it was scarcely surprising that he displayed a deep interest in the matter even to the extent, at least according to some, of taking advantage of the opening for his own ends. He took official charge of the post office on 12th April and four days later he was writing to the neurotic and aristocratic Earl of Shrewsbury, who as Secretary of State for the Southern Department was responsible for relations with France, enclosing 'papers that came in the French mail.' On 6th June a proclamation prohibiting trade and correspondence with France was promulgated, but evidently this was not very effective in stopping treasonable letters, for in the early autumn a big Jacobite plot against William III was discovered from letters passing between Scotland and France; Shrewsbury instructed Wildman that in consequence 'his Majesty thinks that all interchange of letters should cease.' Later, however, the King had second thoughts or was persuaded that it was impracticable for the time being, for after Lord Griffin, one of the principal conspirators, had given himself up, Wildman was told by Shrewsbury that 'the King thinks it unnecessary to continue the stop upon the ports any longer' and ordered that 'the packet boats may go now as formerly even to Calais until you break off entirely that way of sending letters.' On 5th December Shrewsbury again wrote to Wildman complaining that letters written by a spy had got into the Dover post and asking him to intercept any letters addressed to a certain lady in Cockpit Alley and a certain gentleman in Bruges. A week later Shrewsbury wrote that he had had a reliable account of 'great abuses' at Dover, of how 'all manner of persons' were allowed to travel freely between Dover and Calais on the packet boat, and of the corrupt character of the master of the packet boat, a former postmaster. Wildman was warned to prevent so grave a misuse of the packet boats in future. Finally in January, 1690, Shrewsbury notified the Postmaster-General that a certain Francis Williamson had been arrested while in bed at Dover on suspicion of carrying treasonable letters to France, including an invitation to King James to return, and demanded an explanation of how he came to be in possession of a personal letter of recommendation from Wildman himself. We do not possess Wildman's reply, but under the stimulus of all this hectoring the Postmaster-General produced a scheme of reform.

Wildman's scheme was to avoid the necessity of transmitting through France so heavy a correspondence—which consisted largely of letters and bills of exchange for Spain, Portugal, and Italy—by the institution of a packet boat service direct from Falmouth to Corunna in Spain. Shrewsbury was delighted with the plan, and on 13th February notified the Lords of the Treasury of what he called 'Wildman's proposal' 'for detecting and suppressing dangerous correspondence with France,' and recommended it to their immediate consideration. A regular service of packet boats to Corunna was duly started, and although our Dutch allies broke the attempted blockade by still posting their letters to Spain by way of France, Wildman's plan unquestionably damaged our enemies and was at the same time a profitable new enterprise for the English post office. Before the scheme came into full effect Shrewsbury was again writing to Wildman about some freshly intercepted letters at Dover which disclosed correspondence between 'disaffected' persons in England and the national enemies in France. At this point the correspondence ceases, partly no doubt because of the introduction of the Corunna packets but also because Shrewsbury himself, who had displayed such an assiduous interest in the matter, had resigned from office in a burst of valetudinarian frenzy. It is characteristic of the gullibility with which Lord Macaulay and earlier historians of the eighteenth century swallowed Jacobite propaganda that they believed that this conscientious and sensitive minister resigned because he had himself been carrying on a clandestine correspondence with James II in France.

Among Wildman's other duties in connexion with the overseas posts was the obligation to see that extra services were made available whenever the King went abroad or his generals were on campaign. In August, 1689, he was instructed to secure a special packet boat to carry passengers and mails between Liverpool and

Carrickfergus in Ireland—the port where William's troops were to land ten months later to fight and defeat King James at the battle of the Boyne. But this did not prove sufficient and two packet boats between England and Ireland were demanded by the authorities in 1690, while in February, 1691, the Secretary at War complained that the boats should have been sent from Carrickfergus to Lochryan in Scotland when the winds interrupted the Liverpool service. The King's letters to Holland and Flanders also demanded the provision of extra ships: recruits going to Holland had to be provided with free travel in the packet boats; and while the King was on his way to and from Ireland an additional postal service to Chester and Holyhead had to be maintained. Another expense which fell upon the Postmaster-General beyond that of all these royal services was occasioned by the activities of the French privateers in the English Channel during the war. For the packet boats were extremely vulnerable, and even if they were rescued a substantial sum had to be paid in salvage money.

The Secretaries of State saw that the Postmaster-General fulfilled all his obligations to the Government. They insisted that special messengers should ply backwards and forwards daily with the King's letters when he was travelling and that any of his correspondence which went astray should at once be fetched back; they dilated on the need for regularity in the packet boat services to Ireland and Holland; and they warned Wildman that when the packet boats were all on one side of the water he must hire extra boats to carry the royal mail. Under the impact of so many instructions and complaints Wildman none the less maintained his customary equanimity. In February, 1691, one Secretary of State wrote to the other telling him how angry Queen Mary was because letters took such a long time to reach Whitehall from Holland and added that although she had ordered him to give Major Wildman a severe rebuke, 'I do not find it does him any good.'

If Wildman himself was thus kept up to the mark by the monarchs and their ministers, he in his turn had equally intractable servants to control in the form of post office officials. Historically postal officials have invariably been obstreperous and in those revolutionary days they were noticeably so. Twelve days after he took charge of the post office Wildman's suspicions were aroused about some of his postmasters in the north: 'I find some have waylaid the post for Scotland about Durham and Newcastle' he wrote on 24th April 1689, 'or else they have bribed a postmaster and broke open the Scotch mail and bag; and by comparing the charge of letters on the postmaster of Edinburgh with his return I find eight letters were taken out of the Scotch mail.' A month later warrants had to be issued to a couple of high officials of the post office 'to search for treasonable and seditious libels and papers about the persons and in the chambers and warehouses of all carriers, waggoners, pack-horse men and hagglers on the Western and Northern roads.' Complaints had to be investigated about the loyalty of various postmasters, including the one at Bristol. In July, 1690, Wildman was obliged to dismiss the postmaster of East Grinstead, who refused a horse to the express messenger who was bringing the news of the victory of the Boyne. At the same time petitions poured in from former postmasters and other officials who claimed that they had been penalized by the Stuarts. On the instructions of the House of Commons Wildman had to find pensions or sinecures for the earlier pioneers of cheap posts. Some of these were entirely proper. Clement Oxenbridge, who reduced the fee for long distance letters from sixpence to threepence and, according to one account, was unjustly dismissed by Cromwell, had to be given £300 a year sinecure; and Docwra, the father of the penny post in London, received a £500 a year pension.

Among the other suppliants for bounty or profit from the post office was an eccentric as curious as Wildman himself in an age full of odd personalities—Sir Samuel Morland. Morland had spent his early years in peaceful research as a Fellow of Magdalene College, Cambridge; he had emerged on to the political plane as one of John Thurloe's secretaries. He was sent by Cromwell's Secretary of State as an envoy to remonstrate with the Duke of Savoy over his persecution of his subjects, the Piedmontese Protestants, a persecution which had aroused Oliver's wrath and inspired Milton's poetry. But as the Interregnum neared its close, Morland laid aside the diplomatic activities and mathematical studies which he had been pursuing in Geneva and began intriguing with the Royalists, to whom he boasted that 'he had poisoned Cromwell in a posset [sweetmeat] and that Thurloe had a lick of it.' Arriving at Breda in time to greet the rising star of Charles II, he came back to

England to be rewarded for his pains with a baronetcy and a £500 pension on the post office. But he distinguished himself less for his tergiversations in the political field than for his inventiveness in an age deeply susceptible to every form of novelty. Morland is said to have been the originator of the ear-trumpet and to have helped to perfect one of the earliest fire engines. He also designed a perpetual almanac and a poor man's sundial. Specializing in hydrostatics and hydraulics, he produced one of the first plunger pumps and dabbled in the improvement of the watercourses at Windsor Park and the gardens of Versailles. He wrote books on cryptography and compound interest; and he also found the time to marry four wives. No doubt it was his inventiveness which attracted the attention of the indolent but curious Charles II. For we are told that about 1664 the King personally ordered special rooms and machines to be prepared at the General Post Office for the testing of Morland's devices for opening letters without disclosing that the seals had been broken. The test was a triumphant success, and in all Morland perfected four 'machines for intelligence,' as he called them. One of them enabled a letter sealed either with wax or wafer to be opened 'without umbrage to the writer.' The second would make an exact copy of any seal. The third imitated any writing so convincingly that the writer himself could not tell the copy from the original. And the fourth would take copies of any letters in a minute even if they were written on both sides of the paper. With the aid of his royal patronage Morland sold his machines to the post office, but they were all destroyed in the Great Fire of London, so that by 1688 as a lame, blind and impecunious old man he was trying to sell their secrets once more. He and his partner, Dr. Robert Gorge, first offered them to the Court of Venice; then more patriotically they were offered through Shrewsbury to King William III, who, however, 'made a very honourable answer that Sir Sam should be considered but he thought that the secrets ought to die with him as too dangerous to be encouraged.' Wildman, to whom Morland next brought his wares, was less scrupulous. The deal was closed and a certain Mr. Brockett was set to work to rebuild the machines on the instructions of Morland and with the money advanced by Wildman. The instruments 'just then brought to perfection' (according to the account of Dr. Gorge) were duly completed and employed by Wildman for opening, copying, and resealing any letters which took his fancy as they passed through the post office. These wonderful machines were not, however, to be handed down to future Postmasters-General; for, according to Dr. Gorge, 'rather than that his successors should make use of them Wildman so embezzled and spoilt them that little use could be made of what was left.'

So much for Wildman's administration of the post office. During the first year of the reign at any rate he also played an active part in national politics. The Convention Parliament was one in which he might well be happy. Much of its time was devoted to exempting from an Act of Indemnity the 'evil counsellors' of James II, the men who had harassed and punished Wildman and his associates. The same Parliament confiscated the estates of Judge Jeffreys, reversed the attainder of Sir Thomas Armstrong, found a large pension for Robert Ferguson, and prepared a bill to enable the trustees of the late Duke of Buckingham (of whom Wildman was one) to sell his estates and pay his debts. Wildman was made the chairman of a committee to inquire into the misdemeanours of Philip Burton and Richard Graham, who were the solicitors employed by the Crown during the Rye House plot trials. This committee got down to its work with evident relish. On 23rd May 1689 Wildman presented its first report to the House of Commons. The findings were that Burton and Graham had during the years 1679–1688 received over £42,000 and had endeavoured 'to procure accusations against divers subjects, including Lord Delamere and Major Wildman, offering a very great reward. . . . It is the opinion of the committee that they have by their malicious indictments, informations and presentation of Quo Warrantos openly endeavoured the subversion of the Protestant religion and the government of this realm, and wasted many thousands of pounds of the public revenues thereof in the prosecutions and solicitations.' The unfortunate solicitors, who, after all, were merely doing their duty according to their lights, were made to appear at the bar of the House and duly punished by fine and imprisonment. Wildman also served on committees to consider a bill to reverse the verdict on Titus Oates, to relieve the orphans of the City of London, and to investigate the origins of a weavers' tumult. He also represented the Commons in a conference with the Lords over the Bill of Rights.

The reason for this conference was a dispute which had arisen

T

between the two Houses over a clause in the Bill, a controversy in which Wildman had taken a leading part. The clause proposed by the Lords with the King's approval named the Electress of Hanover, a Protestant granddaughter of James I, as next in the succession to the English throne after William and Mary and Mary's sister Anne. Bishop Burnet, who had sponsored the Bill in the House of Lords, records that:

'Wildman and all the republican party opposed it . . . their secret reason seemed to be a design to extinguish monarchy and therefore to substitute none, beyond the three that were named, that so the succession might quickly come to an end.'

Be that as it may, the clause was unanimously rejected in the Commons and the conference between the Houses broke down so completely that the Bill had to be dropped until the next session. It was then passed without the clause to which Wildman and his friends objected.

The first session of the Convention Parliament concluded in August with some ill-feeling between the King and the Commons. The atmosphere did not improve when the House reassembled in October. Wildman was now one of the most prominent members of the Commons. In October he became a member of the Committee of Privileges and in December of the Committee of the Public Revenues. In November he was given leave to appear as a witness before the House of Lords Committee which was investigating who were the advisers and prosecutors of the 'murders' of Russell and Algernon Sidney. Finally it was he who presented an address of the Commons to William III demanding the arrest of Shales, the Commissary General, whom they held responsible for the mismanagement of the Irish war then in progress and for the sufferings and shortages of the English Army in Ireland. Even this summary does not exhaust the activities of Wildman as set out in the journals of the House of Commons. It is no wonder that Wildman was proud of the Convention of 1689. In an anonymous pamphlet which he wrote at the time in his best rhetorical style he claimed:

'The proceedings of the late Parliament were so fair, so prudent, so necessary and so advantageous to the nation, to the Protestant interest in general, and in particular the Church of England that all true Englishmen must acknowledge they owe to the then representatives of the nation, their privileges, their liberties, their lives, their religion, their present and future security from Popery, slavery and arbitrary power. . . . Now we may call ourselves the freeborn subjects of England . . . fully secured forever from the heavy and insupportable yoke of arbitrary power'; 'A change of government,' he added, 'would mean civil war and a French invasion.'

Unfortunately for Wildman, William III, 'the mildest and moderatest Prince that ever sat upon the English throne' (as Wildman called him), did not accept this point of view. During the autumn session of 1689 the majority in the House proceeded with their vendetta against the Tories, but the Tories stood their ground. The House of Commons was soon torn asunder by disputes over domestic affairs, whilst the Jacobites still dominated Ireland and the war with France was only half begun. King William thought of throwing up the sponge and retiring to his native Holland, but he changed his mind and instead dissolved Parliament.

Wildman was not re-elected to the new House of Commons although his son was returned again by Wootton Bassett. Just one year after the Revolution the Tories returned to power with a majority and Wildman retired into the background. His son took only a modest part in this Parliament; the unique record of his services is that he was a member of a committee dealing with the markets of the City of London. This was a Parliament in which a left-wing Postmaster-General could scarcely feel at home. Halifax, the prop of the Glorious Revolution, had resigned from his position as Lord Privy Seal; Delamere and Mordaunt (the latter now confusingly known as the Earl of Monmouth), Wildman's two close associates alike in the Revolution and in the Duke of Monmouth's rebellion, had been dismissed from the Treasury Board; and all the extremist Whigs were now in opposition in the House of Commons. Some Whigs, as was the custom in those days, went further than mere opposition and toyed with conspiracy; and where conspiracy was on the boil, Wildman could not resist dipping his fingers, preferably without burning them. The opportunity for conspiracy arose partly because James II and his supporters were still active in France and Ireland and partly because discontents in Scotland were still unresolved.

The Scottish nobility and gentry had contributed almost

nothing to the revolution of 1688, but they had gained substantially from it. A Scottish Convention had boldly declared that James II had 'forfeited' his throne because of his crimes and had then elected William and Mary in his place; Scotland, in contrast to England, had thereby decided in favour of an elective monarchy, the next best alternative, as Wildman had always believed, to a republican constitution. In return the majority in the Convention had required from William III the abolition of the Scottish bishoprics. To this he consented, but he hesitated to agree to the introduction of a full Presbyterian system of church government. His aim in domestic politics was always to compromise between the opposing parties and he was reluctant to go to extremes if it could be avoided. Consequently when it came to choosing his Scottish ministers, William passed over the claims of Sir James Montgomery, who had supported his election to the throne with vigour in the Convention and was reckoned the leader of the out-and-out Presbyterians. Sir James, 'a gentleman of good parts, but of a most unbridled heat and of a restless ambition,' was not prepared to take this oversight lightly; he proceeded to organize a Presbyterian opposition which foregathered in the taverns and was known as 'the Club' and devoted himself to stirring up trouble against William, not being too nice as to his means or his agents. In December, 1689, he visited London to see what he could do. He came at an opportune moment. The Jacobites were hopeful; the Whigs were cast down. Through Robert Ferguson, the non-conformist ex-clergyman, now well set on the road to Jacobitism and Roman Catholicism, Neville Payne, a fanatic devotee of James II, and a highly dubious character known equally as Simpson and Jones, he opened negotiations with the Jacobites. To them Sir James promised he would bring over various Scottish lords and other eminent Presbyterians into the service of James. At the same time he managed to acquire some influence with the English Whigs, especially those former exiles in Amsterdam—such as Wildman—who were going about London muttering over King William's sullenness, imperiousness and straining of his prerogatives. Even the Earl of Monmouth, of whom Wildman was a particular crony and who resented his dismissal by William, was attracted by Montgomery's schemings. Exactly who was committed and how far is uncertain. But it is known that in

January of the following year a letter was sent to James II inviting him to conclude a treaty whereby in return, among other things, for the full establishment of Presbyterianism in Scotland he was to be given aid from many unexpected but not unwelcome quarters in his efforts to regain his throne. The invitation was dispatched by the hand of Simpson, who was accompanied by Captain Francis Williamson, the same man to whom Wildman had issued a pass, for which, as has already been stated, he was severely reprimanded by the Secretary of State. Williamson, says Bishop Burnet, 'got some persons, of whom it was not proper to show a suspicion, to answer for him.' At Dover he was arrested in his bed; but Simpson reached France with the invitation and later returned with twelve thousand pounds and 'large assurances' from James II.

Thus fortified, Sir James Montgomery with his friends, the Earl of Annandale and the Earl of Arran, spent the rest of the winter in preparing for the next meeting of the Scottish Parliament, at which they hoped to overthrow King William's Government and, with the help of their new Jacobite allies, to establish the rule of the Kirk and win personal power for themselves and the opportunity to enjoy the estates and titles so liberally promised by the exiled King. Ferguson's busy pen was enlisted in the writing of a pamphlet on the *Scots' Grievances*, and instructions went out to the followers of James II in Scotland to take the oaths to the usurper so as to secure an opposition majority in the coming Parliament. The Jacobites hoped that King William would then either be 'obliged to grant the extravagant demands of Sir James Montgomery and his party or to suffer the army (in Scotland) which consisted of nearly ten thousand men, to be undone for want of pay.' This ingenious and over-elaborate scheme failed, however, ignominiously. King William's Commissioner took the wind out of Montgomery's sails by himself agreeing to set up a Presbyterian Church of Scotland. And 'the Club' and the Jacobites, unable to secure a majority, at once fell apart. A leading Jacobite confessed to James II that 'never did men make a more miserable figure in any assembly than your friends did in this,' while the Earl of Annandale bluntly observed that 'the measure of getting the Parliament dissolved being broke, we broke amongst ourselves, and every one looked to their own safety.'

Indeed it was not surprising that by the summer of 1690 the cry of 'every man for himself' went up, for on 30th June 1690 William III inflicted a decisive military defeat on his father-in-law at the Battle of the Boyne, and, although the Anglo-Dutch navy suffered a rebuff at the Battle of Beachy Head, the victory on land outweighed the defeat at sea. It became clear to all that James had lost his best chance of restoration. And Montgomery, Annandale, and the rest hastened to London to lay their confessions at the feet of Queen Mary, each hoping to arrive there first so as to incriminate the others and save his own life. As usual, it was the underlings who paid the penalty. Ferguson was arrested and his lodgings searched, but insufficient evidence was found to convict him, and eventually he escaped to join the Jacobites in France. One minor conspirator died raving mad in prison. Neville Payne, who was arrested in Scotland, was twice put to the torture, as the law of that land permitted, but would confess nothing and inculpate no one. In the end he was thrown into Edinburgh castle where he long lay 'utterly forgotten even by those for whom he had endured more than the bitterness of death.'

The Montgomery conspiracy was examined in all its aspects by the Council of Nine whom King William had left to advise Queen Mary in his government of the country during his absence in Ireland. The Council consisted of five Tories and four Whigs who were invariably at loggerheads with each other. Among them was the Earl of Monmouth, now restored to favour, and the future first Duke of Marlborough; but William had recommended Mary mainly to rely on the Marquess of Caermarthen, who as Earl of Danby had been both Chief Minister and a prisoner of State during the reign of Charles II. Caermarthen, now known as the 'White Marquess' because of the extreme pallor of his complexion, due, it was said, to a digestive complaint that puzzled the entire College of Physicians, was hated alike by the Whigs and the Jacobites. Still very ambitious, assiduous, and a devoted family man, he held the important post of Lord President of the Council, and because he was both an able statesman and unquestionably loyal to the revolutionary settlement both William and Mary paid regard to his advice. From the first he took a deep interest in the Montgomery plot and it was his conviction that Wildman was mixed up in it. In a series of letters to William III, Caermarthen stressed this belief.

In his first letter on the subject he pointed out that he had no private motives for his accusations against Wildman:

'I am sorry' (he wrote on 13th June 1690) 'that my son's interest seeming to interfere with Major Wildman's makes it less fit for me to reflect upon his actings: but there are divers passages which make it highly probable that Mr. Wildman is privy to whatever has been acting against the Government in Scotland, and particularly by his burning very many of his papers, as he did certainly the same night after Ferguson and his papers were seized; with whom I find he used to be constantly in private twice or thrice every week. His proceedings also with Sir Samuel Morland, which are too tedious to trouble Your Majesty withal and about which he gave Sir Samuel a particular strict charge that I should know nothing [are also suspicious]. Upon the whole matter I do truly believe him to be a very dangerous man to the Government; and that neither Your Majesty's nor the Queen's letters do escape his search if he can get to them: insomuch that I am in my conscience of opinion that of all the hands in England the Post Office ought the least to be trusted in his—especially at this time.'

On 16th June he wrote:

'I cannot but also acquaint Your Majesty with a private discourse of my Lord Monmouth's to me on the 14th ... it was that he did then believe we should in a few hours from that time hear that five thousand French foot were landed in Scotland. ... The news (he said) had been brought by a man who came post out of Scotland in forty-eight hours and had rid[den] himself almost dead; but, he said, he did not know the man nor how to enquire after him: and upon further discourse he said he had told Your Majesty that he would endeavour to get what intelligence he could out of Scotland for your service ... but that he would be torn to pieces before he would name any persons. ... In short—although I hope he wishes well to Your Majesty I believe him to be abused by Wildman: and he was in as much disorder as I ever saw, when Ferguson's papers were searched, and went about a dozen times to his lodging, where Wildman was all the time.'

Ten days later Caermarthen wrote to tell William that Monmouth had had a letter from Scotland about Atholl, Arran, and Annandale (three of Montgomery's associates) absconding, and added that it was remarkable that no one had received a letter from Scotland for the previous twelve days except Monmouth 'from whence everybody concludes Wildman's foul play.' He added that he thought that Wildman and Ferguson could probably explain how the Scottish 'Club' had entered into an alliance with James II 'as appears from Crone's confession [Crone was one of the minor conspirators] who names Montgomery and two others that he had forgotten.' Eight months later Caermarthen produced still further evidence of Wildman's complicity in the Scottish plot; Neville Payne, he said, had told him that Ferguson had obtained his pardon from James II and that 'Wildman was a well-wisher to their cause.'

It is difficult for the impartial biographer at this distance of time to decide how far Caermarthen's accusations, on his own showing interested accusations, against Wildman were well founded. On the one hand, none of the prominent Scottish conspirators who confessed their crimes so copiously and named their fellow-plotters so eagerly, made mention of Wildman. And we appear to be better informed about the basis of Wildman's dealings with Morland than Caermarthen was. On the other hand, Crone and Payne were in a position to know whether Wildman was involved. Wildman was certainly an old, though scarcely friendly, associate of Ferguson. And Wildman was undoubtedly mixed up in a suspicious manner with the Williamson-Simpson mission to France.

However, Caermarthen's complaints against the Postmaster-General did not stop at that point; he had another grievance against him which was shared by the Queen herself. In order apparently to increase his credit in the Council of Nine and to cast doubt upon the trustworthiness of the Tories, the eccentric Earl of Monmouth had, over a period of months, been producing for the edification of the King and Queen a number of intercepted letters conveying secret information to an address in Amsterdam; these letters were written in white ink. Caermarthen assured the King that these were all 'sham letters,' forged either in order to put the Tory members of the Council of Nine under suspicion of betraying State secrets to their enemies or to 'put a value upon Mr. Wildman's great diligence in your service at this time.' Queen Mary's view, which she recorded in a letter to her husband dated 7th July 1690, was that Wildman wrote these letters himself:

'I asked Mr. Russell what he thought of those letters, who told me that they were certainly writt by Wildman. I asked what could be the meaning; he said, to amuse us or to give suspicion that some of the company betrayed us; for, he said, Wildman was of the Commonwealth party, and his whole design was to make stirs, in hopes by that means to bring it about. . . . That is their opinion, and indeed is now mine; for I see plainly that while Monmouth was away, there came none of these letters. . . . Wildman said the people were gone, but now they (the letters) begin to come again.'

Besides Edward Russell, who was a Whig member of the Council of Nine, the Earl of Marlborough also had suspicions of Wildman. His concern over Wildman's conduct of the postal services is proved by the fact that a number of Wildman's official papers as Postmaster-General are still to be found in the Blenheim Palace archives. Marlborough said 'he would only write by expresses since he had reason to believe that Major Wildman had exact impressions of most people's seals, and that he makes use of his art.'* And so, as we know, Wildman had, and did.

In spite of these far-reaching accusations against Wildman, made by the most powerful people in the kingdom, it was not until February, 1691, long after William's return from Ireland to England that Wildman was dismissed from the office of Postmaster-General. By that date William had left England again, this time for Holland, accompanied by the Earl of Nottingham, who was one of the two Secretaries of State. Queen Mary was now thoroughly aroused by the constant delays in the posts from Holland. She ordered Wildman to be reprimanded, but found this did no good. And on 24th February it became known in London that King William had sent orders from Holland that Wildman was to be dismissed. Three days later Henry Sidney, who was King William's other Secretary of State and had been left behind in London, wrote to his master:

'The displacing Major Wildman is all the discourse of the Town, and generally people are very well satisfied with it and so they are with the choice the Queen hath made to succeed him.'

---

* In fact a letter from Morland to Wildman about his inventions is at Blenheim. How Marlborough got hold of it is not known, but it may be an early fruit of Marlborough's private intelligence service which proved so profitable in the reign of Queen Anne.

One report that went the rounds was that Wildman had been removed because it had been discovered that he was engaged in a correspondence with the Louvenstein party in Amsterdam, that is, with the Dutch republican opponents of William III. Other rumours were that he had been intriguing with the Scottish Covenanters in order to establish a republican government there and that 'some letter of his had been discovered in Holland, wherein he accused His Majesty of breach of his word already promising to stick by the fanatic interest, which he did not.'

If Wildman had indeed been detected in a republican conspiracy against the throne, he bore himself bravely. Upon his dismissal he was full of complaints which he insisted that he would lay before the King upon his return from Holland. But there is no trace in the official correspondence during the winter of 1690–91 of such fresh accusations. It seems much more likely that Wildman was dismissed mainly because of his failure to provide an efficient and regular postal service, particularly with Scotland and Holland. William had, of course, taken into full consideration the charges made against Wildman by the Queen and leading members of the Council of Nine during the previous summer. But if he were satisfied that Wildman had conspired with the Jacobites, the Covenanters or the Dutch Republicans, he did not disclose his verdict to the world nor did he have Wildman punished in any way other than by depriving him of his office. It is, however, quite possible that King William determined to ignore charges which could never have been fully substantiated. For William III was an outstanding statesman, single-minded and above pettiness. Many more influential and important Whigs and Tories than John Wildman flirted with notions of conspiracy in the years following the revolution of 1688; among them was the great Marlborough himself. Caermarthen stood virtually alone in unflinching loyalty to the new rulers.

During these early years of William and Mary's reign Wildman had maintained his close connexions with the City of London authorities which dated from the time he wrote his pamphlet on *London's Liberties* in 1651, and indeed from that earlier day when as a young advocate he supported the London Levellers against Oliver Cromwell. On 12th December 1689 Wildman had been made a freeman of the City; on 13th January 1690 he was chosen alderman; and on 2nd March 1692 he became a Deputy-Lieutenant of Middlesex. On 29th October 1692, Lord Mayor's Show Day, King William III, with becoming graciousness and discretion, knighted Major John Wildman in the Guildhall. We catch one last and appropriate glimpse of Sir John Wildman in December of the same year sitting on a City of London committee to search for precedents and to 'consider what is fit to be done to preserve their liberties.'

Six months later, on Sunday, 4th June 1693, Sir John Wildman, Alderman of the City of London, sometime Postmaster-General of England, plotter alike against Charles I, Cromwell, Charles II, James II and William III, died peacefully in his bed at the age of seventy. The body of this self-confessed sceptic is buried in the church of St. Andrew, Shrivenham, Berkshire. Alongside the high altar and upon the chancel floor the curious may read of the history and merits of the Wildman family. As Sir John Wildman's only son had no male heir of his body, he copied the Roman practice of adoption, choosing John Chute, later first Earl of Barrington, as his heir. The Barrington family survives to our own day; but it retains, alas, no mementoes of the republican plotter of the seventeenth century.

BIBLIOGRAPHY AND NOTES

This book was started more than ten years ago. During the war unfortunately a great many of my notes were destroyed and, as the libraries have been closed, it has been impossible to check all the references. In some cases, therefore, I have been compelled to indicate the source in general terms so that the diligent student may recover the exact references in due course, if he wishes.

In the following bibliography the abbreviations in square brackets are those that I have used in the notes on the various chapters; those notes are not intended to be comprehensive but only to disclose sources which are not plainly indicated in the text. The bibliography gives only the more important works upon which this book is based.

SELECT BIBLIOGRAPHY

(1) MANUSCRIPT SOURCES

British Museum: Add. MSS. 22919, 27872, 38704, 38847.
Egerton MSS. 2543, 2648.
Harleian MSS. 6845.
Lansdowne MSS. 1152A.
Bodleian Library: Clarendon MSS., vols. 52–62.
Rawlinson MSS. A40.
Carte MSS. 103
Public Record Office: State Papers Domestic.
Chancery Records.
Blenheim Archives: Wildman correspondence.

(2) WILDMAN'S PAMPHLETS

The Case of the Army Stated (1647).
A Call to All the Soldiers of the Army (1647).
Putney Projects (1647).
The Law's Subversion (1647).
The Triumph Stained (1648).
London's Liberties (1650, reprinted 1681).
A Letter from an Officer of the Army in Ireland (?) (about 1654).
The Leveller (?) (1659).
Ten Seasonable Queries (1688).
Memorial of English Protestants (1688).
A Letter to a Friend (1689).
Good Advice before it be Too Late (1689).
A Defence of the Proceedings of the late Parliament in England (1689).

BIBLIOGRAPHY AND NOTES

Unpublished:

'A Brief Discourse concerning the Business of Intelligence' (1660) (ed. Firth in *English Historical Review*, xiii).

(3) ORIGINAL SOURCES

AUBREY, J., *Brief Lives* (ed. Clark) (1890).
BALCARRES, C. L., *Memoirs touching the Revolution in Scotland* (Bannatyne Club, 1868).
BLENCOWE, R. W., *Sydney Papers* (1825).
BURNET, G., *History of My Own Time* (ed. Routh) (1833).
BURTON, T., *Diary* (ed. J. T. Rutt) (1828).
CALAMY, E., *An Historical Account of My Own Life* (ed. J. T. Rutt) [Calamy, *Autobiography*] (1829).
Calendar of Clarendon State Papers (various editors) [*C.S.P.* (Clarendon)].
Calendar of the Proceedings of the Committee for Compounding, 1643–1660.
Calendar of State Papers (Domestic) [*C.S.P. (Dom.)*].
CLARENDON, EARL OF, *State Papers* (ed. Scrope and Monkhouse), (1767–1787) [*Clarendon State Papers*].
CLARKE, W., Selections from the Papers (ed. Firth), four vols. (1891–1901). (See also under WOODHOUSE.)
Commons, House of, Journals, vols. vii–x [*C.J.*].
DALRYMPLE, J., *Memoirs* (1790) [Dalrymple].
ERSKINE, J., *Journal* (ed. W. Macleod) (1893).
FOXCROFT, H., *A Supplement to Burnet's History* (1902).
GREY, A., *Debates*, ix (1769).
GREY, F., *The Secret History of the Rye House Plot* (1754).
(?) HALIFAX, FIRST MARQUESS, *Seasonable Address* (1681) (Somers's Tracts, ed. Scott, viii, 222).
Historical Manuscripts Commission Reports [*H.M.C.*]:

  Beaufort MSS.
  Braye MSS.
  Buccleuch MSS.
  Downshire MSS.
  Egmont MSS.
  House of Lords MSS.
  Leeds MSS.
  Loder Symonds MSS.
  Ormonde MSS.
  Stopford Sackville MSS.

LILBURNE, J., *Regal Tyranny Discovered* (1647).
— *An Impeachment of High Treason against Oliver Cromwell* (1649).
— *Legal and Fundamental Liberties* (1649).
LUDLOW, E., *Memoirs* (ed. Firth) (1894) [Ludlow].
LUTTRELL, N., *A Brief Historical Relation* (1857).

BIBLIOGRAPHY AND NOTES

MARVELL, A., *Poems and Letters* (ed. Margoliouth) (1927).
MASTERSON, G., *Truth's Triumph* (1648).
NEVILE, H., *Plato Redivivus* (1681).
NICHOLAS, E., *Correspondence* (ed. Warner) (1886–1897).
OVERTON, R., *In Defence of the Act of Pardon* (1649).
PEPYS, S., *Diary* (ed. Wheatley) (1899).
RERESBY, J., *Memoirs* (ed. A. Browning) (1936).
SIDNEY, A., *Discourse Concerning Government* (1698). (See also under BLENCOWE.)
SPRAT, T., *A True Account and Declaration of the Horrid Conspiracy* (1685).
State Trials (ed. Howell), vols. v–x.
THURLOE, J., *A Collection of State Papers* (ed. Birch) (1742) [Thurloe].
WHITELOCKE, B., *Memorials of English Affairs* (1682) [Whitelocke].
WOOD, A., *Athenae Oxonienses* (1691).

(4) SECONDARY AUTHORITIES

ABBOTT, W. C., 'Conspiracy and Dissent,' in *American Historical Review*, xiv (1908–1909).
— 'The Long Parliament of Charles II,' in *English Historical Review*, xxi [E.H.R.]
AIRY, O., *Charles II* (1904).
BURGHCLERE, LADY, *George Villiers, Second Duke of Buckingham* (1903).
BURRAGE, C., 'Fifth Monarchy Movement,' in *English Historical Review*, xxv.
Cambridge Modern History, iv.
CHRISTIE, W. D., *A Life of Anthony Ashley Cooper* (1871).
CLARK, G. N., *The Dutch Alliance and the War against French Trade* (1923).
— *The Later Stuarts* (1934).
DAVIES, G., 'The Army and the Downfall of Richard Cromwell' (*Huntingdon Library Bulletin No. 7*).
— *The Early Stuarts* (1936).
Dictionary of National Biography, article on Wildman by C. H. Firth: articles on Marten, Nevile, etc. [D.N.B.].
D'OYLEY, E., *Monmouth* (1938).
EWALD, A. C., *The Life and Times of Algernon Sidney* (1873).
FEA, A., *King Monmouth* (1902).
FEILING, K., *A History of the Tory Party, 1640–1714* (1924).
FERGUSON, J., *Robert Ferguson the Plotter* (1887).
FIRTH, C. H., 'Cromwell and the Insurrection of 1655,' in *English Historical Review*, iii (1889).
— 'Thurloe and the Post Office,' in *English Historical Review* (1898).
— *The Last Years of the Protectorate* (1909).
FISHER, H. A. L., *The Republican Tradition in Europe* (1911).
GARDINER, S. R., *History of the Great Civil War* (1901).
— *History of the Commonwealth and Protectorate* (1901).

BIBLIOGRAPHY AND NOTES

GOOCH, G. P., *Political Thought from Bacon to Halifax* (1915).

GOOCH, G. P., and LASKI, H., *The History of English Democratic Ideas in the Seventeenth Century* (1927).

GUIZOT, F. P. G., *History of Richard Cromwell and the Restoration* (trans. Scoble) (1856) [Guizot].

HOLLIS, T., 'Life of Nevile' (prefaced to *Plato Redivivus*) (1763).

IRELAND, W. W., *Life of Henry Vane* (1905).

JORDAN, W. K., *The Development of Religious Toleration in England* (1936).

JOYCE, H., *The History of the British Post Office* (1893).

KITCHIN, G., *Sir Roger L'Estrange* (1913).

LINDSAY, A. D., *The Essentials of Democracy* (1929).

LODGE, R., *History of England, 1660–1702* (1910).

MASSON, D., *The Life of John Milton (1859–1894)* [Masson].

MUDDIMAN, J. G., *Trial of King Charles* (1928).

OGG, D., *England in the Reign of Charles II* (1934).

PEASE, T. C., *The Leveller Movement* (1916).

POLLOCK, J., *The Popish Plot* (1903).

ROGERS, E., *Some Account of the Life and Opinions of a Fifth Monarchy Man* (1867).

RUSSELL-SMITH, H. F., *Harrington and his Oceana* (1914).

SCOTT, E., *The Travels of the King* (1907).

SHARPE, R. R., *London and the Kingdom* (1894).

TAIT, James, *The Mediaeval English Borough* (1936).

TOLAND, J., *Life of Harrington* (prefaced to *Oceana*) (1700).

— *Tetradymus* (1720).

WILLCOCK, J., *A Scots Earl of Covenanting Times* (1907).

WOODHOUSE, A. S. P., *Puritanism and Liberty* (1938) [Woodhouse] (includes reprints of Clarke Papers, etc.).

REFERENCES

CHAPTER I

Page 7.—For Wildman's advice to his son see the epitaph in St. Andrew's, Shrivenham.

Page 9.—For Wildman's early military career see G. Masterson, *Truth's Triumph*, pp. 15 *seq.*, and Clarke Papers cit. *D.N.B.*

Page 10.—For Wildman as a doctor see *C.S.P.* (*Dom.*), 1683–4, 177. For Ireton's statement see Lansdowne MSS. 1152A, f. 285. Wade's character of Wildman is in Harleian MSS. 6845, ff. 251–296.

Page 17.—Some of the lawsuits in which Wildman was concerned are in the Chancery records in the Public Record Office; they are of little historical significance.

Page 18.—*H.M.C.* 13, iv, 391 for the statement that Wildman was the son-in-law of Lord Lovelace. For John Wildman, junior, see Add. MSS. 38704, f. 51, and his epitaph in Shrivenham church.

CHAPTER II

Pages 20 *seq.*—For the rise of the republican movement in England see, besides the standard works of Firth, Gardiner, Gooch and Laski, and Masson, Professor Woodhouse's edition of the Clarke Papers called *Puritanism and Liberty*; H. A. L. Fisher's *Republican Tradition in Europe*; C. Firth's edition of Ludlow's *Memoirs*—Introduction. For a comparison with the rise of the republican movement in France see A. Sorel, *L'Europe et la Révolution*, i, 60–63.

Page 21.—For the statement about the Short and Long Parliaments see Gooch, *Political Thought from Bacon to Halifax*, 78. For Henry Marten see Aubrey, *Brief Lives* (ed. Clark), ii, 44–47.

Page 22.—For Marten-Wildman connexions in Berkshire see Loder Symonds MSS., *H.M.C.* 13, iv, 391–2.

Page 23.—The Anglican vicar was Robert Abbot, vicar of Cranford. Stowe MSS. 184, f. 27 cit. W. K. Jordan, *Development of Religious Toleration in England*.

CHAPTER III

Page 30.—In this chapter both Firth's and Woodhouse's editions of the Clarke Papers have been used and also A. D. Lindsay, *Essentials of Democracy*, for a discussion of political theory.

Page 39.—This broadsheet, *A Call to All the Soldiers of the Army by the Free People of England*, is reprinted in Woodhouse, pp. 439–443.

REFERENCES

CHAPTER IV

Pages 49 *seq.*—For the Smithfield meeting see G. Masterson's *Truth's Triumph* (1647); B. Whitelocke, *Memorials* (1682), 288–289; Wildman, *The Triumph Stained* (1647); *A Perfect Diurnall* (1647); *A Plea from the Tower* (1647); *A Whip for the House of Lords* (1647).

CHAPTER V

Page 60.—For this meeting see Lilburne, *Legal and Fundamental Liberties* (1649), reprinted in Woodhouse, 342–355.
Page 62.—For this debate see Clarke Papers in Woodhouse, 125 *seq.*
Page 65.—For the trial of Charles I see Muddiman, *Trial of King Charles.*
Page 66.—For the accusations of Wildman by Blancher, see *C.S.P.* (*Dom.*), 1668–9, 424–6.

CHAPTER VI

Pages 69/70.—For Overton's and Lilburne's statements see R. Overton, *In Defiance of the Act of Pardon* (1649), and Lilburne, *An Impeachment of High Treason against Oliver Cromwell and his son-in-law Henry Ireton* (1649). For Wildman's appointments see *C.S.P.* (*Dom.*), *1649–50*, 154, and Clarke Papers cit. *D.N.B.*
Page 72.—For Wildman's investments see *C.S.P.* (*Compounding*), passim.
Page 73.—For the history of the Common Council see R. R. Sharpe, *London and the Kingdom*, ii, passim; J. Tait, *The Mediaeval English Borough*, 256–259, 306 *seq.*
Pages 77/81.—For the Epworth affair see *C.S.P.* (*Dom.*), *1652–3*, 373–6; *ibid.*, *1654*, pp. 309–10; *H.M.C.*, XII, ix, 506–7; T. Burton, *Diary*, i, 199–200; W. Dugdale, *Imbanking and Draining*, chap. xxvii; Ernle, *English Farming Past and Present*, 115; Lipson, *Economic History of England*, ii, 375; Tomlinson, *Hatfield Chace* (1882), 264 *seq.* For the Gloucester negotiations, see *H.M.C.*, XII, ix, 506–7.

CHAPTER VII

Pages 83–84.—For Wildman's parliamentary candidature see *H.M.C.*, *Egmont*, i, 546; *C.S.P.* (*Dom.*), *1654*, 310; Ludlow, i, 380.
Page 86.—For Wildman's broadsheet see B.M. 669, f. 19, No. 21 *C.S.P.* (*Dom.*), *1653–4*, 302.
Pages 89–93.—For Wildman's plot see Thurloe, iv, 147–149, 153, vi, 829–830; Ludlow, i, 418; Whitelocke, *Memorials*, 618–620; *Clarke Papers*, iii, 23–25; Firth, *E.H.R.*, iii, 333 *seq.* I assume 'Edston' is 'Easton'.
Page 94.—For Parker's escape see *Clarke Papers*, iii, 24–25.

REFERENCES

CHAPTER VIII

Pages 95 *seq.*—For Sexby see *Clarendon State Papers*, iii, 272, etc.; W. D. Macrae, *Clarendon*, vi, 80–81; *Nicholas Papers*, ii, 299, etc.
Page 98.—For the sequestration of Wildman's estates see Thurloe, iv, 179, 215, 333, 340, etc.
Pages 98–102.—For Wildman's relations with the Royalists and release see S.P. 181/125, ff. 195, 232, 320; *Clarendon State Papers*, iii, 300; *C.S.P. (Clarendon)*, iii, 135, 138, 142; *C.S.P. (Dom.)*, *1655–6*, 395; *Clarke Papers*, iii, 67; *Nicholas Papers*, iv, 16; Ludlow, i, 434.
Pages 99–100.—Sexby's letter to Wildman is in Thurloe, v, 37.

CHAPTER IX

Page 105.—Howard's petition is in *C.S.P. (Clarendon)*, iii, 145
Page 106.—Sexby's letter of 10th August 1656 is transcribed from Rawlinson MSS. A40, ff. 661–663.
Pages 107–110.—For Wildman's negotiations with Charles II and the Sindercombe plot see Clarendon MSS., vol. 52, ff. 369–370, 53, f. 47, 59 and 250–252; *C.S.P. (Clarendon)*, iii, 152–153, 269, 317, 325, 335, 342, 378, 383.
Page 112.—Wildman's statements to the Spanish Ministers are in *Nicholas Papers*, iv, 16.
Page 113.—For the Gravesend incident see *C.S.P. (Clarendon)*, iii, 375.
Page 115.—Wildman's letters to Talbot are in vol. 57 of the Clarendon MSS. in the Bodleian.
Page 119.—For Howard's accusations and Hyde's reply see *C.S.P. (Clarendon)*, iii, 407–409, 419, iv, 73, 98. For a defence of Willis see *English Historical Review*, 1928, pp. 33–65.

CHAPTER X

Page 123.—Marvell's letter is in Add. MSS. 22919, f. 78.
Page 124.—For the plot to put James in place of his brother see *Clarendon State Papers*, iii, 457 *seq.*; E. Scott, *Travels of the King*, 383–385.
Page 126.—Hyde's views on Wildman in 1659 are in *C.S.P. (Clarendon)*, iv, 136–137, 149, 162; *Clarendon State Papers*, iii, 428.
Pages 126 *seq.*—For Wildman's relations with the Royalists in 1659 see Clarendon MSS., vol. 60, ff. 292–293, 346–349, 560–561, 563; vol. 61, ff. 53–54 (a); *Clarendon State Papers*, iii, 442, 456–458; *C.S.P. (Clarendon)*, iv, 172, 178, 179, 205–206, 215; *H.M.C.*, X, vi, 197.

CHAPTER XI

Page 130.—For Nehemiah Bourne's letter see *Clarke Papers*, iii, 210–213; and for the downfall of Richard Cromwell in general see *Clarke*

REFERENCES

Papers, iii, 187–193; *C.J.*, vii, 631–632; Guizot, *Richard Cromwell*, i, 116–117; Ludlow, ii, 61, 67. Whitelocke, *Memorials*, 677; *Cambridge Modern History*, iv, 480.

Page 130.—For Nevile see Wood, *Athenae*, iv, 409–411; T. Hollis, 'Life of Nevile,' prefaced to *Plato Redivivus* (1763).

Page 131.—For *A Letter from an Officer of the Army in Ireland* see Toland, *Commonwealth of Oceana*, xviii.

Page 136.—*The Leveller* is in Thomason tracts E 968 (11) and *Harleian Miscellany*, iv, 543–550.

Page 140.—The French ambassador's statement is in Guizot. For Wildman's petition see Clarendon MSS. 61, f. 37, 62, ff. 14–15.

Page 142.—For the Covent Garden club see Clarendon MSS., vol. 62, ff. 25–26, S.P. 29/41, f. 95, S.P. 29/46, f. 63; H. F. Russell-Smith, *Harrington and his Oceana*, 124.

CHAPTER XII

Pages 145 *seq.*—For the Rota club see Aubrey, *Brief Lives* (ed. Clark), i, 228 *seq.*; Russell-Smith, *Harrington and his Oceana*; Toland, introduction to *Oceana*.

Page 148.—For the constitutional committee see Whitelocke, *Memorials*, 692.

Page 149.—For Wildman and Windsor see *C.S.P.* (*Dom.*), *1659–1660*, 58, 60, 131, 196, 299, 321; *C.S.P.* (*Clarendon*), iv, 500, 509, 518; *C.J.*, vii, 778; Whitelocke, 692; *A Letter concerning the Securing of Windsor Castle to the Parliament* (1659).

Page 153.—For Massey's report see Clarendon MSS., vol. 71, ff. 266–267; cf. *C.S.P.* (*Clarendon*), iv, 615, and Thurloe, vii, 865–867.

CHAPTER XIII

Page 156.—Hickes's report in *C.S.P.* (*Dom.*), *1660–1661*, 37.

Page 157.—'A brief discourse' is printed by Firth in *E.H.R.* xiii, 527–533.

Page 159.—The learned historian is Professor G. N. Clark.

Page 160.—The quotations are from *State Trials* (ed. Howell), v, 1282 *seq.*

Pages 162–3.—The quotations are from *C.S.P.* (*Dom.*), *1660–1*.

Page 166.—For the Licensing Act and its consequences see W. C. Abbott, 'Conspiracy and Dissent,' in *American Historical Review*, xiv.

Page 167.—For Cantell's report see S.P. 29/23, ff. 126–131.

Page 169.—Ibson's accusations are in S.P. 29/40 under date 2nd August 1661 and S.P. 29/63, f. 15.

REFERENCES

CHAPTER XIV

Page 172.—For the Yarranton plot see *C.S.P.* (*Dom.*), *1661–2*, 143–148, 153, 199, etc.; A. Yarranton, *Full Discovery of the First Presbyterian Sham Plot* (1681); E. Calamy, *Autobiography*.

Page 176.—For the accusations about Nonsuch House see S.P. 29/41, f. 32 *seq.*; S.P. 29/46, f. 66, etc.

Page 178.—Wildman's examination is in Egerton MSS. 2543, f. 65; Harrington's is in Toland, introduction to *Oceana*.

Page 181.—For the story of the Inner Council see *inter alia H.M.C.* (*Beaufort*), XII, 9, 51.

Page 183.—For Lucy Wildman's petitions see S.P. 29/46, f. 67; *C.S.P.* (*Dom.*), *1661–2*, 197, 253–254.

Pages 184 *seq.*—For Wildman's imprisonment see *H.M.C.*, XI, vii, 4; *C.S.P.* (*Dom.*), *1665–6*, 200–201, 288; *C.S.P.* (*Dom.*), *1667*, 20.

Page 185.—For the accusations against Clarendon see *State Trials*, vi, 330.

CHAPTER XV

Page 190.—For Tonge's trial see *State Trials*, vi, 234 *seq.*

Page 192.—For the Yorkshire plot see *C.S.P.* (*Dom.*), *1663–4*, 298 *seq.*

Page 196.—Tyrell's letter on Parker is in S.P. 29/83, f. 206; cf. *C.S.P.* (*Dom.*), *1663–4*, 392.

CHAPTER XVI

Pages 198 *seq.*—For Sidney see A. C. Ewald's *Life* and R. W. Blencowe, *Sydney Papers*, and for Ludlow see Firth's edition of his *Memoirs* and introduction.

Page 201.—For the alleged plot against Albemarle see *C.S.P.* (*Dom.*), *1664–5*, 259 *seq.*

Pages 204–5.—For Buckingham's adventures see Burghclere's *Life* and Add. MSS. 27872, f. 6.

Page 207.—For Wildman and Buckingham see *C.S.P.* (*Dom.*), *1667–8*, 89, 238. Pepys's *Diary*, 4th November 1668.

Page 209.—For Wildman's departure overseas see *C.S.P.* (*Dom.*), *Addenda*, *1660–1670*, 322.

CHAPTER XVII

Page 210.—For Joyce's arrest see Ludlow, ii, 425.

Page 212.—For Wildman and Brian Fairfax see Add. MSS. 27872, f. 24 and verso, and for Wildman as Buckingham's trustee, *H.M.C.*, XI, ii, 306, *C.S.P.* (*Dom.*), *1676–7*, 352.

Page 216.—For Marvell's writings at this time see A. B. Grosart's edition of the prose works, iii, 370, iv, 248, and Margoliouth's edition, i, 180, 188, 195.

Page 217.—For Buckingham's visit to Paris see Burghclere's *Life*, 341–3, and Carte MSS. 103, ff. 225–6.

Page 218.—The Shaftesbury-Wildman story is in Toland, *Tetradymus* (1720), pp. 92–3.

Page 219.—In spite of some defects the best account of the Popish Plot remains that by John Pollock.

Page 222.—For Wildman in 1679 see *H.M.C.* (*Ormonde*), iv, 311, and Halifax (?), *A Seasonable Address* (1681). Miss Foxcroft doubted Halifax's authorship of this pamphlet on internal evidence.

Page 229.—Charles's remark was addressed to Reresby. College's trial is in *State Trials*, viii, 596.

Page 231.—This accusation is in the *Seasonable Address*. Wildman's conversation with Wade is in Harleian MSS. 6845.

Pages 233 *seq.*—Besides the various confessions printed in T. Spratt, *A True Account*, and in *State Trials*, ix and x, the *Calendars of State Papers* (*Domestic*) and Grey's and Ferguson's accounts, I have made use of an unpublished account by Robert West in Add. MSS. 38847, f. 88 *seq.* and Wade's confession in Harleian MSS. 6845 for my story of the Rye House plot.

Page 240.—For forecasts of the 'murder plot' see *C.S.P.* (*Dom.*), 17th April 1678, cit. D'Oyley, *Monmouth*, 124; *C.S.P.* (*Dom.*), *1680–1*, 232; S.P. 29/418, f. 223.

Pages 240–1.—Ferguson's 'confession' is printed in full in James Ferguson, *Robert Ferguson the Plotter*.

Page 244.—For Mrs. Wildman and Becket see *C.S.P.* (*Dom.*), *1683*, 53, 354, 366.

Page 245.—For Doller's statement see *C.S.P.* (*Dom.*), *1683*, p. 368.

Page 246.—For the rumour of the trial at Old Bailey see *C.S.P.* (*Dom.*), *1683*, 315.

Page 247.—For Wildman's imprisonment see *The Proceedings, etc.*, B.M. 515, 12/78; Luttrell, *Diary*, i, 292; *C.S.P.* (*Dom.*), *1683*, 142, 157, 232, 400; *C.S.P.* (*Dom.*), *1683–4*, 38, 49, 89, 177.

Page 248.—For L'Estrange's reports see Kitchen, *L'Estrange*, 333–334; *C.S.P.* (*Dom.*), *1683–4*, 136, 321, in which Wildman is misprinted as Tudman.

Page 249.—For Wade's visit to Vevey see Harleian MSS. 6845.

CHAPTER XIX

Page 251.—For the 'little cabals' see H. C. Foxcroft, *Supplement to Burnet's History*, p. 151.

REFERENCES

Pages 253–4.—Cragg's statements are in *H.M.C.*, XII, vi, 392 *seq.* and Wade's in Harleian MSS. 6845.

Page 257.—Delamere's letter is in Blenheim Palace archives.

Page 258.—For Wade's statement see Harleian MSS. 6845, f. 264; *H.M.C. Stopford Sackville*, i, 23. For Ireton's see Lansdowne MSS. 1152A f. 285 *seq.*

Page 259.—The proclamation of 26th June is in B.M. 8/6 m. 3/7.

Page 262.—Wildman's visit to Germany is recorded by Lord Macaulay; I do not know on what evidence.

Page 262.—For Erskine's adventures see John Erskine, *Journal, 1683–7*, cf. also Calamy, *Autobiography*.

CHAPTER XX

Page 269.—For the conspirators at The Hague see besides Burnet, Ferguson, etc., Albeville's letters in *H.M.C.*, VII, 423–5.

Pages 279 *seq.*—Wildman's speeches and activities are in Grey's *Debates*, ix, 28, 70, 79, 193, 326, and *C.J.*, x, 147, 148, 177, 246, 266, 272, 282, 288, 294–5, etc.

CHAPTER XXI

Page 283.—Wildman's report of conditions in Berkshire is in Grey, *Debates*, ix, 168.

Pages 283–7.—For Wildman and the post office in 1689–91 see *C.S.P.* (*Dom.*), *1689*, 238, 301, 306–7, 313, 344, 354; *ibid. 1689–90*, 28, 74, 389, 425, 462, 450; *ibid. 1690–1*, 10, 45, 80, 116, 119, 129, 273; *H.M.C.*, XI, 7, p. 37; Blenheim Palace MSS. letter from Wildman to Nottingham, 17th February 1691. For the Corunna packet boats see G. N. Clark, *The Dutch Alliance and the War against French Trade* (1923).

Pages 287–9.—For Wildman and Morland see *H.M.C.* (*Buccleuch*), II, i, 49–51; *H.M.C.* (*Downshire*), i, 594–5; letters from Morland to Wildman of 18th June and 18th August 1689 in Blenheim Palace MSS.

Page 289.—For Wildman's report on Burton and Graham see *C.J.*, x, 274–5.

Page 290.—Wildman's pamphlet was called *A Defence of the Proceedings of the late Parliament in England* (1689).

Page 291.—For the Scottish conspiracy see *C.S.P.* (*Dom.*), *1690–1*, 243; Balcarres, *Memoirs*; Dalrymple, *Memoirs*; *Leven and Melville Papers*.

Page 295.—Caermarthen's and Mary's letters to William III about Wildman are printed in Dalrymple; I have corrected his transcripts from the originals in S.P. 8/7 and 8/8.

Page 297.—For Wildman's dismissal see *C.S.P.* (*Dom.*), *1690–1*, 252, 283, 296; Luttrell, *Diary*, ii, 187, 192; S.P. 633/53, f. 36.

Page 298.—For Wildman and London see Luttrell, i, 615; ii, 603, 631; iii, 112.

INDEX

INDEX

INDEX

Russell, Lord John, 232
Russell, Lord William, later Earl
    Russell, 232 *seq.*, 234, 244 *seq.*, 289
Russell-Smith, H. F., quoted, 135
Rye House, 238 *seq.*
Rymer, Ralph, 194

St. John, Oliver, 196
St. Martin's le Grand, 48, 103, 178
St. Nicholas, Mr., 123
St. Nicholas' Island, 183, 184
Saints, Parliament of, 83
Salmon, Colonel Edward, 176, 181,
    215
Saltmarsh, John, 22
Salway, Major Richard, 196, 222
Saunders, Colonel Thomas, 86, 87, 90
Savoy conference, 166, 172
Say, William, 200
Scarborough, 84
Scilly Isles, 184, 196–7, 234
Scot, Thomas, 85, 89, 130, 145, 146,
    152, 161
Scot, Colonel William, 203
Scotland, 201, 251, 291 *seq.*, 298
Scot's Grievances, 293
'Sealed Knot,' the, 117, 143
Sedgemoor, battle of, 258, 263
Seller, John, 189
Sequestration, 71
Sexby, Edward, 25, 32, 88 *seq.*, 95 *seq.*,
    104, 106, 109, 110, 111, 112;
    speech, 32; correspondence with
    Wildman, 97, 99 *seq.*, 106 *seq.*, 111
Shaftesbury, Anthony Ashley Cooper,
    1st Earl of, 123, 208, 213, 215 *seq.*,
    217, 218, 222, 230, 234, 236, 241,
    247
Shales, Henry, 190
Shepherd, Thomas, 235, 245, 246, 248
Shirley, Sir Robert, 101, 106
Shrewsbury, 176
Shrewsbury, Countess of, 204, 207,
    211
Shrewsbury, Charles Talbot, 12th
    Earl of, 207, 284 *seq.*
Shrivenham, 184, 298
Sidney, Algernon, 22, 23, 140, 152,
    198 *seq.*, 214, 217, 222, 224, 225 *seq.*,
    233, 234, 235, 236, 238, 240, 241,
    242, 244, 246 *seq.*, 280, 290
Sidney, Henry, 226, 271, 279, 297

Sieyès, Abbé, 15
Simpson, alias Jones, 292–3, 296
Sindercombe, Miles, 108 *seq.*
Skelton, Sir Bevil, 262, 264, 265
Skinner, Cyriac, 145
Skippon, John, Major-General, 22, 92
Smith, Major William, 119, 177
Smith, Mrs. William, 177
Smithfield, 49, 50, 195
'Solemn Engagement of the Army,' 27
Solemn League and Covenant, 175
Spaniards, 96 *seq.*, 104, 108, 114 *seq.*
Sparry, Ambrose, 173 *seq.*
Sprat, Thomas, Bishop of Rochester,
    212
Stafford, William Howard, Viscount,
    227
Staffordshire, 235
Stapley, John, 119
Stubbe, Henry, 143, 147, 152
Stubbs, Francis, 198
Swiss Republic, 21, 199

Talbot, Father Peter, 97, 113 *seq.*;
    120, 125, 127; correspondence with
    Wildman, 115, 116
Ten Seasonable Queries, 270
Tenure of Kings and Magistrates, 195
Test Act, 210
Thompson, Corporal William, 69
Thurloe, John, 86, 90, 93, 98–9, 107,
    109, 112, 118, 122, 123, 156, 157,
    287
Titus, Captain Silas, 105, 110, 113,
    126–7
Toland, John, quoted, 132–3, 183
Tomlinson, Colonel Matthew, 66
Tonge, Dr., 220 *seq.*, 246
Tonge, Thomas, 166 *seq.*, 219
Toop, John, 109
Trenchard, Sir John, 251
Triumph Stained, The, 52, 54
Truth's Triumph, 54
Tuke, Colonel Samuel, 126
Twyn, John, 195
Tyrconnel, Richard Talbot, Earl of, 146
Tyrell, Thomas, 196

Uniformity, Act of, 182, 187, 191
Utrecht, 262

Valley of Baca, The, 159
Van der Heyden, 169

317

INDEX